AF370450

JAPAN
A COUNTRY STUDY GUIDE

JAPAN
A COUNTRY STUDY GUIDE

ELLOITT LAYTON

Published by

Hawk Press
4836/24, Ansari Road, Daryaganj
New Delhi – 110 002
Phones: 91-11-23278618, 91-11-43667199
E-mail: thehawkpress@gmail.com
www.thehawkpress.com

Contents

Preface

Japan has the world's third-largest economy, having achieved remarkable growth in the second half of the 20th Century after the devastation of the Second World War. Its role in the international community is considerable. It is a major aid donor, and a source of global capital and credit.

More than three quarters of the population live in sprawling cities on the coastal fringes of Japan's four mountainous, heavily-wooded islands. Japan's rapid post-war expansion - propelled by highly successful car and consumer electronics industries - ran out of steam by the 1990s under a mounting debt burden that successive governments have failed to address.

Japan's relations with its neighbours are still heavily influenced by the legacy of Japanese actions before and during the Second World War. Japan has found it difficult to accept and atone for its treatment of the citizens of countries it occupied.

Japan is a fascinating country of economic and business prowess, rich culture, technical wizardry, spatial conundrums and contradictions. Japan held onto the title of the world's second largest economy for more than 40 years from 1968 to 2010. Tokyo, Japan's capital city, is the world's largest metropolitan area, with a population of 32.5 million people. Despite having an area slightly bigger than Germany and smaller than California, Japan is the world's tenth largest country by population, with 127.3 million people.

Japan is a sovereignisland nation in East Asia. Located in the Pacific Ocean, it lies off the eastern coast of the Asian mainland and stretches from the Sea of Okhotsk in the north to the East China Sea and China in the southwest.

The kanji that make up Japan's name mean "sun origin", and it is often called the "Land of the Rising Sun". Japan is a stratovolcanic archipelago consisting of about 6,852 islands. The four largest are Honshu, Hokkaido, Kyushu andShikoku, which make up about ninety-seven percent of Japan's land area and often are referred to as home islands. The country is divided into 47prefectures in eight regions, with Hokkaido being the northernmost prefecture and Okinawa being the southernmost one. The population of 127 million is the world's tenth largest. Japanese people make up 98.5% of Japan's total population. Approximately 9.1 million people live in Tokyo,the capital of Japan.

Archaeological research indicates that Japan was inhabited as early as theUpper Paleolithic period. The first written mention of Japan is in Chinese history texts from the 1st century AD. Influence from other regions, mainlyChina, followed by periods of isolation, particularly from Western Europe, has characterized Japan's history.

The country benefits from a highly skilled workforce and is among the most highly educated countries in the world, with one of the highest percentages of its citizens holding a tertiary education degree. Although Japan has officially renounced its right to declare war, it maintains a modern military with the world's eighth-largest military budget, used for self-defense andpeacekeeping roles. Japan is a developed country with a very high standard of living and Human Development Index. Its population enjoys the highest life expectancy and the third lowest infant mortality rate in the world. Japan is well-known internationally for its major contributions to science and modern-day technology.

This is a reference book. All the matter is just compiled and edited in nature, taken from the various sources which are in public domain.

— Editor

1

Country Profile

Japan has the world's third-largest economy, having achieved remarkable growth in the second half of the 20th Century after the devastation of the Second World War. Its role in the international community is considerable. It is a major aid donor, and a source of global capital and credit.

More than three quarters of the population live in sprawling cities on the coastal fringes of Japan's four mountainous, heavily-wooded islands. Japan's rapid post-war expansion - propelled by highly successful car and consumer electronics industries - ran out of steam by the 1990s under a mounting debt burden that successive governments have failed to address.

Japan's relations with its neighbours are still heavily influenced by the legacy of Japanese actions before and during the Second World War. Japan has found it difficult to accept and atone for its treatment of the citizens of countries it occupied.

FACTS

Japan, Capital: Tokyo

- Population 126.4 million
- Area 377,864 sq km (145,894 sq miles)
- Major language Japanese
- Major religions Shintoism, Buddhism
- Life expectancy 81 years (men), 87 years (women)
- Currency yen

LEADERS

Head of State: Emperor Akihito

Akihito, who has been emperor since 1989, has no political powers but he has played an important role in working to heal the wounds of a war waged across Asia in his own father's name.

His father Emperor Hirohito, who reigned between 1926 and 1989, was once revered as divine but transformed after Japan's defeat to promote peace and democracy.

In 2016, the emperor indicated that he wished to abdicate, out of concern he may become unable to carry out his duties because of old age.

He's expected to give up his throne in late 2018, when he'll be succeeded by his elder son, Crown Prince Naruhito.

Prime minister: Shinzo Abe

Shinzo Abe became Japan's prime minister in 2012 after his Liberal Democratic Party's (LDP) landslide election win.

He was re-elected in 2014. His focus has been on a series of measures - known as "Abenomics" - aimed at boosting Japan's struggling economy.

Mr Abe has said he wants to amend Japan's post-war pacifist constitution, in particular the war-renouncing Article 9 - a goal that has prompted sharp criticism from China.

He previously served as prime minister in 2006 and 2007, but quit after a series of scandals involving his ministers.

MEDIA

Japan's broadcasting scene is competitive and technologically-advanced. While the use of online media and social platforms is ubiquitous, the printed press has a very high readership and is highly trusted.

TIMELINE

A chronology of key events:

1853 - US fleet forces Japan to open up to foreign influence after over 200 years of self-imposed isolation.

1868 - End of centuries of rule by Shogun military caste, Empire of Japan proclaimed, and country enters period of rapid industrialisation and trading dominance over East Asia.

1894-95 - Japan goes to war with China, and its better-equipped forces win victory in just nine months. China cedes Taiwan and permits Japan to trade on mainland.

Capital: Tokyo

1904 - Japan becomes first Asian country in modern times to defeat an European power when it routs Russia in Manchuria.

1910 - Japan annexes Korea after three years of fighting, becoming one of the world's leading powers.

1914 - Japan joins World War I on the side of Britain and her allies, gaining some Pacific islands from Germany at the end of the war.

1918-1922 - Japan tries to establish buffer zone against Bolshevik regime in Russia's Pacific provinces, forced out by British and US diplomatic pressure and domestic opposition.

1923 - Earthquake in Tokyo region kills more than 100,000 people.

British Empire ends 21-year alliance with Japan, signalling Western and US apprehension of Japan's growing power in East Asia.

1925 - Universal male suffrage is instituted. The electorate increases fivefold.

Ultra-nationalism and war

Late 1920s - Extreme nationalism begins to take hold in Japan as world economic depression hits. The emphasis is on a preservation of traditional Japanese values, and a rejection of "Western" influence.

World's oldest monarchy

Royal birth sparks succession debate

1931 - Japanese army invades Chinese province of Manchuria, installs puppet regime.

1932 - Prime Minister Inukai Tsuyoshi killed during failed coup by nationalist army officers. Military holds increasing influence in the country.

1936 - Japan signs alliance with Nazi Germany.

1937 - Japan goes to war with China, capturing Shanghai, Beijing and Nanjing amid atrocities like the "Rape of Nanjing", in which up to 300,000 Chinese civilians were killed.

1939 - Outbreak of Second World War in Europe. With fall of France in 1940, Japan moves to occupy French Indo-China.

Attack on Pearl Harbor

1941 - Japan launches a surprise attack on US Pacific fleet at Pearl Harbor, Hawaii. US and main allies declare war on Japan.

1942 - Japan occupies succession of countries, including Philippines, Dutch East Indies, Burma and Malaya. In June, US aircraft carriers defeat the Japanese at the Battle of Midway. The US begins a strategy of "'island-hopping", cutting the Japanese support lines as its forces advance.

1944 - US forces are near enough to Japan to start bombing raids on Japanese cities.

Atomic attacks

Hiroshima survivors keep memories alive

1945: US drops atomic bomb on Hiroshima

1945: Atom bomb hits Nagasaki

1945 - US planes drop two atomic bombs on Hiroshima and Nagasaki in August. Emperor Hirohito surrenders and relinquishes divine status. Japan placed under US military government. All Japanese military and naval forces disbanded.

1947 - New constitution comes into force, establishes parliamentary system with all adults eligible to vote. Japan renounces war and pledges not to maintain land, sea or air forces for that purpose. Emperor granted ceremonial status.

1951 - Japan signs peace treaty with US and other nations. To this day, there is no peace treaty with Russia, as the legal successor to the Soviet Union.

Independence

1952 - Japan regains independence. US retains several islands for military use, including Okinawa.

1955 - Liberal Democratic Party (LDP) formed. Apart from brief interludes, party governs into 21st century.

1956 - Japan joins United Nations.

1964 - Olympic Games held in Tokyo.

1972 - Japanese prime minister visits China and normal diplomatic relations are resumed. Japan subsequently closes embassy in Taiwan.

Okinawa is returned to Japanese sovereignty, but US retains bases there.

1982 - Japanese car firm Honda opens its first plant in the US.

1989 - Emperor Hirohito dies, succeeded by Akihito.

Aum Shinrikyo cult

Rise of Japanese cults

1993 July - Elections held against a background of bribery scandals and economic decline see the LDP ousted for the first time since 1955. A seven-party coalition takes power.

1993 August - Government issues historic "Kono statement" apologising for Japanese military's war-time use of sex slaves.

1994 - The anti-LDP coalition collapses. An administration supported by the LDP and the Socialists takes over.

Natural and man-made disasters

1995 January - An earthquake hits central Japan, killing thousands and causing widespread damage. The city of Kobe is hardest hit.

1995 March - A religious sect, Aum Shinrikyo, releases the deadly nerve gas sarin on the Tokyo underground railway system. Twelve people are killed and thousands are injured.

1997 - The economy enters a severe recession.

2001 March - A Japanese court overturns compensation order for Korean women forced to work as sex slaves during WW II.

Koizumi at helm

2001 April - Junichiro Koizumi becomes new LDP leader and prime minister.

2001 April - Trade dispute with China after Japan imposes import tariffs on Chinese agricultural products. China retaliates with import taxes on Japanese vehicles and other manufactured goods.

2001 August- Koizumi pays homage at the Yasukuni shrine dedicated to the country's war dead, provoking protests from Japan's neighbours. The memorial also honours war criminals.

Yasukuni shrine

2001 October - Koizumi visits Seoul and offers an apology for the suffering South Korea endured under his country's colonial rule.

2002 September - Koizumi becomes the first Japanese leader to visit North Korea. North Korean leader Kim Jong-il apologises for abductions of Japanese citizens in 1970s and 1980s and confirms that eight of them are dead. Five Japanese nationals return home.

2003 December - Government announces decision to install "purely defensive" US-made missile shield.

Iraq deployment

2004 February - Non-combat soldiers arrive in Iraq in first Japanese deployment in combat zone since World War II.

2005 September - PM Koizumi wins a landslide victory in early general elections.

2006 July - The last contingent of Japanese troops leaves Iraq.

Abe takes over

2006 September - Shinzo Abe succeeds Junichiro Koizumi as prime minister.

2006 December - Parliament approves the creation of a fully-fledged defence ministry, the first since World War II.

2007 April - Wen Jiabao becomes first Chinese prime minister to address the Japanese parliament. Mr Wen says both sides have succeeded in warming relations.

2007 August - On the 62nd anniversary of Japan's surrender in World War II, almost the entire cabinet stays away from the Yasukuni shrine. Prime Minister Abe says he has no plans to visit the shrine for as long as the issue continues to be a diplomatic problem.

Abe steps down

2007 September - Prime Minister Shinzo Abe resigns, is replaced by Yasuo Fukuda.

Shinto religion

2008 June - Japan and China reach a deal for the joint development of a gas field in the East China Sea, resolving a four-year-old dispute.

2008 September - Prime Minister Yasuo Fukuda resigns. Former foreign minister Taro Aso appointed as new premier.

2008 November - General Toshio Tamogami, head of Japan's air force, loses his job after writing an essay seeking to justify Japan's role in the second world war.

2009 February - Economics Minister Kaoru Yosano says Japan is facing worst economic crisis since World War II, after figures show its economy shrank by 3.3% in last quarter.

LDP defeated

2009 August - Opposition Democratic Party of Japan (DPJ) wins general election by a landslide, ending more than 50 years of nearly unbroken rule by the Liberal Democratic Party.

2009 September - DPJ leader Yukio Hatoyama elected PM at head of coalition with Social Democratic Party and People's New Party.

Futenma: Controversial base

2010 June - Prime Minister Hatoyama quits over failure to close US military base on Okinawa. Finance Minister Naoto Kan takes over.

2010 July - Ruling coalition loses majority in elections to the upper house of parliament.

Economic woes

2011 February - Japan is overtaken by China as world's second-largest economy.

2011 March - Huge offshore earthquake and subsequent tsunami devastate miles of shoreline. Damage to the Fukushima nuclear plant causes a radiation leak that leaves extensive areas uninhabitable and contaminates food supplies.

2011 August - Following severe criticism of his handling of the aftermath of the Fukushima nuclear crisis, Prime Minister Naoto Kan steps down. He is succeeded by Yoshihiko Noda.

2011 December - The government announces a relaxation of Japan's self-imposed ban on arms exports. It says the move will allow the country to supply military equipment for humanitarian missions.

2012 June - The lower house of parliament approves a bill to double sales tax, in order to make up the income tax shortfall caused by an ageing population. The governing Democratic Party splits, but retains its lower house majority.

2012 July - Japan restarts the Ohi nuclear reactor, the first since the meltdown at the Fukushima power plant last year, amid local protests.

Islands rows

2012 August - Japan's economic growth slows to 0.3% from 1%

in the second quarter as eurozone crisis hits exports and domestic consumption.

Japan recalls its ambassador to Seoul in protest at a visit to the Liancourt Rocks by South Korean President Lee Myung-bak. Both countries claim the islets, which Japan calls Takeshima and South Korea calls Dokdo.

2012 September - China cancels ceremonies to mark the 40th anniversary of restored diplomatic relations with Japan because of a public flare-up in a dispute over ownership of a group of islands in the East China Sea administered by Japan as the Senkaku Islands and claimed by China as the Diaoyu Islands. Taiwan also claims the islands.

Abe returns

2012 December - Opposition conservative Liberal Democratic Party wins landslide in early parliamentary elections. Former prime minister Shinzo Abe forms government on pledge of stimulating economic growth.

2013 May - Exports rise 10.1% - the fastest annual rate since 2010 - thanks to weaker yen, boosting Prime Minister Abe's economic recovery plan.

2013 July - Prime Minister Abe's coalition wins upper house elections, giving him control of both houses of parliament - a first for a prime minister in six years.

2013 September - Tokyo is chosen to host the 2020 Olympics.

New security strategy

2013 December - Japan approves the relocation of a US military airbase on its southern island of Okinawa. The base, which houses over 25,000 US troops, will be relocated to a less densely populated part of the island.

Japan's cabinet approves a new national security strategy and increased defence spending in a move widely seen as aimed at China.

2014 July - Japan's government approves a landmark change in security policy, paving the way for its military to fight overseas.

A judicial panel recommends that three former executives of the TEPCO utility - which runs the damaged Fukushima nuclear plant - be indicted on criminal charges for their role in the 2011 disaster.

2014 December - The LDP-led government retains its large parliamentary majority in snap elections called by Prime Minister

Shinzo Abe to seek a fresh mandate for his economic policies, after Japan's economy slips back into recession mid-year.

2015 February - Economy re-emerges from recession in last quarter of 2014, although growth remains sluggish.

2015 July - Lower house of parliament backs bills allowing troops to fight overseas for first time since Second World War, prompting protests at home and criticism from China.

2015 August - Japan restarts first nuclear reactor at Sendai plant, under new safety rules following 2011 Fukushima disaster.

2016 April - At least 44 people die and more than 1,000 are injured as a result of two major earthquakes on the southern island of Kyushu.

These and major aftershocks also leave at least 100,000 people displaced.

2016 August - Emperor Akihito indicates his readiness to abdicate in a rare video message to the public.

2017 June - Parliament passes a landmark bill allowing Emperor Akihito to abdicate.

Geography of Japan

Japan is an archipelago of some 6,852 islands located in a volcanic zone on the Pacific Ring of Fire. A nearly continuous series of ocean trenches, volcanic arcs and shifting tectonic plates, the Pacific Ring of Fire accounts for more than 75 percent of the world's active volcanoes and 90 percent of the world's earthquakes.

Japan's four main islands, Honshu, Hokkaido, Kyushu and Shikoku, make up 97 percent of the country's total land area. Honshu is home to Tokyo and many of Japan's other largest cities, including Yokahama, Osaka, Nagoya, Kobe, Kyoto, Kawasaki, Saitama, Hiroshima and Sendai.

Hokkaido, the second largest Japanese island and northernmost prefecture, accounts for nearly a quarter of Japan's arable land. Hokkaido leads Japan's other 46 prefectures in the production of seafood and a host of agricultural products, including soybeans (the key ingredient for tofu and all things miso), wheat, corn, beef and raw milk. Sapporo, Hokkaido's capital and largest city, hosts the annual Sapporo Snow Festival, which regularly draws more than 2 million visitors to the spectacular exhibition of some 400 snow and ice sculptures.

Kyushu, the third largest and most southern of Japan's four main islands, is the site of Japan's most active volcano, Mt. Aso, and several cities with important historical, political and commercial significance, including Nagasaki, Kagoshima and Fukuoka.

Tohoku Earthquake and Tsunami

Few are likely to ever forget the shocking images of the massive wall of Pacific Ocean water that engulfed embankments and effortlessly swept away everything in its path in Japan's Tohoku region in March, 2011. The most powerful earthquake to ever hit Japan, and the world's fifth most powerful quake in modern history, unleashed waves that reached heights up to 40.5 meters or 133 feet in the city of Miyako. The devastation wrought by Japan's Tohoku earthquake and tsunami accounted for 57 percent of total economic damages from natural catastrophes and man-made disasters in 2011.

Japan's Economy, Business and Development

Japan is the world's third largest economy, having ceded the second spot to China in 2010. Since the collapse of the property bubble in 1989, Japan has faced extended periods of economic stagnation, deflation and relatively high unemployment, at least compared to the nearly full employment Japanese companies managed to sustain for much of the post-WWII era. Among other issues, Japan's economic performance has been constrained by weak domestic demand and a rigid labor market that has limited risk taking and entrepreneurial activity.

Despite Japan's challenging domestic economic environment, many Japanese companies have continued to perform well on the world stage. As of 2011, Japan counted 68 companies in the Fortune/ CNN Money Global 500 ranking of the world's largest corporations. Japanese companies in the top 100 of the Fortune ranking include: Toyota Motor, Hitachi, Honda Motor, Nissan Motor, Panasonic, Sony and Toshiba. Japan's corporate sector has continued to push the technology envelope in fields such as robotics, medical devices, clean energy, satellite communications and spacecraft, water processing and other high tech industries.

Toyota became the world's largest car company in 2009, before losing a bit of ground to unprecedented product recalls. Nintendo's innovative Wii marked a virtual revolution in the large, global market for gaming and family entertainment products.

Japanese Society, Language and Culture

Japanese society is strikingly homogenous. Ethnic Japanese account for 98.5 percent of the country's sizeable population. While different areas of Japan, particularly the central Kansai region encompassing Osaka, Kyoto and Kobe, are known for having distinctive, colorful local dialects, the whole country essentially speaks the same language.

Traditional Japanese society and culture stress the values of harmony, consensus decision-making and social conformity. "The nail that sticks out gets hammered down" is a common Japanese saying and guideline of social behavior.

Japan's Aging, Shrinking Population

Japan's population has been aging and shrinking at an alarming rate due to the combination of a disproportionately large elderly population, one of the lowest fertility rates of any developed, OECD country and minimal net immigration. Japan's fertility rate of roughly 1.2 children born for every Japanese woman is well below the replacement level of 2.1 children per woman that is needed to maintain the existing population level. By 2050, the population of Japan has been forecasted to contract by more than 25 percent to about 95 million people.

International Relations and Foreign Policy

Japan has deliberately elected to take a largely passive stance toward involvement in international conflicts and disputes for most of its post-WWII history. Article 9 of The Constitution of Japan, adopted on November 3, 1946, renounces going to war or "the use of force as a means of settling international disputes." In lieu of a conventional military, Japan established the Japan Self-Defense Forces (also known as the SDF, JSDF or Jietai) as an extension of the Japanese police force and a strictly defensive mechanism to provide for the country's national security and assist with national emergencies.

Japan first deployed the SDF abroad in 1991 when it dispatched minesweepers to the Persian Gulf after fighting ceased in the 1991 Gulf War. Since Japan enacted the International Peace Cooperation Law in 1992, the Japanese government has deployed the SDF on certain overseas missions to support the U.N.'s international peacekeeping operations.

Japan largely relies on the U.S. for protection against external threats. Under the 1960 Treaty of Mutual Cooperation and Security between Japan and the U.S., the U.S. has agreed to defend Japan if the country or any of its territories come under attack. Roughly 40,000 U.S. military personnel and civilians in defense roles are stationed or employed on U.S. military bases located across Japan.

The majority of U.S. military personnel in Japan are stationed on the main island of Okinawa Prefecture in Japan's Ryukyu Islands, where U.S. military bases occupy about 18 percent of the territory. Japan pays roughly $2 billion as annual host-nation support to cover the costs and defense services of the U.S. military presence in Japan.

2

History

It is widely accepted that first human habitation in the Japanese archipelagocan be traced back to prehistoric times. The Jômon period, named after its "cord-marked" pottery, was followed by the Yayoi in the first millennium BC, when new technologies were introduced from continental Asia. During this period, in the first century AD, the first known written reference to Japan was recorded in the Chinese *Book of Han*. Between the fourth century and the ninth century, Japan's many kingdoms and tribes gradually came to be unified under a centralized government, nominally controlled by the Emperor. Theimperial dynasty established at this time continues to reign over Japan to this day. In 794, a new imperial capital was established at Heian-kyô (modernKyoto), marking the beginning of the Heian period, which lasted until 1185. The Heian period is considered a golden age of classical Japanese culture. Japanese religious life from this time and onwards was a mix of Buddhism, and native religious practices known as Shinto.

Over the following centuries the power of the Emperor and the imperial court gradually declined and passed to the military clans and their armies of samuraiwarriors. The Minamoto clan under Minamoto no Yoritomo emerged victorious from the Genpei War of 1180–85. After seizing power, Yoritomo set up his capital in Kamakura and took the title of *shôgun*. In 1274 and 1281, theKamakura shogunate withstood two Mongol invasions, but in 1333 it was toppled by a rival claimant to the shogunate, ushering in the Muromachi period. During the Muromachi period regional warlords called *daimyô* grew in power at the expense of the shogun. Eventually, Japan descended into a period of civil war. Over the course of the late sixteenth century, Japan was reunified under the leadership of the *daimyô* Oda Nobunaga and his successor Toyotomi Hideyoshi. After Hideyoshi's death in 1598, Tokugawa Ieyasu came to power and was appointed shogun by the Emperor. The Tokugawa shogunate, which governed from Edo (modern Tokyo), presided over a prosperous and peaceful era known as the Edo period (1600–1868). The Tokugawa shogunate imposed a strict class system on Japanese society and cut off almost all contact with the outside world.

The American Perry Expedition in 1853–54 ended Japan's seclusion; this in turn contributed to the fall of the shogunate and the return of power to the Emperor in 1868. The new national leadership of the following Meiji periodtransformed their isolated, underdeveloped island country into an empire that closely followed Western models and became a world power.

Although democracy developed and modern civilian culture prospered during the Taishô period (1912–26), Japan's powerful military had great autonomy and overruled Japan's civilian leaders in the 1920s and 1930s.

The military invaded Manchuria in 1931, and from 1937 the conflict escalated into a prolonged war with China. Japan's attack on Pearl Harbor in December 1941 led to war with the United States and its allies. Japan's forces soon became overextended, but the military held out in spite of Allied air attacks that inflicted severe damage on population centers. Japan's unconditional surrender was announced by EmperorHirohito on 15 August 1945 following the atomic bombings of Hiroshima and Nagasaki and the Soviet invasion of Manchuria.

The Allies occupied Japan until 1952, during which a new constitution was enacted in 1947 that transformed Japan into aconstitutional monarchy. After 1955, Japan enjoyed very high economic growth, and became a world economic powerhouse. Since the 1990s, economic stagnation has been a major issue. An earthquake and tsunami in 2011 caused massive economic dislocations and a serious nuclear power disaster.

GEOGRAPHICAL BACKGROUND

The mountainous Japanese archipelago stretches north to south 3,000/ km off the east of the Asian continent at the convergence of four tectonic plates; it has about forty active volcanoes and experiences about 1,000 earthquakes a year. The steep, craggy mountains that cover two-thirds of its surface are prone to quick erosion from fast-flowing rivers and to mudslides.

They thus have hampered internal travel and communication and driven the population to rely on transportation along coastal waters. There is a great variety to its regions' geographical features and weather patterns, with a rainy season in most parts in early summer. Volcanic soil that washes along the 13% of the area that makes up the coastal plains provides fertile land, and the mainly temperate climate allows long growing seasons, which with the diversity of flora and fauna provide rich resources able to support the density of the population.

PREHISTORIC AND ANCIENT JAPAN

Paleolithic and Jômon period

Land bridges (when world sea level was lower during the Ice Ages) have periodically linked the Japanese archipelago to the Asian continent at Korea in the southwest,Sakhalin in the north and over the Ryukyu isles with a landbridge to Taiwan andSundaland in the south. The earliest firm evidence of human habitation is of early Upper Paleolithic hunter-gatherers from 40,000 years ago, when Japan was separated from the continent. Edge-ground axes dating to 32–38,000 years ago, found in 224 sites in Honshu and Kyushu, are unlike anything found in neighbouring areas of continental Asia, and have been proposed as evidence for the first *Homo sapiens* in Japan; watercraft appear to have been in use in this period.Radiocarbon dating has shown that the earliest fossils in Japan date back to around 32,000-27,000 years ago; for example in the case of Yamashita Cave 32,100 ± 1,000 BP, in Sakitari Cave cal 31,000–29,000 BP, in Shiraho Saonetabaru Cave c. 27,000 BP among others.

The Jômon period of prehistoric Japan spans from about 12,000 BC (in some cases dates as early as 14,500 BC are given) to about 800 BC. Japan was inhabited by a hunter-gatherer culture that reached a considerable degree of sedentism and cultural complexity. The name "cord-marked" was first applied by the American scholar Edward S. Morse who discovered shards of pottery in 1877 and subsequently translated it into Japaneseas *jômon*. The pottery style characteristic of the first phases of Jômon culture was decorated by impressing cords into the surface of wet clay.

Yayoi period

New technologies and modes of living took over from the Jômon culture, spreading from northern Kyushu. The date of the change was until recently thought to be around 400 BC, but radio-carbon evidence suggests a date up to 500 years earlier, between 1,000 and 800 BC. The period was named after a district in Tokyo where a new, unembellished style of pottery was discovered in 1884. Though hunting and foraging continued, the Yayoi period brought a new reliance on agriculture. Bronze and iron weapons and tools were imported from China and Korea; such tools were later also produced in Japan. The Yayoi period also saw the introduction of weaving and silk production, glassmaking and new techniques of woodworking.

The Yayoi technologies originated on the Asian mainland. There is debate among scholars as to what extent their spread was accomplished by means of migration or simply a diffusion of ideas, or a combination of both. The migration theory is supported by genetic and linguistic studies. Hanihara Kazurô has suggested that the annual immigrant influx from the continent ranged from 350 to 3,000. Modern Japanese are genetically more similar to the Yayoi people than to the Jômon people – though more so in southern Japan than in the north – whereas the Ainu bear significant resemblance to the Jômon people. It took time for the Yayoi people and their descendants to fully displace or intermix with the Jômon, who continued to exist in northern Honshu until the eighth century AD.

The population of Japan began to increase rapidly, perhaps with a 10-fold rise over the Jômon. Calculations of the population size have varied from 1.5 to 4.5 million by the end of the Yayoi. Skeletal remains from the late Jômon period reveal a deterioration in already poor standards of health and nutrition, in contrast to Yayoi archaeological sites where there are large structures suggestive of grain storehouses. This change was accompanied by an increase in both the stratificationof society and tribal warfare, indicated by segregated gravesites and military fortifications. Yoshinogari site, a large moated village of the period, began to be excavated by archaeologists in the late-1980s.

During the Yayoi period, the Yayoi tribes gradually coalesced into a number of kingdoms. The earliest written work of history to mention Japan, the *Book of Han* completed around 82 AD, states that Japan, referred to as Wa, was divided into one hundred kingdoms. A later Chinese work of history, the *Wei Zhi*, states that by 240 AD one powerful kingdom had gained ascendancy over the others.

According to the *Wei Zhi*, this kingdom was called Yamatai, though modern historians continue to debate its location and other aspects of its depiction in the *Wei Zhi*. Yamatai was said to have been ruled by the female monarch Himiko.

Kofun period (c. 250–538)

During the subsequent Kofun period, most of Japan gradually unified under a single kingdom. The symbol of the growing power of Japan's new leaders was the *kofun* burial mounds they constructed from around 250 onwards. Many were of massive scale, such as the Daisenryô Kofun (ja), a 486 m-long keyhole-shaped burial mound that took huge teams of laborers fifteen years to complete. The *kofun* were often surrounded by and filled with numerous *haniwa* clay sculptures, often in the shape of warriors and horses.

The center of the unified state was Yamato in the Kinai region of central Japan.The rulers of the Yamato state were a hereditary line of Emperors who still reign as the world's longest dynasty. The rulers of the Yamato extended their power across Japan through military conquest, but their preferred method of expansion was to convince local leaders to accept their authority in exchange for positions of influence in the government. Many of the powerful local clans who joined the Yamato state became known as the *uji*.

These leaders sought and received formal diplomatic recognition from China, and Chinese accounts record five successive such leaders as the Five kings of Wa. Craftsmen and scholars from China and the Three Kingdoms of Korea played an important role in transmitting continental technologies and administrative skills to Japan during this period.

CLASSICAL JAPAN

Asuka period (538–710)

The Asuka period began in 538 with the introduction of the Buddhist religion from the Korean kingdom of Baekje. Since then, Buddhism has coexisted with Japan's native Shinto religion, in what is today known as Shinbutsu-shûgô. The period draws its name from the *de facto* imperial capital, Asuka, in the Kinai region.

The Buddhist Soga clan took over the government in 587 and controlled Japan from behind the scenes for nearly sixty years. Prince Shôtoku, an advocate of Buddhism and the Soga cause who was of partial Soga descent, served as regent and *de facto* leader of Japan from 594 to 622. Shôtoku authored the Seventeen-article constitution, a Confucian-inspired code of conduct for officials and citizens, and attempted to introduce a merit-based civil service called the Cap and Rank System. In 607 A.D., Shôtoku offered a subtle insult to China by opening his letter with the phrase, "The sovereign of the land where the sun rises is sending this mail to the sovereign of the land where the sun sets" as seen in the kanji characters for Japan (Nippon) thus indicating that sun's full strength originates with Japan and China receives the waning sun. and by 670 a variant of this expression, *Nihon,* established itself as the official name of the nation, which has persisted to this day.

In 645, the Soga clan were overthrown in a coup launched by Prince Naka no Ôe andFujiwara no Kamatari, the founder of theFujiwara clan. Their government devised and implemented the far-reaching Taika Reforms. The reforms nationalized all land in Japan, to be distributed equally among cultivators, and ordered the compilation of a household registry as the basis for a new system of taxation. Subsequently, the Jinshin War of 672, a bloody conflict between Prince Ôama and his nephew Prince Ôtomo, two rivals to the throne, became a major catalyst for further administrative reforms. These reforms culminated with the promulgation of the Taihô Code, which consolidated existing statutes and established the structure of the central government and its subordinate local governments. These legal reforms created the *ritsuryô* state, a system of Chinese-style centralized government that remained in place for half a millennium.

Nara period (710–794)

In 710, the government constructed a grandiose new capital at Heijô-kyô (modern Nara) modeled on Chang'an, the capital of the Chinese Tang dynasty. The first two books produced in Japan appeared during this period, the *Kojiki* and *Nihon Shoki*, which contain chronicles of legendary accounts of early Japan and its creation myth, which explains the imperial line being descendants of the gods. The latter half of the eighth century also saw the compilation of the *Man'yôshû*, widely considered the finest collection of Japanese poetry.

During this period, Japan suffered a series of natural disasters, including wildfires, droughts, famines, and outbreaks of disease, such as a smallpox epidemic that killed over a quarter of the population. Emperor Shômu (r. 724–49) feared his lack of piousness had caused the trouble and so increased the government's promotion of Buddhism, including the construction of the Tôdai-ji Temple. The funds to build this temple were raised in part by the influential Buddhist monkGyôki, and once completed it was used by the Chinese monk Ganjin as an ordination site. Japan nevertheless entered a phase of population decline that continued well into the subsequent Heian period.

Heian period (794–1185)

In 784, the capital moved briefly to Nagaoka-kyô, then again in 794 to Heian-kyô(modern Kyoto), which remained the capital until 1868. Political power within the court soon passed to the Fujiwara clan, a family of court nobles who grew increasingly close to the imperial family through intermarriage. In 858, Fujiwara no Yoshifusa had himself declared *sesshô* ("regent") to the underage Emperor. His sonFujiwara no Mototsune created the office of *kampaku*, which could rule in the place of an adult reigning Emperor. Fujiwara no Michinaga, a skilled statesman who became *kampaku* in 996, governed during the height of the Fujiwara clan's powerand had four of his daughters married to Japanese Emperors. The Fujiwara clan held on to power until 1086, when Emperor Shirakawa ceded the throne to his son Emperor Horikawa but continued to exercise political power, establishing the practice of cloistered rule, by which the reigning Emperor would function as a figurehead while real power was held by a retired predecessor behind the scenes.

Throughout the Heian period, the power of the imperial court declined. The court became so self-absorbed with power struggles, and with the artistic pursuits of court nobles, that it neglected the administration of government outside the capital. The nationalization of land undertaken as part of the *ritsuryô* state decayed as various noble families and religious orders succeeded in securing tax-exempt status for their private *shôen* manors. By the eleventh century, more land in Japan was controlled by *shôen* owners than by the central government. The imperial court was thus deprived of the tax revenue to pay for its national army. In response, the owners of the *shôen* set up their own armies of samurai warriors.Two powerful noble families that had descended from branches of the imperial family, the Taira and Minamoto clans, acquired large armies and many *shôen* outside the capital. The central government began to employ these two warrior clans to help suppress rebellions and piracy. Although Japan's population stabilized during the late-Heian period after hundreds of years of decline, this was accompanied by the growth of a new class of slaves composed of poor farmers, debtors, and criminals sold into bondage.

During the early Heian period, the imperial court successfully consolidated its control over the Emishi people of northern Honshu. Ôtomo no Otomaro was the first man the court granted the title of *seii tai-shôgun* ("Great Barbarian Subduing General"). In 802, seii tai-shôgun Sakanoue no Tamuramaro subjugated the Emishi people, who were led by Aterui. By 1051, members of the Abe clan, who occupied key posts in the regional government, were openly defying the central authority. The court requested the Minamoto clan to engage the Abe clan, whom they defeated in the Former Nine Years War. The court, thus, temporarily reasserted its authority in northern Japan. Following another civil war – the Later Three-Year War – Fujiwara no Kiyohira took full power; his family, the Northern Fujiwara, controlled northern Honshu for the next century from their capital Hiraizumi.

In 1156, a dispute over succession to the throne erupted and the two rival claimants (Emperor Go-Shirakawa and Emperor Sutoku) hired the Taira and Minamoto clans in the hopes of securing the throne by military force. During this war, the Taira clan led by Taira no Kiyomori defeated the Minamoto clan. Kiyomori used his victory to accumulate power for himself in Kyoto and even installed his own grandson Antoku as Emperor. The outcome of this war led to the rivalry between the Minamoto and Taira clans. As a result, the dispute and power struggle between both clans led to the Heiji Rebellion in 1160. In 1180, Taira no Kiyomori was challenged by an uprising led by Minamoto no Yoritomo, a member of the Minamoto clan whom Kiyomori had exiled to Kamakura. Though Taira no Kiyomori died in 1181, the ensuing bloody Genpei Warbetween the Taira and Minamoto families continued for another four years. The victory of the Minamoto clan was sealed in 1185, when a force commanded by Yoritomo's younger brother, Minamoto no Yoshitsune, scored a decisive victory at the naval Battle of Dan-no-ura. Yoritomo and his retainers, thus, became the *de facto* rulers of Japan.

Heian culture

During the Heian period, the imperial court was a vibrant center of high art and culture. Its literary accomplishments include the poetry collection *Kokinshû* and the *Tosa Diary*, both associated with the poet Ki no Tsurayuki, as well as Sei Shônagon's collection of miscellany

The Pillow Book, and Murasaki Shikibu's *Tale of Genji*, considered the supreme masterpiece of Japanese literature.

The development of the kana written syllabaries was part of a general trend of declining Chinese influence during the Heian period. The Japanese missions toTang dynasty of China, which began in the year 630, ended during the ninth century and thereafter more typically Japanese forms of art and poetry developed. A major architectural achievement, apart from Heian-kyô itself, was the temple of Byôdô-in built in 1053 inUji.

MEDIEVAL JAPAN

Kamakura period (1185–1333)

Upon the consolidation of power, Minamoto no Yoritomo chose to rule in consort with the imperial court in Kyoto. Though Yoritomo set up his own government in Kamakura in the Kantô region located east of Japan, its power was legally authorized by the Imperial court in Kyoto in several occasions. In 1192, the Emperor declared Yoritomo *seii tai-shôgun* (*Eastern Barbarian Subduing Great General*), abbreviated *shôgun*. Later (in Edo period), the word *bakufu* (originally means a general's house or office, literally a "tent office") came to be used to mean a government headed by a shogun. The English term *shogunate* refers to the *bakufu*. Japan remained largely under military rule until 1868.

Legitimacy was conferred on the shogunate by the Imperial court, but the shogunate were the *de facto* rulers of the country. The court maintained bureaucratic and religious functions, and the shogunate welcomed participation by members of the aristocratic class. The older institutions remained intact in a weakened form, and Kyoto remained the official capital. This system has been contrasted with the "simple warrior rule" of the later Muromachi period.

While the Ise branch (ja) of the Taira, which had fought against Yoritomo, was extinguished, other branches, as well as theHôjô, Chiba, Hatakeyama and other families descended from the Taira, continued to thrive in eastern Japan, with some (notably the Hôjô) attaining high positions in the Kamakura shogunate. Yoshitsune was initially harbored by Fujiwara no Hidehira, the grandson of Kiyohira and the de facto ruler of northern Honshu. In 1189, after Hidehira's death, his successor Yasuhira attempted to curry favor with Yoritomo by attacking Yoshitsune's home. Although Yoshitsune was killed, Yoritomo still invaded and conquered the Northern Fujiwara clan's territories. In subsequent centuries, Yoshitsune would become a legendary figure, portrayed in countless works of literature as an idealized tragic hero.

After Yoritomo's death in 1199, the office of shogun weakened. Behind the scenes, Yoritomo's wife Hôjô Masako became the true power behind the government. In 1203, her father, Hôjô Tokimasa, was appointed regent to the shogun, Yoritomo's sonMinamoto no Sanetomo. Henceforth, the Minamoto shoguns became puppets of the Hôjô regents, who wielded actual power.

The regime which Yoritomo had established and which was kept in place by his successors was decentralized and feudalistic in structure, in contrast with the earlier ritsuryô state. Yoritomo selected the provincial governors, known under the titles of*shugo* or *jitô*, from among his close vassals, the *gokenin*. The Kamakura shogunate allowed its vassals to maintain their own armies and to administer law and order in their provinces on their own terms.

In 1221, the retired Emperor Go-Toba instigated what became known as the Jôkyû War, a rebellion against the shogunate, in an attempt to restore political power to the court. The rebellion was a failure, and led to Go-Toba himself being exiled toOki Island, along with two other Emperors, the retired Emperor Tsuchimikado and Emperor Juntoku, who were exiled to Tosa Province and Sado Island respectively. The shogunate further consolidated its political power relative to the Kyoto aristocracy.

The samurai armies of the whole nation were mobilized in 1274 and 1281 to confront two full-scale invasions launched byKublai Khan of the Mongol Empire. Though outnumbered by an enemy equipped with superior weaponry, the Japanese fought the Mongols to a standstill in Kyushu on both occasions until the Mongol fleet was destroyed by typhoons called*kamikaze*, meaning "divine wind". In spite of the Kamakura shogunate's victory, the defense so depleted its finances that it was unable to provide compensation to its vassals for their role in the victory. This had permanent negative consequences for the shogunate's relations with the samurai class.

Discontent among the samurai proved decisive in ending the Kamakura shogunate. In 1333, Emperor Go-Daigo launched a rebellion in the hope of restoring full power to the imperial court. The shogunate sent General Ashikaga Takauji to quell the revolt, but Takauji and his men instead joined forces with Emperor Go-Daigo and overthrew the Kamakura shogunate.

Japan nevertheless entered a period of prosperity and population growth starting around 1250. In rural areas, the greater use of iron tools and fertilizer, improved irrigation techniques, and double-cropping increased productivity and rural villages grew. Fewer famines and epidemics allowed cities to grow and commerce to boom. Buddhism, which had been largely a religion of the elites, was brought to the masses by prominent monks, such as Hônen (1133–1212), who established Pure Land Buddhism in Japan, and Nichiren (1222–82), who founded Nichiren Buddhism. Zen Buddhism spread widely among the samurai class.

Literary developments of the late-Heian and Kamakura periods

Waka poetry flourished in the late Heian and early Kamakura periods.

The aristocrat Fujiwara no Shunzei was "the leading poet of [his] day" and on a request from Emperor Go-Shirakawacompiled the *Senzai Wakashû* the seventh imperial collection. Donald Keene noted that Shunzei was "the most eminent poet since Tsurayuki to have been charged with the compilation of an imperial collection". The anthology, commissioned in 1183 but not completed until 1188, after the defeat of the Taira, contained poems by Taira adherents who had been officially denounced as enemies of the throne, as a gesture to calm the vengeful spirits of the Taira. It also contained poems by thirty-three female poets, the most women recognized by any of the late-Heian imperial collections. Teika, Shunzei's son, would become even more important: his *Hyakunin Isshu* made him "the arbiter of the poetic tastes of most Japanese even as late as the twentieth century". His later work copying manuscripts was of such importance that Keene noted that "what we know of the literature of Teika's day and earlier is mainly what he thought was worthy of preservation." He also served on the committee that compiled the eighth imperial anthology, the *Shin Kokin Wakashû,*and along with the itinerant monk Saigyô and Emperor Go-Toba, is considered one of the best poets represented in the collection. More poems by Saigyô were included in the collection than those of any other poet. and centuries laterMatsuo Bashô selected him as the representative poet of the *waka* genre.

The third shogun, Minamoto no Sanetomo, was the first distinctive new poet of the Kamakura period, and he studied the art under Teika's tutelage. Among Sanetomo's admirers include Kamo no Mabuchi and Saitô Mokichi.

Zen monks were associated with the composition of poetry in Chinese, and at least one Zen monk, Shôtetsu, was notable for his contributions to the *waka* medium. After Shôtetsu, however, *waka* composition became an oddity until modern times.

The Kamakura period saw an explosion in the popularity of a new genre: the "war tale" (*gunki monogatari*), whose early representative works include the *Hôgen Monogatari*, *Heiji Monogatari* and *Heike Monogatari*. The latter work, which recounted the rise and fall of the Taira clan, has been described as "the Japanese epic", and the twentieth century novelist and essayist Kafû Nagai called it "a unique and immortal Japanese *épopée*." These works were at least partly indebted to earlier Heian works such as the *Shômonki* and *Mutsu Waki* , bare historical chronicles of battles fought against Taira no Masakado and the Earlier Nine Years' War, narrated in a non-literary style of classical Chinese as opposed to the mixed Sino-Japanese vernacular of the later Kamakura works.

Muromachi period (1333–1568)

Takauji and many other samurai soon became dissatisfied with Emperor Go-Daigo'sKenmu Restoration, an ambitious attempt to monopolize power in the imperial court. Takauji rebelled after Go-Daigo refused to appoint him shogun. In 1338, Takauji captured Kyoto and installed a rival member of the imperial family to the throne,Emperor Kômyô, who did appoint him shogun. Go-Daigo responded by fleeing to the southern city of Yoshino, where he set up a rival government. This ushered in a prolonged period of conflict between the Northern Court and the Southern Court.

Takauji set up his shogunate in the Muromachi district of Kyoto. However, the shogunate was faced with the twin challenges of fighting the Southern Court and of maintaining its authority over its own subordinate governors. Like the Kamakura shogunate, the Muromachi shogunate appointed its allies to rule in the provinces, but increasingly these men styled themselves as feudal lords — called *daimyôs* — of their domains and they often refused to obey the shogun. The Ashikaga shogun who was most successful at bringing the country together was Takauji's grandson Ashikaga Yoshimitsu, who came to power in 1368 and remained influential until his death in 1408. Yoshimitsu expanded the power of the shogunate and in 1392, brokered a deal to bring the Northern and Southern Courts together and end the civil war. Henceforth, the shogunate kept the Emperor and his court under tight control.

During the final century of the Ashikaga shogunate the country descended into another, more violent period of civil war. This started in 1467 when the Ônin Warbroke out over who would succeed the ruling shogun. The *daimyôs* each took sides and burned Kyoto to the ground while battling for their preferred candidate. By the time the succession was settled in 1477, the shogun had lost all power over the*daimyô*, who now ruled hundreds of independent states throughout Japan.During this Warring States period, *daimyôs* fought among themselves for control of the country. Some of the most powerful *daimyôs* of the era were Uesugi Kenshin,Takeda Shingen, and Date Masamune. One enduring symbol of this era was the ninja, skilled spies and assassins hired by *daimyôs*. Few definite historical facts are known about the secretive lifestyles of the ninja, who became the subject of many legends. In addition to the*daimyôs*, rebellious peasants and "warrior monks" affiliated with Buddhist temples also raised their own armies.

Amid this on-going anarchy, a Chinese ship was blown off course and landed in 1543 on the Japanese island of Tanegashima, just south of Kyushu. The threePortuguese traders on board were António Mota, Francisco Zeimoto, and presumably Fernão Mendes Pinto. They were the first Europeans to set foot in Japan. Soon European traders would introduce many new items to Japan, most importantly the musket. By 1556, the *daimyôs* were already using about 300,000 muskets in their armies. The Europeans also brought Christianity, which soon came to have a substantial following in Japan. The Jesuit missionary Francis Xavierdisembarked in Kyushu in 1549.

Muromachi culture

In spite of the war, Japan's relative economic prosperity, which had begun in the Kamakura period, continued well into the Muromachi period. By 1450 Japan's population stood at ten million, compared to six million at the end of the thirteenth century. Commerce flourished, including considerable trade with China and Korea. Because the *daimyôs* and other groups within Japan were minting their own coins, Japan began to transition from a barter-based to a currency-based economy. During the period, some of Japan's most representative art forms developed, including ink wash painting,*ikebana* flower arrangement, the tea ceremony, Japanese gardening, *bonsai*, and *Noh* theater. Though the eighth Ashikaga shogun, Yoshimasa, was an ineffectual political and military leader, he played a critical role in promoting these cultural developments.

EARLY MODERN PERIOD

Azuchi–Momoyama period (1568–1600)

During the second half of the 16th century Japan gradually reunified under two powerful warlords, Oda Nobunaga andToyotomi Hideyoshi. The period takes its name from Nobunaga's headquarters, Azuchi Castle, and Hideyoshi's headquarters, Momoyama Castle.

Nobunaga was the *daimyô* of the small province of Owari. He burst onto the scene suddenly in 1560 when, during the Battle of Okehazama, his army defeated a force several times its size led by the powerful *daimyô* Imagawa Yoshimoto.Nobunaga was renowned for his strategic leadership and his ruthlessness. He encouraged Christianity to incite hatred toward his Buddhist enemies and to forge strong relationships with European arms merchants. He equipped his armies with muskets and trained them with innovative tactics. He promoted talented men regardless of their social status, including his peasant servant Toyotomi Hideyoshi, who became one of his best generals.

The Azuchi–Momoyama period began in 1568 when Nobunaga seized Kyoto and thus effectively brought an end to the Ashikaga shogunate. He was well on his way towards his goal of reuniting all Japan in 1582 when one of his own officers,Akechi Mitsuhide, killed him during an abrupt attack on his encampment. Hideyoshi avenged Nobunaga by crushing Akechi's uprising and emerged as Nobunaga's successor. Hideyoshi completed the reunification of Japan by conqueringShikoku, Kyushu, and the lands of the Hôjô family in eastern Japan. He launched sweeping changes to Japanese society, including the confiscation of swords from the peasantry, new restrictions on *daimyôs*, persecutions of Christians, a thorough land survey, and a new law effectively forbidding the peasants and samurai from changing their social class. Hideyoshi's land survey designated all those who were cultivating the land as being "commoners", an act which effectively granted freedom to most of Japan's slaves.

As Hideyoshi's power expanded he dreamed of conquering China and launched two massive invasions of Korea starting in 1592. Hideyoshi failed to defeat the Chinese and Korean armies on the Korean Peninsula and the war ended only after his death in 1598.

In the hope of founding a new dynasty, Hideyoshi had asked his most trusted subordinates to pledge loyalty to his infant sonToyotomi

Hideyori. Despite this, almost immediately after Hideyoshi's death, war broke out between Hideyori's allies and those loyal to Tokugawa Ieyasu, a *daimyô* and a former ally of Hideyoshi. Tokugawa Ieyasu won a decisive victory at theBattle of Sekigahara in 1600, ushering in 268 uninterrupted years of rule by the Tokugawa clan.

Edo period (1600–1868)

The Edo period was characterized by relative peace and stability under the tight control of the Tokugawa shogunate, which ruled from the eastern city of Edo(modern Tokyo). In 1603, Emperor Go-Yôzei declared Tokugawa Ieyasu shogun, and Ieyasu abdicated two years later to groom his son as the second shogun of what became a long dynasty. Nevertheless, it took time for the Tokugawas to consolidate their rule. In 1609, the shogun gave the *daimyô* of Satsuma Domainpermission to invade the Ryukyu Kingdom for perceived insults towards the shogunate; the Satsuma victory began 266 years of Ryukyu's dual subordination to Satsuma and China. Ieyasu led the Siege of Osaka that ended with the destruction of the Toyotomi clan in 1615. Soon after the shogunate promulgated the Laws for the Military Houses, which imposed tighter controls on the *daimyôs*,and the alternate attendance system, which required each *daimyô* to spend every other year in Edo. Even so, the *daimyôs* continued to maintain a significant degree of autonomy in their domains. The central government of the shogunate in Edo, which quickly became the most populous city in the world, took counsel from a group of senior advisors known as *rôjû* and employed samurai as bureaucrats. The Emperor in Kyoto was funded lavishly by the government but was allowed no political power.

The Tokugawa shogunate went to great lengths to suppress social unrest. Harsh penalties, including crucifixion, beheading, and death by boiling, were decreed for even the most minor offenses, though criminals of high social class were often given the option of *seppuku* ("self-disembowelment"), an ancient form of suicide that now became ritualized. Christianity, which was seen as a potential threat, was gradually clamped down on until finally, after the Christian-led Shimabara Rebellion of 1638, the religion was completely outlawed. To prevent further foreign ideas from sowing dissent, the third Tokugawa shogun, Iemitsu, implemented the *sakoku* ("closed country") isolationist policy under which Japanese people were not allowed to travel abroad, return from overseas, or build ocean-going vessels.The only Europeans allowed on Japanese soil were the Dutch, who were granted a single trading post on the island of Dejima. China and Korea were the only other countries permitted to trade, and many foreign books were banned from import.

During the first century of Tokugawa rule, Japan's population doubled to thirty million, due in large part to agricultural growth; the population remained stable for the rest of the period. The shogunate's construction of roads, elimination of road and bridge tolls, and standardization of coinage promoted commercial expansion that also benefited the merchants and artisans of the cities. City populations grew, but almost ninety percent of the population continued to live in rural areas. Both the inhabitants of cities and of rural communities would benefit from one of the most notable social changes of the Edo period: increased literacy and numeracy. The number of private schools greatly expanded, particularly those attached to temples and shrines, and raised literacy to thirty percent. This may have been the world's highest rate at the time and drove a flourishing commercial publishing industry, which grew to produce hundreds of titles per year. In the area of numeracy – approximated by an index measuring people's ability to report an exact rather than a rounded age (age-heaping method), and which level shows a strong correlation to later economic development of a country – Japan's level was comparable to that of north-west European countries, and moreover, Japan's index came close to the 100 percent mark throughout the nineteenth century. These high levels of both literacy and numeracy were part of the socio-economical foundation for Japan's strong growth rates during the following century

Culture and philosophy

The Edo period was a time of prolific cultural output. Haiku, whose greatest master is generally considered Matsuo Bashô(1644–94), rose as a major form of poetry. Forms of theatre developed, such as the flamboyant kabuki drama and*bunraku* puppet theatre, the latter of which reached its height of through the plays of Chikamatsu Monzaemon (1653–1725). Members of the wealthy merchant class who patronized this poetry and theater were said to live hedonistic lives, which came to be called *ukiyo* ("floating world"). They often paid for the services of courtesans and geisha entertainers, most of whom also served as prostitutes in designated red-light districts such as Yoshiwara in Edo. This lifestyle inspired*ukiyo-zôshi* popular novels and *ukiyo-e* art, the latter of which were often woodblock prints that progressed to greater sophistication and use of multiple printed colors.

Decline and fall of the shogunate

By the late eighteenth and early nineteenth centuries, the shogunate showed signs of weakening. The dramatic growth of agriculture that had characterized the early Edo period had ended and the government handled the devastatingTenpô famines poorly. Peasant unrest grew and government revenues fell. The shogunate cut the pay of the already financially distressed samurai, many of whom worked side jobs to make a living. Discontented samurai were soon to play a major role in engineering the downfall of the Tokugawa shogunate.

At the same time, the people drew inspiration from new ideas and fields of study. Dutch books brought into Japan stimulated interest in Western learning, called *rangaku* or "Dutch learning". The physician Sugita Genpaku, for instance, used concepts from Western medicine to help spark a revolution in Japanese ideas of human anatomy. The scholarly field of*kokugaku* or "National Learning", developed by scholars such as Motoori Norinaga and Hirata Atsutane, promoted what it asserted were native Japanese values. For instance, it criticized the Chinese-style Neo-Confucianism advocated by the shogunate and emphasized the Emperor's divine authority, which the Shinto faith taught had its roots in Japan's mythic past, which was referred to as the "Age of the Gods".

The arrival in 1853 of a fleet of American ships commanded by CommodoreMatthew C. Perry threw Japan into turmoil. The US government aimed to end Japan's isolationist policies. The shogunate had no defense against Perry's gunboats and had to agree to his demands that American ships be permitted to acquire provisions and trade at Japanese ports. The US, Great Britain, Russia, and other Western powers imposed what became known as "unequal treaties" on Japan which stipulated that Japan must allow citizens of these countries to visit or reside on Japanese territory and must not levy tariffs on their imports or try them in Japanese courts.

The shogunate's failure to oppose the Western powers angered many Japanese, particularly those of the southern domains of Chôshû and Satsuma. Many samurai there, inspired by the nationalist doctrines of the kokugaku school, adopted the slogan of *sonnô jôi* ("revere the Emperor, expel the barbarians"). The two domains then went on to form an alliance. In August 1866, soon after becoming shogun,

Tokugawa Yoshinobu, struggled to maintain power as civil unrest continued. In November 1867, Yoshinobu officially tendered his resignation to the Emperor and he formally stepped down ten days later. The Chôshû and Satsuma domains in 1868 convinced the young Emperor Meiji and his advisors to issue a rescript calling for an end to the Tokugawa shogunate. The armies of Chôshû and Satsuma soon marched on Edo and the ensuing Boshin War led to the eventual fall of the shogunate.

MODERN JAPAN

Meiji period (1868–1912)

The Emperor was restored to nominal supreme power, and in 1869, the imperial family moved to Edo, which was renamed Tokyo ("eastern capital"). However, the most powerful men in the government were former samurai from Chôshû and Satsuma rather than the Emperor, who was fifteen in 1868. These men, known as the Meiji oligarchs, oversaw the dramatic changes Japan would experience during this period. The leaders of theMeiji government, who are regarded as some of the most successful statesmen in human history, desired Japan to become a modern nation-state that could stand equal to the Western imperialist powers. Among them were Ôkubo Toshimichi and Saigô Takamorifrom Satsuma, as well as Kido Takayoshi, Ito Hirobumi, and Yamagata Aritomo from Chôshû.

Political and social changes

The Meiji government abolished the Neo-Confucian class structure, and replaced the feudal domains of the *daimyôs* with prefectures. It instituted comprehensive tax reform and lifted the ban on Christianity. Major government priorities included the introduction of railways, telegraph lines, and a universal education system.

The Meiji government promoted widespread Westernization and hired hundreds of advisers from Western nations with expertise in such fields as education, mining, banking, law, military affairs, and transportation to remodel Japan's institutions.The Japanese adopted the Gregorian calendar, Western clothing, and Western hairstyles. One leading advocate of Westernization was the popular writerFukuzawa Yukichi. As part of its Westernization drive, the Meiji government enthusiastically sponsored the importation of Western science, above all medical science. In 1893, Kitasato

Shibasaburô established the Institute for Infectious Diseases, which would soon become world-famous, and in 1913, Hideyo Noguchiproved the link between syphilis and paresis. Furthermore, the introduction of European literary styles to Japan sparked a boom in new works of prose fiction. Characteristic authors of the period included Futabatei Shimei and Mori Ôgai,although the most famous of the Meiji era writers was Natsume Sôseki, who wrote satirical, autobiographical, and psychological novels combining both the older and newer styles. Ichiyô Higuchi, a leading female author, took inspiration from earlier literary models of the Edo period.

Government institutions developed rapidly in response to Freedom and People's Rights Movement, a grassroots campaign demanding greater popular participation in politics. The leaders of this movement included Itagaki Taisuke and Ôkuma Shigenobu. Itô Hirobumi, the first Prime Minister of Japan, responded by writing the Meiji Constitution, which was promulgated in 1889. The new constitution established an elected lower house, the House of Representatives, but its powers were restricted. Only two percent of the population were eligible to vote, and legislation proposed in the House required the support of the unelected upper house, the House of Peers. Both the cabinet of Japan and the Japanese military were directly responsible not to the elected legislature but to the Emperor. Concurrently, the Japanese government also developed a form of Japanese nationalism under which Shinto became the state religion and the Emperor was declared a living god. Schools nationwide instilled patriotic values and loyalty to the Emperor.

Rise of imperialism and the military

In December 1871, a Ryukyuan ship was shipwrecked on Taiwan and the crew were massacred. In 1874, using the incident as a pretext, Japan launched a military expedition to Taiwan to assert their claims to the Ryukyu Islands. The expedition featured the first instance of the Japanese military ignoring the orders of the civilian government, as the expedition set sail after being ordered to postpone.

Yamagata Aritomo, who was born a samurai in the Chôshû Domain, was a key force behind the modernization and enlargement of the Imperial Japanese Army, especially introduction of national conscription. The new army was put to use in 1877 to crush the Satsuma Rebellion of discontented samurai in southern Japan led by the former Meiji leader Saigo Takamori.

The Japanese military played a key role in Japan's expansion abroad. The government believed that Japan had to acquire its own colonies to compete with the Western colonial powers. After consolidating its control over Hokkaido and annexing the Ryukyu Kingdom, it next turned its attention to China and Korea. In 1894, Japanese and Chinese troops clashed in Korea, where they were both stationed to suppress the Donghak Rebellion. During the ensuing First Sino-Japanese War, Japan's highly motivated and well-led forces defeated the more numerous and better-equipped military of Qing China.The island of Taiwan was thus ceded to Japan in 1895, and Japan's government gained enough international prestige to allow Foreign Minister Mutsu Munemitsu to renegotiate the "unequal treaties". In 1902 Japan signed an important military alliance with the British.

Japan next clashed with Russia, which was expanding its power in Asia. The Russo-Japanese War of 1904–05 ended with the dramatic Battle of Tsushima, which was another victory for Japan's military. Japan thus laid claim to Korea as a protectorate in 1905, followed by full annexation in 1910.

Economic modernization and labor unrest

During the Meiji period, Japan underwent a rapid transition towards an industrial economy. Both the Japanese government and private entrepreneurs adopted Western technology and knowledge to create factories capable of producing a wide range of goods. By the end of the period, the majority of Japan's exports were manufactured goods. Some of Japan's most successful new businesses and industries constituted huge family-owned conglomerates called *zaibatsu*, such as Mitsubishi and Sumitomo. The phenomenal industrial growth sparked rapid urbanization. The proportion of the population working in agriculture shrank from 75 percent in 1872 to 50 percent by 1920.

Japan enjoyed solid economic growth at this time and most people lived longer and healthier lives. The population rose from 34 million in 1872 to 52 million in 1915. Poor working conditions in factories led to growing labor unrest, and many workers and intellectuals came to embrace socialist ideas. The Meiji government responded with harsh suppression of dissent. Radical socialists plotted to assassinate the Emperor in the High Treason Incident of 1910, after which the Tokkôsecret police force was established to root out left-wing agitators. The government also introduced social legislation in 1911 setting maximum work hours and a minimum age for employment.

TAISHÔ PERIOD (1912–1926)

Emperor Taishô's short reign saw Japan develop stronger democratic institutions and grow in international power. TheTaishô political crisis opened the period with mass protests and riots organized by Japanese political parties. These succeeded in forcing Katsura Tarô to resign as prime minister.

This and the rice riots of 1918 increased the power of Japan's political parties over the ruling oligarchy. The Seiyûkai and Minseitô parties came to dominate politics by the end of the so-called "Taishô democracy" era. The franchise for the House of Representatives had been gradually expanded since 1890, and in 1925 universal male suffrage was introduced. However, the same year also saw passage of the far-reaching Peace Preservation Law that prescribed harsh penalties for political dissidents.

Japan's participation in World War I on the side of the Allies sparked unprecedented economic growth and earned Japannew colonies in the South Pacific seized from Germany. After the war Japan signed the Treaty of Versailles and enjoyed good international relations through its membership in the League of Nations and participation in international disarmament conferences. The Great Kantô earthquake in September 1923 left over 100,000 dead, and combined with the resultant fires destroyed the homes of more than three million.

The growth of popular prose fiction, which began during the Meiji period, continued into the Taishô period as literacy rates rose and book prices dropped. Notable literary figures of the era included short story writer Ryûnosuke Akutagawaand the novelist Haruo Satô. Jun'ichirô Tanizaki, described as "perhaps the most versatile literary figure of his day" by the historian Conrad Totman, produced many works during the Taishô period influenced by European literature, though his 1929 novel *Some Prefer Nettles* reflects deep appreciation for the virtues of traditional Japanese culture. At the end of the Taishô period, Tarô Hirai, known by his penname Edogawa Ranpo, began writing popular mystery and crime stories.

Shôwa period (1926–1989)

Emperor Hirohito's sixty-three-year reign from 1926 to 1989 is the longest in recorded Japanese history. The first twenty years were characterized by the rise of extreme nationalism and a series of expansionist wars. After suffering defeat in World War II, Japan was occupied by foreign powers for the first time in its history, and then re-emerged as a major world economic power.

Manchurian Incident and the Second Sino-Japanese War

Left-wing groups had been subject to violent suppression by the end of the Taishô period, and radical right-wing groups, inspired by fascism and Japanese nationalism, rapidly grew in popularity. The extreme right became influential throughout the Japanese government and society, notably within the Kwantung Army, a Japanese army stationed in China along the Japanese-owned South Manchuria Railroad. During the Manchurian Incident of 1931, radical army officers bombed a small portion of the South Manchuria Railroad and, falsely attributing the attack to the Chinese, invaded Manchuria. The Kwantung Army conquered Manchuria and set up the puppet government of Manchukuo there without permission from the Japanese government. International criticism of Japan following the invasion led to Japan withdrawing from the League of Nations.

Prime Minister Tsuyoshi Inukai of the Seiyûkai Party attempted to restrain the Kwantung Army and was assassinated in 1932 by right-wing extremists. Because of growing opposition within the Japanese military and the extreme right to party politicians, who they saw as corrupt and self-serving, Inukai was the last party politician to govern Japan in the pre-World War II era. In February 1936 young radical officers of the Imperial Japanese Army attempted a coup d'état. They assassinated many moderate politicians before the coup was suppressed. In its wake the Japanese military consolidated its control over the political system and most political parties were abolished when the Imperial Rule Assistance Association was founded in 1940.

Japan's expansionist vision grew increasingly bold. Many of Japan's political elite aspired to have Japan acquire new territory for resource extraction and settlement of surplus population. These ambitions led to the outbreak of the Second Sino-Japanese War in 1937. After their victory in the Chinese capital, the Japanese military committed the infamous Nanking Massacre. The Japanese military failed to defeat the Chinese government led by Chiang Kai-shek and the war descended into a bloody stalemate that lasted until 1945. Japan's stated war aim was to establish the Greater East Asia Co-Prosperity Sphere, a vast pan-Asian union under Japanese domination. Hirohito's role in Japan's foreign wars remains a subject of controversy, with various historians portraying him as either a powerless figurehead or an enabler and supporter of Japanese militarism.

The United States opposed Japan's invasion of China and responded with increasingly stringent economic sanctions intended to deprive Japan of the resources to continue its war in China. Japan reacted by forging an alliance with Germany and Italy in 1940, known as the Tripartite Pact, which worsened its relations with the US. In July 1941, the United States, the United Kingdom, and the Netherlands froze all Japanese assets when Japan completed its invasion of French Indochina by occupying the southern half of the country, further increasing tension in the Pacific.

World War II

In late 1941, Japan's government, led by Prime Minister and General Hideki Tojo, decided to break the US-led embargo through force of arms. On December 7, 1941, the Imperial Japanese Navy launched a surprise attack on the American fleet at Pearl Harbor, Hawaii. This brought the US into World War II on the side of theAllies. Japan then successfully invaded the Asian colonies of the United States, the United Kingdom, and the Netherlands, including the Philippines, Malaya, Hong Kong,Singapore, Burma, and the Dutch East Indies.

In the early stages of the war, Japan scored victory after victory. The tide began to turn against Japan following the Battle of Midway in June 1942 and the subsequentBattle of Guadalcanal, in which Allied troops wrested the Solomon Islands from Japanese control. During this period the Japanese military was responsible for such war crimes as mistreatment of prisoners of war, massacres of civilians, and the use of chemical and biological weapons. The Japanese military earned a reputation for fanaticism, often employingbanzai charges and fighting almost to the last man against overwhelming odds. In 1944 the Imperial Japanese Navy began deploying squadrons of *kamikaze* pilots who crashed their planes into enemy ships.

Life in Japan became increasingly difficult for civilians due to stringent rationing of food, electrical outages, and a brutal crackdown on dissent. In 1944 the US Army captured the island of Saipan, which allowed the United States to begin widespreadbombing raids on the Japanese mainland. These destroyed over half of the total area of Japan's major cities. The Battle of Okinawa, fought between April and June 1945, was the largest naval operation of the war and left 77,166

Japanese soldiers and more than 140,000 Okinawans dead, suggesting that the plannedinvasion of mainland Japan would be even bloodier. The Japanese superbattleship *Yamato* was sunk en route to aid in the Battle of Okinawa.

However, on August 6, 1945, the US dropped an atomic bomb over Hiroshima, killing over 90,000 people. This was the first nuclear attack in history. On August 9 theSoviet Union declared war on Japan and invaded Manchukuo, and Nagasaki was struck by a second atomic bomb. The unconditional surrender of Japan was announced by Emperor Hirohito and communicated to the Allies on August 14, andbroadcast on national radio on the following day, marking the end of Imperial Japan's ultranationalist ideology, and was a major turning point in Japanese history.

Occupation of Japan

Japan experienced dramatic political and social transformation under the Allied occupation in 1945–1952. US General Douglas MacArthur, the Supreme Commander of Allied Powers, served as Japan's *de facto* leader and played a central role in implementing reforms, many inspired by the New Deal of the 1930s.

The occupation sought to decentralize power in Japan by breaking up the *zaibatsu*, transferring ownership of agricultural land from landlords to tenant farmers, and promoting labor unionism. Other major goals were the demilitarization and democratization of Japan's government and society. Japan's military was disarmed,its colonies were granted independence,the Peace Preservation Law and Tokkô were abolished, and the International Military Tribunal of the Far East tried war criminals. The cabinet became responsible not to the Emperor but to the elected National Diet. The Emperor was permitted to remain on the throne, but was ordered torenounce his claims to divinity, which had been a pillar of the State Shinto system. Japan's new constitution came into effect in 1947 and guaranteed civil liberties, labor rights, and women's suffrage, and through Article 9, Japan renounced its right to go to war with another nation.

The San Francisco Peace Treaty of 1951 officially normalized relations between Japan and the United States. The occupation ended in 1952, although the US continued to administer a number of the Ryukyu Islands, with Okinawa being the last to be returned in 1972. The US continues to operate military bases throughout the Ryukyu Islands, mostly on Okinawa, as part of the US-Japan Security Treaty.

Postwar growth and prosperity

Shigeru Yoshida served as prime minister in 1946–47 and 1948–54, and played a key role in guiding Japan through the occupation. His policies, known as the Yoshida Doctrine, proposed that Japan should forge a tight relationship with the United States and focus on developing the economy rather than pursuing a proactive foreign policy. Yoshida'sLiberal Party merged in 1955 into the new Liberal Democratic Party (LDP), which went on to dominate Japanese politics for the remainder of the Shôwa period.

Though the Japanese economy was in bad shape in the immediate postwar years, an austerity program implemented in 1949 by finance expert Joseph Dodge ended inflation.The Korean War (1950–53) was a major boon to Japanese business. In 1949 the Yoshida cabinet created the Ministry of International Trade and Industry (MITI) with a mission to promote economic growth through close cooperation between the government and big business. MITI sought successfully to promote manufacturing and heavy industry, and encourage exports. The factors behind Japan's postwar economic growth included technology and quality control techniques imported from the West, close economic and defense cooperation with the United States, non-tariff barriers to imports, restrictions on labor unionization, long work hours, and a generally favorable global economic environment. Japanese corporations successfully retained a loyal and experienced workforce through the system of lifetime employment, which assured their employees a safe job.

By 1955, the Japanese economy had grown beyond prewar levels and it had become the second largest in the world by 1968. The GNP expanded at an annual rate of nearly 10% from 1956 until the 1973 oil crisis slowed growth to a still-rapid average annual rate of just over 4% until 1991. Life expectancy rose and Japan's population increased to 123 million by 1990. Ordinary Japanese people became wealthy enough to purchase a wide array of consumer goods. During this period, Japan became the world's largest manufacturer of automobiles and a leading producer of electronics. Japan signed the Plaza Accord in 1985 to depreciate the US dollar against the yen and other currencies. By the end of 1987, theNikkei stock market index had doubled and the Tokyo Stock Exchange became the largest in the world. During the ensuing economic bubble, stock and real-estate loans grew rapidly.

Japan became a member of the United Nations in 1956 and further cemented its international standing in 1964, when it hosted the Olympic

Games in Tokyo. Japan was a close ally of the United States during the Cold War, though this alliance did not have unanimous support from the Japanese people. As requested by the United States, Japan reconstituted its army in 1954 under the name Japan Self-Defense Forces (JSDF), though some Japanese insisted that the very existence of the JSDF was a violation of Article 9 of Japan's constitution. In 1960, hundreds of thousands protested against amendments to the US-Japan Security Treaty. Japan successfully normalized relations with the Soviet Union in 1956, despite an ongoing dispute over the ownership of the Kuril Islands, and with South Korea in 1965, despite an ongoing dispute over the ownership of the islands of Liancourt Rocks. In accordance with US policy, Japan recognized theRepublic of China on Taiwan as the legitimate government of China after World War II, though Japan switched its recognition to the People's Republic of China in 1972.

Among cultural developments, the immediate post-occupation period became a golden age for Japanese cinema. The reasons for this include the abolition of government censorship, low film production costs, expanded access to new film techniques and technologies, and huge domestic audiences at a time when other forms of recreation were relatively scarce.

Heisei period (1989–present)

Emperor Akihito's reign began upon the death of his father, Emperor Hirohito. The economic bubble popped in 1989, and stock and land prices plunged as Japan entered a deflationary spiral. Banks found themselves saddled with insurmountable debts that hindered economic recovery. Stagnation worsened as the birthrate declined far below replacement level.The 1990s are often referred to as Japan's Lost Decade. Economic performance was frequently poor in the following decades and the stock market never returned to its pre-1989 highs. Japan's system of lifetime employment largely collapsed and unemployment rates rose. The faltering economy and several corruption scandals weakened the LDP's dominant political position. Japan was nevertheless governed by non-LDP prime ministers only in 1993–96 and 2009–12.

Japan's dealing with its war legacy has strained international relations. China and Korea have found official apologies, such as those of the Emperor in 1990 and the Murayama Statement of 1995, inadequate or insincere. Nationalist politics have exacerbated this, such as denial of the Nanking Massacre and other war crimes; revisionist history textbooks, which have provoked protests in East Asia, and frequent visits by Japanese politicians to Yasukuni Shrine, where convicted war criminals are enshrined. Legislation in 2015 expanding the military's role overseas was criticized as a "war bill".

In spite of Japan's economic difficulties, this period also saw Japanese popular culture, including video games, anime, and manga, become worldwide phenomena, especially among young people.

On March 11, 2011, one of the largest earthquakes recorded in Japan occurred in the northeast. The resulting tsunami damaged the nuclear facilities in Fukushima, which experienced a nuclear meltdown and severe radiation leakage. In the 21st century there have been increasing reports on the prevalence of sexlessness among the Japanese, including its byproducts such as a decreasing population.

SOCIAL CONDITIONS

Social stratification in Japan became pronounced during the Yayoi period. Expanding trade and agriculture increased the wealth of society, which was increasingly monopolized by social elites. By 600 AD, a class structure had developed which included court aristocrats, the families of local magnates, commoners, and slaves. Over 90% were commoners, who included farmers, merchants, and artisans. During the late Heian period, the governing elite centered around three classes. The traditional aristocracy shared power with Buddhist monks and samurai, though the latter became increasingly dominant in the Kamakura and Muromachi periods. These periods witnessed the rise of the merchant class, which diversified into a greater variety of specialized occupations.

Women initially held social and political equality with men, and archaeological evidence suggests a prehistorical preference for female rulers in western Japan. Female Emperors appear in recorded history until the Meiji Constitutiondeclared strict male-only ascension in 1889. Chinese Confucian-style patriarchy was first codified in the 7th–8th centuries with the *ritsuryô* system, which introduced a patrilineal family register with a male head of household.Women until then had held important roles in government which thereafter gradually diminished, though even in the late Heian period women wielded considerable court influence. Marital customs and many laws governing private property remained gender neutral.

For reasons that are unclear to historians the status of women rapidly deteriorated from the fourteenth century and onwards. Women of all social classes lost the right to own and inherit property and were increasingly viewed as inferior to men.

Hideyoshi's land survey of the 1590s further entrenched the status of men as dominant landholders. During the US occupation following World War II , women gained legal equality with men, but faced widespread workplace discrimination.

A movement for women's rights led to the passage of an equal employment law in 1986, but by the 1990s women held only 10% of management positions.

Hideyoshi's land survey of the 1590s designated all who cultivated the land as commoners, an act which granted effective freedom to most of Japan's slaves.

The Tokugawa shogunate rigidified long-existent class divisions, placing most of the population into a Neo-Confucian hierarchy of four occupations, with the ruling elite at the top, followed by the peasants who made up 80% of the population, then artisans, and merchants at the bottom.

Court nobles, clerics, outcasts, entertainers, and workers of the licensed quarters fell outside this structure.Different legal codes applied to different classes, marriage between classes was prohibited, and towns were subdivided into different class areas.

The social stratification had little bearing on economic conditions: many samurai lived in poverty and the wealth of the merchant class grew throughout the period as the commercial economy developed and urbanization grew. The Edo-era social power structure proved untenable and gave way following the Meiji Restoration to one in which commercial power played an increasingly significant political role.

Although all social classes were legally abolished at the start of the Meiji period, income inequality greatly increased.New economic class divisions were formed between capitalist business owners who formed the new middle class, small shopkeepers of the old middle class, the working class in factories, rural landlords, and tenant farmers. The great disparities of income between the classes dissipated during and after World War II, eventually declining to levels that were among the lowest in the industrialized world. Some postwar surveys indicated that up to 90% of Japanese self-identified as being middle class.

Populations of workers in professions considered unclean, such as leatherworkers and those who handled the dead, developed in the 15th and 16th centuries into hereditary outcast communities.

These people, later called *burakumin*, fell outside the Edo-period class structure and suffered discrimination that lasted after the class system was abolished.Though activism has improved the social conditions of those from *burakumin* backgrounds, discrimination in employment and education lingered into the 21st century.

3

Geography

Japan is an island nation in East Asia comprising a volcanic archipelagoextending along the continent's Pacific coast. It lies between 24° to 46° north latitude and from 123° to 146° east longitude. Japan is southeast of theRussian Far East, separated by the Sea of Okhotsk; slightly east of theKorean Peninsula, separated by the Sea of Japan; and east-northeast ofChina and Taiwan, separated by the East China Sea. The closest neighboring country to Japan is Russia.

Overview

The major islands, sometimes called the "Home Islands", are (from north to south) Hokkaido, Honshu (the "mainland"), Shikoku and Kyushu.

There are 6,852 islands in total, including the Nansei Islands, the Nanpo Islands andislets, with 430 islands being inhabited and others uninhabited. In total, as of 2006, Japan's territory is 377,923.1 km² (145,916.9 sq mi), of which 374,834 km² (144,724 sq mi) is land and 3,091 km² (1,193 sq mi) water.

Location: Eastern Asia, island chain between the North Pacific Ocean and theSea of Japan, east of the Korean Peninsula.

Map references: Asia, Oceania

Area:

- *total*: 377,915 km²
- *land*: 364,485 km²
- *water*: 13,430 km²
- *notes*: Includes the Bonin Islands, Daitô Islands, Minami-Tori-

shima, Okinotorishima, the Ryukyu Islands, and the Volcano Islands. Ownership of the Senkaku Islands and Liancourt Rocks(Japanese:*Takeshima*, Korean:*Dokdo*) is in dispute.

Land boundaries: the ocean

Coastline: 29,751 km (18,486 mi)

Maritime claims:

- *territorial sea*: 12 nmi (22.2 km; 13.8 mi); between 3 and 12 nmi (5.6 and 22.2 km; 3.5 and 13.8 mi) in the international straits — La Pérouse (or Sôya Strait), Tsugaru Strait, Osumi, and Eastern and Western Channels of the Korea or Tsushima Strait.
- *exclusive economic zone*: 200 nmi (370.4 km; 230.2 mi)
- *contiguous zone*: 24 nmi (44.4 km; 27.6 mi)

Climate: varies from tropical in south to cool temperate in north

Terrain: mostly rugged and mountainous, can easily be compared to Norway, both having about 70% of their land in the mountains.

Natural resources: small deposits of coal, oil, iron, and minerals. Major fishing industry.

Land use:

- *arable land*: 11.65%
- *permanent crops*: 0.83%
- *other*: 87.52% (2012)

Irrigated land: 25,000 km² (2010)

Total renewable water resources: 430 km³ (2011)

Freshwater withdrawal (domestic/industrial/agricultural):

- *total*: 90.04 km³/yr (20%/18%/62%)
- *per capita*: 714.3 m³/yr (2007)

COMPOSITION, TOPOGRAPHY AND GEOGRAPHY

About 73% of Japan is mountainous, with a mountain range running through each of the main islands. Japan's highest mountain isMount Fuji, with an elevation of 3,776 m (12,388 ft). Japan's forest cover rate is 68.55% since the mountains are heavily forested. The only other developed nations with such a high forest cover percentage are Finland andSweden.

Since there is little level ground, many hills and mountainsides at lower elevations around towns and cities are often cultivated. As Japan is situated in a volcanic zone along the Pacific deeps, frequent low-intensity earth tremors and occasional volcanic activity are felt throughout the islands. Destructive earthquakes occur several times a century. Hot springs are numerous and have been exploited as aneconomic capital by the leisure industry.

The mountainous islands of the Japanese archipelago form a crescent off the eastern coast of Asia. They are separated from the mainland by the Sea of Japan, which historically served as a protective barrier. The country consists of four major islands: Hokkaido,Honshu, Shikoku, and Kyushu; with more than 6,500 adjacent smaller islands and islets ("island" defined as land more than 100 m in circumference), including the Izu Islands andOgasawara Islands in the Nanpô Islands, and the Satsunan Islands, Okinawa Islands, andSakishima Islands of the Ryukyu Islands.

The national territory also includes the Volcano Islands (Kazan Retto) such as Iwo Jima, located some 1,200 kilometers south of mainlandTokyo. A territorial dispute with Russia, dating from the end of World War II, over the two southernmost of the Kuril Islands, Etorofu andKunashiri, and the smaller Shikotan Island andHabomai Islands northeast of Hokkaido remains a sensitive spot in Japanese–Russian relations(as of 2005). Excluding disputed territory, the archipelago covers about 377,000 square kilometers. No point in Japan is more than 150 kilometers from the sea.

The four major islands are separated by narrow straits and form a natural entity. The Ryukyu Islands curve 970 kilometers southward from Kyûshû.

The distance between Japan and the Korean Peninsula, the nearest point on the Asian continent, is about 200 kilometers at the Korea Strait. Japan has always been linked with the continent through trade routes, stretching in the north towardSiberia, in the west through the Tsushima Islands to the Korean Peninsula, and in the south to the ports on the south China coast.

The Japanese islands are the summits of mountain ridges uplifted near the outer edge of the continental shelf. About 73 percent of Japan's area is mountainous, and scattered plains and intermontane basins (in which the population is concentrated) cover only about 27 percent. A long chain of mountains runs down the middle of the archipelago, dividing it into two halves, the "face", fronting on the Pacific Ocean, and the "back", toward the Sea of Japan. On the Pacific side are steep mountains 1,500 to 3,000 meters high, with deep valleys and gorges.

Central Japan is marked by the convergence of the three mountain chains — the Hida, Kiso, and Akaishi mountains — that form the Japanese Alps (Nihon Arupusu), several of whose peaks are higher than 3,000 meters. The highest point in the Japanese Alps is Mount Kita at 3,193 meters. The highest point in the country is Mount Fuji (Fujisan, also erroneously called Fujiyama), a volcano dormant since 1707 that rises to 3,776 meters above sea level in Shizuoka Prefecture. On the Sea of Japan side are plateaus and low mountain districts, with altitudes of 500 to 1,500 meters.

None of the populated plains or mountain basins are extensive in area. The largest, the Kantô Plain, where Tokyo is situated, covers only 13,000 square kilometers. Other important plains are the Nôbi Plain surrounding Nagoya, the Kinai Plain in the Osaka–Kyoto area, the Sendai Plain around the city of Sendai in northeastern Honshû, and the Ishikari Plain on Hokkaidô. Many of these plains are along the coast, and their areas have been increased by reclamation throughout recorded history.

The small amount of habitable land has prompted significant human modification of the terrain over many centuries. Land was reclaimed from the sea and from river deltas by building dikes and drainage, and rice paddies were built on terraces carved into mountainsides. The process continued in the modern period with extension of shorelines and building of artificial islands for industrial and port development, such as Port Island in Kobe and the new Kansai International Airport in Osaka Bay. Hills and even mountains have been razed to provide flat areas for housing.

Rivers are generally steep and swift, and few are suitable for navigation except in their lower reaches. Most rivers are less than 300 kilometers in length, but their rapid flow from the mountains provides a valuable, renewable resource: hydroelectric power generation. Japan's hydroelectric power potential has been exploited almost to capacity. Seasonal variations in flow have led to extensive development of flood control measures. Most of the rivers are very short. The longest, the Shinano River, which winds through Nagano Prefecture to Niigata Prefecture and flows into the Sea of Japan, is only 367 kilometers long. The largest freshwater lake is Lake Biwa, northeast of Kyoto.

Extensive coastal shipping, especially around the Seto Inland Sea (Seto Naikai), compensates for the lack of navigable rivers. The Pacific coastline south of Tokyo is characterized by long, narrow, gradually shallowing inlets produced by sedimentation, which has created many natural harbors. The Pacific coastline north of Tokyo, the coast of Hokkaidô, and the Sea of Japan coast are generally unindented, with few natural harbors.

In November 2008, Japan filed a request to expand its claimed continental shelf. In April 2012, the U.N. Commission on the Limits of the Continental Shelf recognized around 310,000 square kilometres (120,000 sq mi) of seabed aroundOkinotorishima, giving Japan priority over access to seabed resources in nearby areas. According to U.N. Commission on the Limits of the Continental Shelf, the approved expansion is equal to about 82% of Japan's total land area. The People's Republic of China and South Korea have opposed Japan's claim because they view Okinotorishima not as an island, but a group of rocks.

CLIMATE

Most regions of Japan, such as much of Honshu, Shikoku and Kyushu, belong to the temperate zone with humid subtropical climate(Köppen climate classification *Cfa*) characterized by four distinct seasons. However, its climate varies from cool humid continental climate (Köppen climate classification *Dfb*) in the north such as northern Hokkaido, to warm tropical rainforest climate(Köppen climate classification *Af*) in the south such as Ishigaki in the Yaeyama Islands.

The two primary factors influences in Japan's climate are a location near the Asian continent and the existence of major oceanic currents. Two major ocean currents affect Japan: the warm Kuroshio Current (Black Current; also known as the Japan Current); and the coldOyashio Current (Parent Current; also known as the Okhotsk Current). The Kuroshio Current flows northward on the Pacific side of Japan and warms areas as north as the South Kantô region; a small branch, the Tsushima Current, flows up the Sea of Japan side. The Oyashio Current, which abounds in plankton beneficial to coldwater fish, flows southward along the northern Pacific, cooling adjacent coastal areas. The intersection of these currents at 36 north latitude is a bountiful fishing ground.

Its varied geographical features divide Japan into six principal climatic zones.

- Hokkaido : Belonging to the humid continental climate, Hokkaido has long, cold winters and cool summers. Precipitation is not great.

- Sea of Japan : The northwest seasonal wind in winter gives heavy snowfall, which south of Tohoku mostly melts before the beginning of spring. In summer it is a little less rainy than the Pacific area but sometimes experiences extreme high temperatures due to the foehn wind phenomenon.

- Central Highland : A typical inland climate gives large temperature variations between summers and winters and between days and nights. Precipitation is lower than on the coast due to rain shadow effects.

- Seto Inland Sea : The mountains in the Chûgoku and Shikoku regions block the seasonal winds and bring mild climate and many fine days throughout the year.

- Pacific Ocean : The climate varies greatly between the north and the south but generally winters are significantly milder and sunnier than those of the side that faces the Sea of Japan. Summers are hot and humid due to the southeast seasonal wind. Precipitation is very heavy in the south, and heavy in the summer in the north. The climate of the Ogasawara Island chain in the Pacific Ocean ranges from a humid subtropical climate (Köppen climate classification *Cfa*) to tropical savanna climate (Köppen climate classification *Aw*) with temperatures being warm to hot all year round.

- Ryukyu Islands : The climate of these islands ranges from humid subtropical climate (Köppen climate classification *Cfa*) in the north to tropical rainforest climate (Köppen climate classification *Af*) in the south with warm winters and hot summers. Precipitation is very high, and is especially affected by the rainy season and typhoons.

Japan is generally a rainy country with high humidity. Because of its wide range of latitude, seasonal winds and different types of ocean currents, Japan has a variety of climates, with a latitude range of the inhabited islands from 24° to 46° north, which is comparable to the range between Nova Scotia and The Bahamas in the east coast of North America. Tokyo is at about 35 degrees north latitude, comparable to that of Tehran, Athens, or Las Vegas.

Regional climatic variations range from humid continental in the northern island ofHokkaido extending down through northern Japan to the Central Highland, then blending with and eventually changing to a humid subtropical climate on the Pacific Coast and ultimately reaching tropical rainforest climate on the Yaeyama Islands of the Ryukyu Islands. Climate also varies dramatically with altitude and with location on the Pacific Ocean or on the Sea of Japan.

Northern Japan has warm summers but long, cold winters with heavy snow. Central Japan in its elevated position, has hot, humid summers and moderate to short winters with some areas having very heavy snow, and southwestern Japan has long, hot, humid summers and mild winters. The generally humid, temperate climate exhibits marked seasonal variation such as the blooming of the spring cherry blossoms, the calls of the summer cicada and fall foliage colors that are celebrated in art and literature.

The climate from June to September is marked by hot, wet weather brought by tropical airflows from the Pacific Ocean and Southeast Asia. These airflows are full of moisture and deposit substantial amounts of rain when they reach land. There is a marked rainy season, beginning in early June and continuing for about a month.

It is followed by hot, sticky weather. Five or six typhoons pass over or near Japan every year from early August to early October, sometimes resulting in significant damage. Annual precipitation averages between 1,000 and 2,500 mm (40 and 100 in) except for the areas such as Kii Peninsula and Yakushima Island which is Japan's wettest place with the annual precipitation being one of the world's highest at 4,000 to 10,000 mm.

Maximum precipitation, like the rest of East Asia, occurs in the summer months except on the Sea of Japan coast where strong northerly winds produce a maximum in late autumn and early winter. Except for a few sheltered inland valleys during December and January, precipitation in Japan is above 25 millimetres (1 in) of rainfall equivalent in all months of the year, and in the wettest coastal areas it is above 100 millimetres (4 in) per month throughout the year.

In winter, the Siberian High develops over the Eurasian land mass and the Aleutian Low develops over the northern Pacific Ocean. The result is a flow of cold air southeastward across Japan that brings freezing temperatures and heavy snowfalls to the central mountain ranges facing the Sea of Japan, but clear skies to areas fronting on the Pacific.

Mid June to mid July is generally the rainy season in Honshu, Shikoku and Kyushu, excluding Hokkaidô since the seasonal rain front or *baiu zensen* dissipates in northern Honshu before reaching Hokkaido. In Okinawa, the rainy season starts early in May and continues until mid June. Unlike the rainy season in mainland Japan, it rains neither everyday nor all day long during the rainy season in Okinawa. Between July and October, typhoons, grown from tropical depressions generated near the equator, can attack Japan with furious rainstorms.

The warmest winter temperatures are found in the Nanpô and Bonin Islands, which enjoy a tropical climate due to the combination of latitude, distance from the Asian mainland, and warming effect of winds from the Kuroshio, as well as the Volcano Islands (at the latitude of the southernmost of the Ryukyu Islands, 24° N). The coolest summer temperatures are found on the northeastern coast of Hokkaidô in Kushiro and Nemuro Subprefectures.

Sunshine, in accordance with Japan's uniformly heavy rainfall, is generally modest in quantity, though no part of Japan receives the consistently gloomy fogs that envelope the Sichuan Basin or Taipei. Amounts range from about six hours per day in the Inland Sea coast and sheltered parts of the Pacific Coast and Kantô Plain to four hours per day on the Sea of Japan coast of Hokkaidô. In December there is a very pronounced sunshine gradient between the Sea of Japan and Pacific coasts, as the former side can receive less than 30 hours and the Pacific side as much as 180 hours. In summer, however, sunshine hours are lowest on exposed parts of the Pacific coast where fogs from the Oyashio current create persistent cloud cover similar to that found on the Kuril Islands and Sakhalin.

As an island nation, Japan has the 7th longest coastline in the world. A few prefectures are landlocked: Gunma,Tochigi, Saitama, Nagano, Yamanashi, Gifu, Shiga, and Nara. As Mt. Fuji and the coastal Japanese Alps provide a rain shadow, Nagano and Yamanashi Prefectures receive the least precipitation in Honshu, though this still exceeds 900 millimetres (35 in) annually. A similar effect is found in Hokkaido, where Okhotsk Subprefecture receives as little as 750 millimetres (30 in) per year. All other prefectures have coasts on the Pacific Ocean, Sea of Japan, Seto Inland Sea or have a body of salt water connected to them. Two prefectures — Hokkaido and Okinawa — are composed entirely of islands.

The hottest temperature ever measured in Japan, 41.0 °C (105.8 °F), occurred in Shimanto, Kochi on August 12, 2013.

ENVIRONMENTAL ISSUES

Environment - current issues: In the 2006 environment annual report, the Ministry of Environment reported that current major issues are: global warming and preservation of the ozone layer, conservation of the atmospheric environment, water and soil, waste management and recycling, measures for chemical substances, conservation of the natural environment and the participation in the international cooperation.

Environment - international agreements:

Party to: Antarctic-Environmental Protocol, Antarctic Treaty, Biodiversity, Climate Change, Desertification, Endangered Species, Environmental Modification, Hazardous Wastes (Basel Convention), Law of the Sea, Marine Dumping, Ozone Layer Protection (Montreal Protocol), Ship Pollution (MARPOL 73/78), Tropical Timber 83, Tropical Timber 94, Wetlands (Ramsar Convention), Whaling

Signed and ratified: Climate Change-Kyoto Protocol

NATURAL HAZARDS

Ten percent of the world's active volcanoes — forty in the early 1990s (another 148 were dormant) — are found in Japan, which lies in a zone of extreme crustal instability. As many as 1,500 earthquakes are recorded yearly, and magnitudes of 4 to 7 are common. Minor tremors occur almost daily in one part of the country or another, causing slight shaking of buildings. Major earthquakes occur infrequently; the most famous in the twentieth century was the great Kantô earthquake of 1923, in which 130,000 people died. Undersea earthquakes also expose the Japanese coastline to danger from tsunamis.

On March 11, 2011 Japan was subject to a devastating magnitude 9.0 earthquake and a massive tsunami as a result. The March 11 quake was the largest ever recorded in Japan and is the world's fourth largest earthquake to strike since 1900, according to the U.S. Geological Service. It struck offshore about 371 kilometres (231 mi) northeast of Tokyo and 130 kilometres (81 mi) east of the city of Sendai, and created a massive tsunami that devastated Japan's northeastern coastal areas. At least 100 aftershocks registering a 6.0 magnitude or higher have followed the main shock. At least 15,000 people died as a result.

Japan has become a world leader in research on causes and prediction of earthquakes. The development of advanced technology has permitted the construction of skyscrapers even in earthquake-prone areas. Extensive civil defence efforts focus on training in protection against earthquakes, in particular against accompanying fire, which represents the greatest danger.

Another common hazard are several typhoons that reach Japan from the Pacific every year and heavy snowfall during winter in the snow country regions, causing landslides, flooding, and avalanches.

REGIONS

Japan is informally divided into eight regions. Each contains several prefectures, except the Hokkaido region, which covers only Hokkaido Prefecture.

The region is not an official administrative unit, but has been traditionally used as the regional division of Japan in a number of contexts: for example, maps and geography textbooks divide Japan into the eight regions, weather reports usually give the weather by region, and many businesses and institutions use their home region as part of their name (Kinki Nippon Railway, Chûgoku Bank, Tohoku University, etc.). While Japan has eight High Courts, their jurisdictions do not correspond to the eight regions.

EXTREME POINTS

This is a list of the extreme points of Japan, the points that are farther north, south, east or west than any other location.

Japan

1. Northernmost point
   * Benten-jima, Wakkanai, Hokkaido – *45°31′353 N, 141°55′093 E*
   * Including land currently disputed with Russia: Cape Kamuiwakka), Etorufu *–45°33′N, 148°45′E*
2. Southernmost point: Okinotorishima – *20°25′N, 136°04′E*
3. Westernmost point: Yonaguni – 24°272 N, *122°592 E*
4. Easternmost point: Minami-Tori-shima – 24°182 N, *153°582 E*

Japan (main islands)

* Northernmost point: Cape Sôya, Wakkanai, Hokkaido – *45°31′N, 141°56′E*
* Southernmost point: Cape Sata on Ôsumi Peninsula, Minamiôsumi, Kagoshima – *30°59′N, 130°39′E*
* Westernmost point: Kôsakibana , Sasebo (formerly Kosaza), Nagasaki – 33°13′N, *129°33′E*

- Easternmost point: Cape Nosappu), Nemuro, Hokkaido –
  43°22'N, *145°492 E*

Elevation extremes

- Lowest point: Hachirôgata – -4 m
- Highest point: Mount Fuji – 3,776 m

ANTIPODES

The only part of Japan with antipodes over land are the Ryukyu Islands, though the islands off the western coast of Kyûshû are close.

The northernmost antipodal island in the Ryukyu Island chain, Nakanoshima, is opposite the Brazilian coast near Capão da Canoa. The other islands south to the Straits of Okinawa correspond to southern Brazil, with Gaja Island being opposite the outskirts of Santo Antônio da Patrulha, Takarajima with Jua, Amami Ôshima covering the villages of Carasinho and Fazenda Pae João, Ginoza, Okinawa withPalmas, Paraná, the Kerama Islands with Pato Branco, Tonaki Island with São Lourenço do Oeste, and Kume Island corresponding toPalma Sola. The main Daitô Islands correspond to near Guaratuba, with Oki Daitô Island nearApiaí.

The Sakishima Islands beyond the straits are antipodal to Paraguay, from the Brazilian border almost to Asunción, with Ishigaki overlapping San Isidro de Curuguaty, and the uninhabited Senkaku Islands surrounding Villarrica.

LAND AND LANDSCAPE OF JAPAN

Most Japanese live in the sprawling urban areas that seem to go on forever, but once they end they give way to beautiful countryside. Forests cover about two-thirds of Japan. About 41 percent of the trees in the forests have been planted in nice neat rows, and 44 percent of the planted tree are cedars. The heavily indented coastline extends for 16,654 miles.

The less developed side of Japan that faces the Sea of Japan is often referred as the "backside of Japan" as opposed to more developed "front side" that faces the Pacific. East Japan refers mainly to the Tokyo-Yokohama, Mount Fuji, Japan Alps area. West Japan refers to everything south of Kyoto and Osaka on Honshu, plus the northern part of Kyushu. The area around Tokyo is called Kanto (a reference to Kanto Plain which Tokyo is part of); the region that embraces

Osaka, Kyoto and Kobe is called Kansai (or Kinki). Tohuko describes northern Honshu.

The Japanese countryside landscape, sometimes called the satoyama, is structured like a fine patchwork quilt or tile mosaic. An amazing variety of land-use patterns are jumbled together in a complicated manner.

The individual patches are all small in area, and often isolated from others of their kind. Each type of land-use pattern contains its own distinctive set of tree species. The result is that a wide diversity of trees, shrubs and woody vines can be found within a very limited area. [Source: Kevin Short, Daily Yomiuri, October 5, 2011]

Paul Theroux wrote in The Daily Beast: Japan is almost without hinterland. Its population lives mainly on its coast. The mountains are for tunneling through, not residing on. And where there is open landscape, as in the low rolling hills of Hokkaido, it is thinly settled. From the carriage window, as the train travels north from Tokyo, through Sendai and the coastal towns of Minamisanriku, Kesennuma, Okuma, and others — the ones now swept away — the Japanese can be seen living in unusual urban density, the low, snug houses cheek by jowl, traversed by narrow lanes, as they have been throughout history. My sense is that they have been able to live closely together because of their elaborate good manners, mutual respect, self-sufficiency, and work ethic. A less polite society would require more space or higher fences or guard dogs. [Source: Paul Theroux, The Daily Beast, March 20, 2011]

"With this acute sense of limited land and few natural resources, and the hostility of nature, they have taken pains to put off the evil day by manipulating their weird geography, even if it means a disfigurement. The result makes the strange Japanese landscape even weirder: it is the most possessed-looking place imaginable, its awkward-seeming features ordered and buttressed, the human hand visible everywhere. The notion of control and containment, which dominates Japanese life, dominates the landscape. Rivers are cemented into place, embankments are tiers of concrete blocks; sidewalks and bridges exist in the most unlikely places. The 33-mile Seikan Tunnel that links Honshu to Hokkaido under the Tsugaru Strait is the world's longest railway tunnel. The watchtowers and sea walls all over the coast reinforce the look of Japan as a fortress in the sea. It is, of course, an illusion. [Ibid]

Japan's Island Arcs

Japan is an archipelago that forms an arc in the Pacific Ocean to the east of the Asian continent. The land comprises four large islands named (in decreasing order of size) Honshu, Hokkaido, Kyushu, and Shikoku, together with many smaller islands. The Pacific Ocean lies to the east while the Sea of Japan and the East China Sea separate Japan from the Asian continent.

The four main islands account for 90 percent of Japan's land area. The four major islands of Japan are: 87,800-square-mile Honshu, or the "mainland," where Tokyo, Osaka and Kyoto are found; 30,150-square-mile Hokkaido, the northernmost of the large islands; 14,100-square-mile Kyushu, the volcanically-active southernmost large island; and 7,050-square-mile Shikoku, a rustic island on the Inland Sea between Honshu and Kyushu.

Japan is comprised of island arcs. An island arc is a string of volcanic islands in a curving arc-like pattern above a deep ocean trench. It is formed by magmatic activity after one oceanic tectonic plate subducts another one.

Island arcs serve as nests for earthquakes and volcanoes. They are scattered throughout Southeast Asia, the Pacific Rim and the Caribbean Sea. In Japan, four island arcs converge on an area extending from Hokkaido through Honshu to Kyushu, to create a complex formation that has rarely occurred throughout the Earth's history. This formation makes the country always under threat from disasters. [Source: Yomiuri Shimbun, July 10, 2012]

"Island arcs are vulnerable to tsunami because their land extends over a small area at relatively low altitudes. They often experience heavy rain and tropical cyclones as many are sandwiched between a continent and the high seas.

However, Japan's island arcs come with unique benefits. Rich river resources have been created by rapid currents that are caused by a radical difference in height between mountainous and low-lying areas.

Magma has produced a leading geothermal area blessed with undersea deposits of precious metals and rare earths raised from deep within the seabed. There are also deposits of an icy natural gas substance called methane hydrate, which was created by high-pressure low-temperature conditions. [Ibid]

"The U.N. Commission on the Limits of the Continental Shelf upheld in April some of Japan's claims on an extended continental shelf in seabed areas around the country.

The elevated seabed from the Shikoku basin and the maritime area to the south of Okinotorishima, the southernmost island of Japan — about 1,700 kilometers from Tokyo — is a remnant of the island arc that was active in the past. Due to the concentration of island arcs, Japan could obtain a continental shelf equivalent to 80 percent of its national land area. [Ibid]

Coastline and Rivers of Japan

Japan has 32,000 kilometers of coast. Much of Japan's outer coastline consists of alternating stretches of rock shore and beach , with protected bays, marshes and mud flats here and there. Around cities and towns the coastal areas are highly developed. There are not many nice beaches near the cities. The nicest ones in remote places. Many places have been reclaimed from the sea.

Japan's coastline is quite varied. In some places, such as Kujukurihama in Chiba Prefecture, there are long sandy beaches continuing fairly straight and uninterrrupted for 60 kilometers or so, while the coast of Nagasaki Prefecture is an example of an area characterized by peninsulas and inlets and offshore islands (like the Goto archipelago and the islands of Tsushima and Iki, which are part of that prefecture).

There are also accidented areas of the coast with many inlets and steep cliffs caused by the submersion of part of the former coastline due to changes in the Earth's crust. [Source: Web-Japan, Ministry of Foreign Affairs, Japan]

"There are 32,000 rivers, streams and lakes. Because Japan is so mountainous it doesn't really have any navigable rivers except near the seas.

Most of Japan's rivers flow very fast, their waters reaching the ocean not long after leaving mountain valleys and basins. An example of the "steepness" of river flows is the Kurobe River, which joins the Sea of Japan after flowing only 83 kilometers from its source in the Japan Alps at an altitude of over 2,900 meters. [Ibid]

"Japan's longest river is the Shinano River, which flows 367 kilometers from the mountains of the Chubu region through Niigata Prefecture to the Sea of Japan. Second in length is the Tone River, which flows through the Kanto Plain to the Pacific Ocean, and third in length is the Ishikari River in Hokkaido, at 268 kilometers. The many rivers descending from mountainous areas have done much to mold Japan's topography, creating large and small valleys and basins and producing fan-shaped deltas near the points where they flow into the sea.

Most of the country's plains are small. The largest is the Kanto Plain, which includes parts of Tochigi, Ibaraki, Gunma, Saitama, Chiba, Tokyo, and Kanagawa prefectures. Other relatively large areas of flat land are the Echigo Plain (Niigata Prefecture), the Ishikari Plain (Hokkaido), and the Nobi Plain (Aichi and Gifu prefectures).

Beginning about 250 miles south of Kyushu are the Ryukyu islands, which includes Okinawa. North of Hokkaido are a few islands than run up to the Sakhalin islands, which Japan is currently trying to get back from Russia.

Mountains, Volcanoes and Earthquakes in Japan

Hokkaido's Daisetsuzan mountain About three-fourths of Japan's land surface is mountainous. The Chubu Region of central Honshu is known as "the roof of Japan" and has many mountains which are more than 3,000 meters high.

Japan's highest mountain is Mt. Fuji (3,776 meters) on the border of Yamanashi and Shizuoka Prefectures. Japan's secondhighest peak is Kitadake in Yamanashi Prefecture, at 3,192 meters, and its thirdhighest peak is Hotakadake at 3,190 meters, on the border between Nagano and Gifu Prefectures. Mt. Fuji Japan's highest peak, Mt. Fuji, is seen here from Lake Kawaguchi in April. It remains covered in snow until June. [Source: Web-Japan, Ministry of Foreign Affairs, Japan]

"As it is situated along the circum-Pacific volcanic belt, Japan has several volcanic regions — usually considered to number seven "from the far north to the far south. Of the total number of volcanoes, approximately 80 are active, including Mt. Mihara on Izu Oshima island, Mt. Asama on the border between Nagano and Gunma Prefectures, and Mt. Aso in Kumamoto Prefecture.

Japan has almost 1/10 of the world's approximately 840 active volcanoes, even though it has only about 1/400 of the world's land area. Mt. Fuji, which has been dormant since its last eruption in 1707, is by no means incapable of erupting again in our lifetimes. Though volcanoes can cause great harm through large eruptions, they also contribute an incalculable tourist resource. Touristic areas such as Nikko, Hakone, and the Izu Peninsula, for example, are famous for their hot springs and attractive scenery of volcanic mountains. [Ibid]

"As all these volcanoes attest, the Earth's crust beneath the Japanese archipelago is unstable and full of energy. Thus Japan is among those countries most likely to suffer from earthquakes. Every year there are approximately 1,000 earthquakes which are strong enough to be felt. In January 1995, the Great Hanshin-Awaji Earthquake killed approximately 6,000 people, injured over 40,000, and left 200,000 homeless.

An earthquake in Niigata Prefecture in October 2004 left over 60 people dead and more than 4,700 injured. In March 2011, a magnitude 9 earthquake was recorded off the coast of Sanriku (Tohoku) in the Pacific Ocean, and the ensuing tsunami, more than 10m high in places, hit the coast across a vast region from Tohoku to Kanto. The number of dead and missing after the earthquake and tsunami reached nearly 20,000.

Geographical Names and Japan

In the early 1990s both the U.N.'s conference on Geographical Names and the U.S. Board of Geographic names rejected suggestions by Koreans to the change the name of the body of water between Korea and Japan from the Sea of Japan to the East Sea.

In August 2007, the ninth conference for the standardization of geographical names ruled that the Sea of Japan will remain the Sea of Japan.

South Korea and North Korea wanted the name to be changed to the "East Sea" or the "Sea of Korea," names which they say have been used for more than 2,000 years.

The chairman of the conference said, "I encourage the three countries involved to find a solution acceptable to all of them, taking into account any relevant solutions, or else agree to differ."

North Korea and South Korea joined together to contest the name and argued that the "East Sea" and "Sea of Japan" names to be used concurrently until a common designation could be worked out.

Japan argues that the "Sea of Japan" name has long been established and widely recognized as the name of the sea since the late 18th century.

Geology of Japan

Geologically, Japan is one of the youngest inhabited areas on earth. It regularly experiences volcanic eruptions and earthquakes. Around Tokyo much of the landscape is made up of marine sediments — deposited when the area was occupied by seas — covered by layers of ash from eruptions by Haokone, Mt. Fuji and other volcanoes.

Japan lies on the Pacific Ring of Fire and is home to 108 of the world's 1,500 or so active volcanos, including more than 10 percent of the active volcanos that are a threat to human populations. Volcanos in Japan are ranked A to C in accordance with the degree of their volcanic activity, with A being the most active. Some A volcanos have erupted 400 times a year. Mt. Fuji is classified as an active volcano even though it hasn't erupted since 1707.

Japan is riddled with faults and is located at the junction of four tectonic plates. In the last 75 years, the Japanese archipelago or areas immediately offshore have experienced five earthquakes measuring more than eight on the Richter scale; and 17 measuring more than seven on the Richter scale. It is unusual for a year to go by without three or four earthquakes measuring 6.0 or more.

Japan's First Glaciers Have Been Found

In April 2012, Jiji Press reported: "A Japanese research team has confirmed that large bodies of ice discovered in the Tateyama mountain range in central japan satisfy the definition of glaciers. The bodies of ice, found in three places in Toyama Prefecture, are the first confirmed glaciers in Japan.

Previously, no glacier was known to exist in the region south of the Russian peninsula of Kamchatka. It was learned that the Japanese Society of Snow and Ice reached its conclusion by analyzing research by the Tateyama Caldera Sabo Museum in Tateyama, Toyama Prefecture. Its findings will be reported in the May edition of the society's newsletter.

Snow in valleys and streams at high altitudes remains even during the summer. This snow may cover large bodies of ice, which may be considered glaciers if they move for at least one year. Using the Global Positioning System, the museum tracked the movements of bodies of ice in the Sannomado and Komado valleys of the 2,999-meter-high Mt. Tsurugi and the Gozenzawa snow valley of Mt. Oyama, which is 3,003 meters high.In research conducted in 2010 and 2011, the museum confirmed that the ice moved 10 to 30 centimeters per month.

All three bodies of ice are considered independent glaciers. "I'm very happy [the bodies of ice] have been recognized as glaciers," said museum member Kotaro Fukui, who participated in the study."We will continue our research," he said, noting that there are more bodies of ice that may satisfy the definition of glaciers.

Japan's Southernmost Island

size, latitude comparison with the U.S. The southernmost point of Japan is a heliport on Okinotori Island—about 1,700 kilometers south of Tokyo. The landing pad sits on a 50-meter-wide foundation intended for an unbuilt lighthouse planned built before World War II. Japan claims the waters around the island—an area of 400,000 square kilometers, which is the total land area of Japan.

Okinotori island embraces a coral reef that has a circumference of 11 kilometers during low tide. At high tide just two peaks—including the one with the heliport'sit above the ocean surface. Located in a strategic spot between Taiwan and Guam, it requires regular "maintenance" to keep it from submerging. China claims that Okinotori is a rock not an island and Japan has no right to claim it or the waters around it. It opposes the "maintenance" efforts.

There has been some discussion of employing new technology that creates sand from substances in seawater to help protect Okinotori from erosion. The technology—called the electrodeposition method— uses electrodes with negative charges that attract calcium and magnesium ions and they in turn form sandlike chemical compounds and they in turn attract coral

Twenty-Three Remote Isles Put under State Ownership

The government has placed 23 remote islands under state ownership after finishing necessary legal procedures last August, Chief Cabinet Secretary Osamu Fujimura said. The 23 islands, which are used to determine Japan's exclusive economic zones, do not include remote isles around the Senkaku Islands in the East China Sea off Okinawa Prefecture. China also claims the Senkaku Islands. This time, the designated remote islands include those under the jurisdiction of the village of Ogasawara, Tokyo; Ishigaki, Okinawa Prefecture; and Tsushima, Nagasaki Prefecture.

"Under the Civil Code, unowned land is vested in state coffers. The government has confirmed that the isles had no owners after checking property registers. The government has been strengthening its control over remote islands based on a basic policy decided in 2009 for the purpose of maritime supervision. The state ownership of the 23 isles is in line with this policy. "The Japan Coast Guard has filed the isles as administrative assets for the purpose of contributing to stable maintenance of EEZs," Fujimura said.

"The legal steps were taken based on the National Property Law. As a reason for excluding the remote islands around Senkaku, Fujimura said: "Only remote islets around unowned islands have been placed under state ownership. Senkaku does not fall within that category." Of the three main isles of Senkaku, the state only owns the Taishojima islet. The Kubajima and Uotsurijima islets are privately owned, though they are leased and administered by the state. In a related move, the government announced a list of 39 newly named islands. These islands had been previously unnamed despite being used as reference points to draw Japan's EEZs.

4

Government and Politics

GOVERNMENT OF JAPAN

The government of Japan is a constitutional monarchy in which the power of the Emperor is limited and is relegated primarily to ceremonial duties. As in many other states, the Government is divided into three branches: theExecutive branch, the Legislative branch and the Judicial branch.

The Government runs under the framework established by the Constitution of Japan, adopted in 1947. It is a unitary state, containing forty-sevenadministrative divisions, with the Emperor as its head of state. His role is ceremonial and he has no powers related to Government.

Instead, it is theCabinet, composing of the Ministers of State and the Prime Minister, that directs and controls the Government. The Cabinet is the source of power of the Executive branch, and is formed by the Prime Minister, who is the head of government. He or she is designated by the National Diet and appointed to office by the Emperor.

The National Diet is the legislature, the organ of the Legislative branch. It isbicameral, consisting of two houses with the House of Councillors being theupper house, and the House of Representatives being the lower house.

Its members are directly elected from the people, who are the source ofsovereignty. The Supreme Court and other inferior courts make up the Judicial branch, and they are independent from the executive and the legislative branches.

History

Prior to the Meiji Restoration, Japan was ruled by successive military shoguns. During this period, effective power of the government resided in the Shogun, who officially ruled the country in the name of the Emperor. The Shoguns were the hereditary military governors, with their modern rank equivalent to ageneralissimo. Although the Emperor was the sovereign who appointed the Shogun, his roles were ceremonial and he took no part in governing the country. This is often compared to the present role of the Emperor, whose official role is to appoint the Prime Minister.

The Meiji Restoration in 1868 led to the resignation of Shogun Tokugawa Yoshinobu, agreeing to "be the instrument for carrying out" the Emperor's orders. This event restored the country to Imperial rule and the proclamation of the Empire of Japan. In 1889, the Meiji Constitution was adopted in a move to strengthen Japan to the level of western nations, resulting in the first parliamentary system in Asia. It provided a form of mixed constitutional-absolute monarchy, with an independent judiciary, based on thePrussian model of the time.

A new aristocracy known as the Kazoku was established. It merged the ancient court nobility of the Heian period, the Kuge, and the former Daimyo, feudal lords subordinate to the Shogun. It also established the Imperial Diet, consisting of theHouse of Representatives and the House of Peers. Members of the House of Peers were made up of the Imperial Family, the Kazoku, and those nominated by the Emperor, while members of the House of Representatives were elected by direct male suffrage. Despite clear distinctions between powers of the executive branch and the Emperor in the Meiji Constitution, ambiguity and contradictions in the Constitution eventually led to a political crisis. It also devalued the notion of civilian control over the military, which meant that the military could develop and exercise a great influence on politics.

Following the end of World War II, the Constitution of Japan was adopted as an intention to replace the previous Imperial rule with a form of Western-style liberal democracy.

THE EMPEROR

The Emperor of Japan is the head of the Imperial Family and the ceremonial head of state. He is defined by the Constitution to be "the symbol of the State and of the unity of the people". However, he is not the nominal Chief Executive and he possesses only certain ceremonially important powers. He has no real powers related to the Government as stated clearly in article 4 of the Constitution.

Article 6 of the Constitution of Japan delegates the Emperor the following ceremonial roles:

1. Appointment of the Prime Minister as designated by the Diet.
2. Appointment of the Chief Justice of the Supreme Court as designated by the Cabinet.

While the Cabinet is the source of executive power and most of its power is exercised directly by the Prime Minister, several of its powers are exercised by the Emperor. The powers exercised via the Emperor, as stipulated by Article 7 of the Constitution, are:

1. Promulgation of amendments of the constitution, laws, cabinet orders and treaties.
2. Convocation of the Diet.
3. Dissolution of the House of Representatives.
4. Proclamation of general election of members of the Diet.
5. Attestation of the appointment and dismissal of Ministers of State and other officials as provided for by law, and of full powers and credentials of Ambassadors and Ministers.
6. Attestation of general and special amnesty, commutation of punishment, reprieve, and restoration of rights.
7. Awarding of honors.
8. Attestation of instruments of ratification and other diplomatic documents as provided for by law.
9. Receiving foreign ambassadors and ministers.
10. Performance of ceremonial functions.

The Emperor is known to hold the nominal ceremonial authority. For example, the Emperor is the only person that has the authority to appoint the Prime Minister, even though the Diet has the power to designate the person fitted for the position. One such example can be prominently seen in the 2009 Dissolution of the House of Representatives. The House was expected to be dissolved on the advice of the Prime Minister, but was temporarily unable to do so for the next general election, as both the Emperor and Empress were visiting Canada.

In this manner, the Emperor's modern role is often compared to those of the Shogunate period and much of Japan's history, whereby the Emperor held great symbolic authority but had little political power; which is often held by others nominally appointed by the Emperor himself. Today, a legacy has somewhat continued for a retired Prime Minister who still wields considerable power, to be called a *Shadow Shogun* .

Unlike his European counterparts, the Emperor is not the source of sovereign power and the government does not act under his name. Instead, the Emperor represents the State and appoints other high officials in the name of the State, in which the Japanese people hold sovereignty. Article 5 of the Constitution, in accordance with the Imperial Household Law, allows a regency to be established in the Emperor's name, should the Emperor be unable to perform his duties.

Historically, the Imperial House of Japan is said to be the oldest continuing hereditary monarchy in the world. According to the Kojiki and Nihon Shoki, Japan was founded by the Imperial House in 660 BC by Emperor Jimmu . Emperor Jimmu was the first Emperor of Japan and the ancestor of all of the Emperors that followed. He is, according to Japanese mythology, the direct descendant of Amaterasu , the sun goddess of the native Shinto religion, through Ninigi, his great-grandfather.

The Current Emperor of Japan is Akihito. He was officially enthroned on November 12, 1990. He is styled as *His Imperial Majesty* , and his reign bears the era name of Heisei . Naruhito, the Crown Prince of Japan, is the heir apparent to the Chrysanthemum Throne.

EXECUTIVE

The Executive branch of Japan is headed by the Prime Minister. The Prime Minister is the head of the Cabinet, and is designated by the legislative organ, the National Diet. The Cabinet consists of the Ministers of State and may be appointed or dismissed by the Prime Minister at any time. Explicitly defined to be the source of executive power, it is in practice, however, mainly exercised by the Prime Minister. The practice of its powers is responsible to the Diet, and as a whole, should the Cabinet lose confidence and support to be in office by the Diet, the Diet may dismiss the Cabinet *en masse* with a motion of no confidence.

Prime Minister

The Prime Minister of Japan is designated by the National Dietand serves a term of four years or less; with no limits imposed on the number of terms the Prime Minister may hold. The Prime Minister heads the Cabinet and exercises "control and supervision" of the executive branch, and is the head of government and commander-in-chief of the Japan Self-Defense Forces. The Prime Minister is vested with the power to present bills to the Diet, to sign laws, to declare a state of emergency, and may also dissolve the Diet's House of Representatives at will. He or she presides over the Cabinet and appoints, or dismisses, the other Cabinet ministers.

Both houses of the National Diet designates the Prime Minister with a ballot cast under the run-off system. Under the Constitution, should both houses not agree on a common candidate, then a joint committee is allowed to be established to agree on the matter; specifically within a period of ten days, exclusive of the period of recess. However, if both houses still do not agree to each other, the decision made by the House of Representatives is deemed to be that of the National Diet. Upon designation, the Prime Minister is presented with their commission, and then formally appointed to office by the Emperor. As a candidate designated by the Diet, he or she is required to report to the Diet whenever demanded. The Prime Minister must also be both a civilian and a member of either house of the Diet.

The Cabinet

The Cabinet of Japan consists of the Ministers of State and the Prime Minister. The members of the Cabinet are appointed by the Prime Minister, and under the Cabinet Law, the number of members of the Cabinet appointed, excluding the Prime Minister, must be fourteen or less, but may only be increased to nineteen should a special need arise. Article 68 of the Constitution states that all members of the Cabinet must be civilians and the majority of them must be chosen from among the members of either house of theNational Diet. The precise wording leaves an opportunity for the Prime Minister to appoint some non-elected Diet officials. The Cabinet is required to resign *en masse*while still continuing its functions, till the appointment of a new Prime Minister, when the following situation arises:

1. The Diet's House of Representatives passes a non-confidence resolution, or rejects a confidence resolution, unless the House of Representatives is dissolved within the next ten days.
2. When there is a vacancy in the post of the Prime Minister, or upon the first convocation of the Diet after a general election of the members of the House of Representatives.

Conceptually deriving legitimacy from the Diet, whom it is responsible to, the Cabinet exercises its power in two different ways. In practice, much of its power is exercised by the Prime Minister, while others are exercised nominally by the Emperor.

Article 73 of the Constitution of Japan expects the Cabinet to perform the following functions, in addition to general administration:

1. Administer the law faithfully; conduct affairs of state.
2. Manage foreign affairs.
3. Conclude treaties. However, it shall obtain prior or, depending on circumstances, subsequent approval of the Diet.
4. Administer the civil service, in accordance with standards established by law.
5. Prepare the budget, and present it to the Diet.
6. Enact cabinet orders in order to execute the provisions of this Constitution and of the law. However, it cannot include penal provisions in such cabinet orders unless authorized by such law.
7. Decide on general amnesty, special amnesty, commutation of punishment, reprieve, and restoration of rights.

Under the Constitution, all laws and cabinet orders must be signed by the competent Minister and countersigned by the Prime Minister, before being formally promulgated by the Emperor. Also, all members of the Cabinet cannot be subject to legal action without the consent of the Prime Minister; however, without impairing the right to take legal action.

Ministries

The Ministries of Japan consist of eleven ministries and the Cabinet Office. Each ministry is headed by a Minister of State, which are mainly senior legislators, and are appointed from among the members of the Cabinet by the Prime Minister. The Cabinet Office, formally headed by the Prime Minister, is an agency that handles the day-to-day affairs of the Cabinet. The ministries are the most influential part of the daily-exercised executive power, and since few ministers serve for more than a year or so necessary to grab hold of the organisation, most of its power lies within the senior bureaucrats.

1. Cabinet Office
   * National Public Safety Commission
   * National Police Agency

- Consumer Affairs Agency
- Financial Services Agency
- Fair Trade Commission
- Food Safety Commission
- Imperial Household Agency

2. Manages the Imperial Household.

- Ministry of Internal Affairs and Communications
- Environmental Dispute Coordination Commission
- Fire and Disaster Management Agency
- Ministry of Justice
- Public Security Examination Commission
- Public Security Intelligence Agency
- Public Prosecutors Office
- Ministry of Foreign Affairs
- Reconstruction Agency
- Ministry of Finance
- National Tax Agency
- Ministry of Education, Culture, Sports, Science and Technology (MEXT)
- Agency for Cultural Affairs

3. Promotes Arts and Culture, manages copyrights, as well as funding for cultural events in music, theater, dance, art exhibitions, and film-making, and making improvements to the national language.

- Ministry of Health, Labour, and Welfare
- Pension Service
- Central Labour Relations Commission
- Ministry of Agriculture, Forestry and Fisheries
- Fisheries Agency
- Forestry Agency
- Ministry of Economy, Trade and Industry (METI)
- Agency for Natural Resources and Energy
- Small and Medium Enterprise Agency
- Patent Office

4. Administers the laws relating to patents, utility models, designs, and trademarks.

- Ministry of Land, Infrastructure, Transport and Tourism (MLIT)

- Japan Transport Safety Board
- Japan Tourism Agency
- Japan Meteorological Agency
- Japan Coast Guard
- Ministry of the Environment
- Nuclear Regulation Authority
- Ministry of Defense
- National Security Council
- Self-Defense Forces (Ground / Maritime / Air)

5. As of November 18, 2017.

The Board of Audit is the only unique body of the Government; in which, the Board is totally independent from the Diet and the Cabinet. It reviews government expenditures and submits an annual report to the Diet. Article 90 of theConstitution of Japan and the Board of Audit Act of 1947 gives this body substantial independence from both controls.

LEGISLATIVE

The Legislative branch organ of Japan is the National Diet . It is a bicameral legislature, composing of a lower house, the House of Representatives, and an upper house, the House of Councillors. Empowered by the Constitution to be "the highest organ of State power" and the only "sole law-making organ of the State", its houses are both directly elected under a parallel voting system and is ensured by the Constitution to have no discrimination on the qualifications of each members; whether be it based on "race, creed, sex, social status, family origin, education, property or income". The National Diet, therefore, reflects the sovereignty of the people; a principle of popular sovereignty whereby the supreme power lies within, in this case, the Japanese people.

The Diet responsibilities includes the making of laws, the approval of the annual national budget, the approval of the conclusion of treaties and the selection of the Prime Minister. In addition, it has the power to initiate draft constitutional amendments, which, if approved, are to be presented to the people for ratification in a referendum before being promulgated by the Emperor, in the name of the people. The Constitution also enables both houses to conduct investigations in relation to government, demand the presence and testimony of witnesses, and the production of records, as well as allowing either house of the Diet to demand the presence of the Prime Minister or the other Minister of State, in order to give answers or explanations whenever so required. The Diet is also able to impeach Court judges convicted of criminal or irregular conduct. The Constitution, however, does not specify the voting methods, the number of members of each house, and all other matters pertaining to the method of election of the each members, and are thus, allowed to be determined for by law.

Under the provisions of the Constitution and by law, all adults aged over 18 are eligible to vote, with a secret ballot and auniversal suffrage, and those elected have certain protections from apprehension while the Diet is in session. Speeches, debates, and votes cast in the Diet also enjoy parliamentary privileges. Each house is responsible for disciplining its own members, and all deliberations are public unless two-thirds or more of those members present passes a resolution agreeing it otherwise. The Diet also requires the presence of at least one-third of the membership of either house in order to constitute a quorum. All decisions are decided by a majority of those present, unless otherwise stated by the Constitution, and in the case of a tie, the presiding officer has the right to decide the issue. A member cannot be expelled, however, unless a majority of two-thirds or more of those members present passes a resolution therefor.

Under the Constitution, at least one session of the Diet must be convened each year. The Cabinet can also, at will, convoke extraordinary sessions of the Diet and is required to, when a quarter or more of the total members of either house demands it. During an election, only the House of Representatives is dissolved. The House of Councillors is however, not dissolved but only closed, and may, in times of national emergency, be convoked for an emergency session. The Emperor both convokes the Diet and dissolves the House of Representatives, but only does so on the advice of the Cabinet.

For bills to become Law, they are to be first passed by both houses of the National Diet, signed by the Ministers of State, countersigned by the Prime Minister, and then finally promulgated by the Emperor; however, without specifically giving the Emperor the power to oppose legislation.

House of Representatives

The House of Representatives of Japan is the Lower house, with the members of the house being elected once every four years, or when dissolved, for a four-year term. As of November 18, 2017, it has 465 members. Of these, 176 members are elected from 11 multi-member constituencies by a party-list system of proportional representation, and 289 are elected from single-member constituencies. 233 seats are required for majority. The House of Representatives is the more powerful house out of the two, it is able to overridevetoes on bills imposed by the House of Councillors with a two-thirds majority. It can, however, be dissolved by the Prime Minister at will. Members of the house must be of Japanese nationality; those aged 18 years and older may vote, while those aged 25 years and older may run for office in the lower house.

The legislative powers of the House of Representatives is considered to be more powerful than that of the House of Councillors. While the House of Councillors has the ability to veto most decisions made by the House of Representatives, some however, can only be delayed. This includes the legislation of treaties, the budget, and the selection of the Prime Minister. The Prime Minister, and collectively his Cabinet, can in turn, however, dissolve the House of Representatives whenever intended. While the House of Representatives is considered to be officially dissolved upon the preparation of the document, the House is only formally dissolved by the dissolution ceremony. The dissolution ceremony of the House is as follows:

1. The document is rubber stamped by the Emperor, and wrapped in a purple silk cloth; an indication of a document of state act, done on behalf of the people.

2. The document is passed on to the Chief Cabinet Secretary at the House of Representatives President's reception room.

3. The document is taken to the Chamber for preparation by the General-Secretary.

4. The General-Secretary prepares the document for reading by the Speaker.

5. The Speaker of the House of Representatives promptly declares the dissolution of the House.

6. The House of Representatives is formally dissolved.

It is customary that, upon the dissolution of the House, members will shout the Three Cheers of Banzai .

House of Councillors

The House of Councillors of Japan is the Upper house, with half the members of the house being elected once every three years, for a six-year term. As of November 18, 2017, it has 242 members. Of these, 73 are elected from the 47 prefectural districts, by single non-transferable votes, and 48 are elected from a nationwide list by proportional representation with open lists. The House of Councillors cannot be dissolved by the Prime Minister. Members of the house must be of Japanese nationality; those aged 18 years and older may vote, while those aged 30 years and older may run for office in the upper house.

As the House of Councillors can veto a decision made by the House of Representatives, the House of Councillors can cause the House of Representatives to reconsider its decision. The House of Representatives however, can still insist on its decision by overwriting the veto by the House of Councillors with a two-thirds majority of its members present. Each year, and when required, the National Diet is convoked at the House of Councillors, on the advice of the Cabinet, for an extra or an ordinary session, by the Emperor. A short speech is, however, usually first made by the Speaker of the House of Representatives before the Emperor proceeds to convoke the Diet with his Speech from the throne.

JUDICIAL

The Judicial branch of Japan consist of the Supreme Court, and four other lower courts; the High Courts, District Courts, Family Courts and Summary Courts. Divided into four basic tiers, the Court's independence from the executive and legislative branches are guaranteed by the Constitution, and is stated as: "no extraordinary tribunal shall be established, nor shall any organ or agency of the Executive be given final judicial power"; a feature known as theSeparation of Powers. Article 76 of the Constitution states that all the Court judges are independent in the exercise of their own conscience and that they are only bounded by the Constitution and the laws. Court judges are removable only by public impeachment, and can only be removed, without impeachment, when they are judicially declared mentally or physically incompetent to perform their duties. The Constitution also explicitly denies any power for executive organs or agencies to administer disciplinary actions against judges. However, a Supreme Court judge may be dismissed by a majority in a referendum; of which, must occur during the first general election of the National Diet's House of Representatives following the judge's appointment, and also the first general election for every ten years lapse thereafter.

Trials must be conducted, with judgment declared, publicly, unless the Court "unanimously determines publicity to be dangerous to public order or morals"; with the exception for trials of political offenses, offenses involving the press, and cases wherein the rights of people as guaranteed by the Constitution, which cannot be deemed and conducted privately. Court judges are appointed by the Cabinet, in attestation of the Emperor, while the Chief Justice is appointed by the Emperor, after being nominated by the Cabinet; which in practice, known to be under the recommendation of the former Chief Justice.

The Legal system in Japan has been historically influenced by Chinese law; developing independently during the Edo periodthrough texts such as *Kujikata Osadamegaki*. It has, however, changed during the Meiji Restoration, and is now largely based on the European civil law; notably, the civil code based on the German model still remains in effect. A quasi-jury system has recently came into use, and the legal system also includes a bill of rights since May 3, 1947. The collection ofSix Codes makes up the main body of the Japanese statutory law.

All Statutory Laws in Japan are required to be rubber stamped by the Emperor with the Privy Seal of Japan , and no Law can take effect without the Cabinet's signature, the Prime Minister's countersignature and the Emperor'spromulgation.

Supreme Court

The Supreme Court of Japan is the court of last resort and has the power of Judicial review; as defined by the Constitution to be "the court of last resort with power to determine the constitutionality of any law, order, regulation or official act". The Supreme Court is also responsible for nominating judges to lower courts and determining judicial procedures. It also oversees the judicial system, overseeing activities of public prosecutors, and disciplining judges and other judicial personnel.

High Courts

The High Courts of Japan has the jurisdiction to hear appeals to judgments rendered by District Courts and Family Courts, excluding cases under the jurisdiction of the Supreme Court. Criminal appeals are directly handled by the High Courts, but Civil cases are first handled by District Courts. There are eight High Courts in Japan: the Tokyo, Osaka, Nagoya, Hiroshima, Fukuoka, Sendai, Sapporo, and Takamatsu High Courts.

Penal system

The Penal system of Japan is operated by the Ministry of Justice. It is part of the criminal justice system, and is intended to resocialize, reform, and rehabilitate offenders. The ministry's Correctional Bureau administers the adult prison system, the juvenile correctional system, and three of the women's guidance homes, while the Rehabilitation Bureau operates the probation and the parole systems.

LOCAL GOVERNMENT

The Local Governments of Japan are unitary, in which local jurisdictions largely depend on the national government both administratively and financially. They are established as an act of devolution. Under the Constitution, all matters pertaining to the local self-government is allowed to be determined for by law; more specifically, the Local Autonomy Law.

The Ministry of Internal Affairs and Communications intervenes significantly in local government, as do other ministries. This is done chiefly financially because many local government jobs need funding initiated by national ministries. This is dubbed as the "thirty-percent autonomy".

The result of this power is a high level of organizational and policy standardization among the different local jurisdictions allowing them to preserve the uniqueness of their prefecture, city, or town. Some of the more collectivist jurisdictions, such asTokyo and Kyoto, have experimented with policies in such areas as social welfare that later were adopted by the national government.

Local Authorities

Japan is divided into forty-seven administrative divisions, the prefectures are: one metropolitan district (Tokyo), two urban prefectures (Kyoto and Osaka), forty-three rural prefectures, and one "district", Hokkaidô. Large cities are subdivided into wards, and further split into towns, or precincts, or subprefectures and counties.

Cities are self-governing units administered independently of the larger jurisdictions within which they are located. In order to attain city status, a jurisdiction must have at least 500,000 inhabitants, 60 percent of whom are engaged in urban occupations. There are self-governing towns outside the cities as well as precincts of urban wards. Like the cities, each has its own elected mayor and assembly. Villages are the smallest self-governing entities in rural areas. They often consist of a number of rural hamlets containing several thousand people connected to one another through the formally imposed framework of village administration. Villages have mayors and councils elected to four-year terms.

Structure of Local Government

Each jurisdiction has a chief executive, called a governor in prefectures and a mayor in municipalities. Most jurisdictions also have a unicameral assembly , although towns and villages may opt for direct governance by citizens in a general assembly . Both the executive and assembly are elected by popular vote every four years.

Local governments follow a modified version of the separation of powers used in the national government. An assembly may pass a vote of no confidence in the executive, in which case the executive must either dissolve the assembly within ten days or automatically lose their office. Following the next election, however, the executive remains in office unless the new assembly again passes a no confidence resolution.

The primary methods of local lawmaking are local ordinance and local regulations . Ordinances, similar to statutes in the national system, are passed by the assembly and may impose limited criminal penalties for violations (up to 2 years in prison and/or 1 million yen in fines). Regulations, similar to cabinet orders in the national system, are passed by the executive unilaterally, are superseded by any conflicting ordinances, and may only impose a fine of up to 50,000 yen.

Local governments also generally have multiple committees such as school boards, public safety committees (responsible for overseeing the police), personnel committees, election committees and auditing committees. These may be directly elected or chosen by the assembly, executive or both.

All prefectures are required to maintain departments of general affairs, finance, welfare, health, and labor. Departments of agriculture, fisheries, forestry, commerce, and industry are optional, depending on local needs. The Governor is responsible for all activities supported through local taxation or the national government.

EMPEROR

The Emperor is the symbol of Japan and of the unity of the people, performs the following acts in matters of state, with the advice and approval of the Cabinet, such as the promulgation of amendments of the Constitution, laws, cabinet orders and treaties, the convocation of the Diet, the dissolution of the House of Representatives, the proclamation of general election of members of the Diet, the attestation of the appointment and dismissal of Ministers of State and other officials as provided by laws, and of full powers and credentials of Ambassadors and Ministers, the awarding of honors, the attestation of instruments of ratification and other diplomatic documents as provided by laws, receiving foreign Ambassadors and Ministers and the performance of ceremonial functions, while he has no powers related to government.

He also appoints the Prime Minister and the Chief Justice of the Supreme Court as designated by the Diet and the Cabinet respectively.

In this respect, the position of the Emperor in postwar Japan differs from that in prewar days when the Emperor was the source of sovereign power.

The Imperial Throne is dynastic and succeeded from father to son.

Diet

The National Diet, composed of two houses - the House of Representatives and the House of Councilors, is the highest organ of state power and the sole law-making organ of the State.

The House of Representatives is composed of 480 members, of whom 300 are elected from the single-seat constituencies and 180 by the proportional representation system in which the nation is divided into 11 electoral blocs which according to size return between 6 and 30 members. Their term of office is 4 years, but shall be terminated, before the full term is up, if the House is dissolved.

The total membership of the House of Councilors is 242, of whom 96 are elected by the proportional representation system from a single nationwide electoral district and 146 from 47 prefectural constituencies, each returning 2 to 8 members. Their term of office is 6 years, and a half of the members being elected every 3 years.

Both Houses have the same power with some exceptional cases in which the decision of the House of Representatives precedes that of the House of Councilors.

The Diet begins its 150 day ordinary session from January each year, which may be extended only once by the Diet. The Cabinet may determine to convoke extraordinary sessions whenever necessary.

Cabinet

Executive power is vested in the Cabinet, which consists of the Prime Minister and not more than 17 Ministers of State (including Ministers without portfolio and the Chief Cabinet Secretary) and is collectively responsible to the Diet. The Cabinet has to resign en masse when the post of Prime Minister becomes vacant or when the first session of the Diet is convoked after a general election of members of the House of Representatives. If the House of Representatives passes a non-confidence resolution or rejects a confidence resolution the Cabinet shall resign en masse, unless the House of Representatives is dissolved within ten days.

Prime Minister, who is designated from among the members of the Diet by a resolution of the Diet and appointed by the Emperor, must be a civilian.

Prime Minister appoints the Ministers of States and may dismiss them as he chooses. The Prime Minister, representing the Cabinet, submits bills to the Diet, reports to the Diet on general national affairs and foreign relations, and exercises control and supervision over various administrative branches.

The Cabinet has the Cabinet Office and 11 Ministries, which are established by the respective Establishment Laws and are enumerated in the National Government Organization Law, as well as the Cabinet Secretariat, Cabinet Legislation Bureau, National Personnel Authority, Security Council of Japan, and other Cabinet organs.

There is the Board of Audit which is a constitutionally independent organization to audit the final accounts of the State and other public corporations and agencies.

Judiciary

The whole judicial power is vested in the Supreme Court, and in such inferior courts as High Courts, District Courts, Family Courts and Summary Courts.

No extraordinary court can be established, nor can any organ of the Executive have final judicial power.

The Justices of the Supreme Court, except the Chief Justice who is appointed by the Emperor, are appointed by the Cabinet. The Judges of inferior courts are also appointed by the Cabinet but only from a list of persons nominated by the Supreme Court.

POLITICS OF JAPAN

The politics of Japan is conducted in a framework of a multi-party bicameralparliamentary representative democratic constitutional monarchy whereby theEmperor acts as the ceremonial head of state, and the Prime Minister is the head of government and the head of the Cabinet, which directs the executive branch.

Legislative power is vested in the National Diet, which consists of the House of Representatives and the House of Councillors. Judicial power is vested in theSupreme Court and lower courts, and sovereignty is vested in the Japanese peopleby the Constitution.

Japan is considered a constitutional monarchy with a system ofcivil law.

Government

The Constitution of Japan defines the Emperor to be "the symbol of the State and of the unity of the people". He performs ceremonial duties and holds no real power. Political power is held mainly by the Prime Minister and other elected members of the Diet. The Imperial Throne is succeeded by a member of the Imperial House as designated by the Imperial Household Law.

The chief of the executive branch, the Prime Minister, is appointed by the Emperor as directed by the Diet. He is a member of either house of the Diet and must be a civilian. The Cabinet members are nominated by the Prime Minister, and are also required to be civilian. With the Liberal Democratic Party (LDP) in power, it has been convention that the President of the party serves as the Prime Minister.

POLITICAL PARTIES AND ELECTIONS

Several political parties exist in Japan, however, the politics of Japan have primarily been dominated by the LDP since 1955, with the DPJ playing an important role as opposition several times.

POLICY MAKING

Despite an increasingly unpredictable domestic and international environment, policy making conforms to well established postwar patterns. The close collaboration of the ruling party, the elite bureaucracy and important interest groups often make it difficult to tell who exactly is responsible for specific policy decisions.

Policy development in Japan

After a largely informal process within elite circles in which ideas were discussed and developed, steps might be taken to institute more formal policy development. This process often took place in deliberation councils (*shingikai*). There were about 200 *shingikai*, each attached to a ministry; their members were both officials and prominent private individuals in business, education, and other fields. The *shingikai* played a large role in facilitating communication among those who ordinarily might not meet.

Given the tendency for real negotiations in Japan to be conducted privately (in the *nemawashi*, or root binding, process of consensus building), the *shingikai* often represented a fairly advanced stage in policy formulation in which relatively minor differences could be thrashed out and the resulting decisions couched in language acceptable to all. These bodies were legally established but had no authority to oblige governments to adopt their recommendations. The most important deliberation council during the 1980s was the Provisional Commission for Administrative Reform, established in March 1981 by Prime Minister Suzuki Zenko. The commission had nine members, assisted in their deliberations by six advisers, twenty-one "expert members," and around fifty "councillors" representing a wide range of groups. Its head, Keidanren presidentDoko Toshio, insisted that government agree to take its recommendations seriously and commit itself to reforming the administrative structure and the tax system.

In 1982, the commission had arrived at several recommendations that by the end of the decade had been actualized. These implementations included tax reform, a policy to limit government growth, the establishment in 1984 of the Management and Coordination Agency to replace the Administrative Management Agency in the Office of the Prime Minister, and privatization of the state-owned railroad and telephone systems. In April 1990, another deliberation council, the Election Systems Research Council, submitted proposals that included the establishment of single-seat constituencies in place of the multiple-seat system.

Another significant policy-making institution in the early 1990s were the Liberal Democratic Party's Policy Research Council. It consisted of a number of committees, composed of LDP Diet members, with the committees corresponding to the different executive agencies. Committee members worked closely with their official counterparts, advancing the requests of their constituents, in one of the most effective means through which interest groups could state their case to the bureaucracy through the channel of the ruling party.

POST-WAR POLITICAL DEVELOPMENTS IN JAPAN

Political parties had begun to revive almost immediately after the occupation began. Left-wing organizations, such as theJapan Socialist Party and the Japanese Communist Party, quickly reestablished themselves, as did various conservative parties. The old Rikken Seiyûkai and Rikken Minseitô came back as, respectively, the Liberal Party (Nihon Jiyûtô) and theJapan Progressive Party (Nihon Shimpotô). The first postwar elections were held in 1948 (women were given the franchise for the first time in 1947), and the Liberal Party's vice president, Yoshida Shigeru (1878–1967), became prime minister.

For the 1947 elections, anti-Yoshida forces left the Liberal Party and joined forces with the Progressive Party to establish the new Democratic Party (Minshutô). This divisiveness in conservative ranks gave a plurality to the Japan Socialist Party, which was allowed to form a cabinet, which lasted less than a year. Thereafter, the socialist party steadily declined in its electoral successes. After a short period of Democratic Party administration, Yoshida returned in late 1948 and continued to serve as prime minister until 1954.

Even before Japan regained full sovereignty, the government had rehabilitated nearly 80,000 people who had been purged, many of whom returned to their former political and government positions. A debate over limitations on military spending and the sovereignty of the Emperor ensued, contributing to the great reduction in the Liberal Party's majority in the first post-occupation elections (October 1952). After several reorganizations of the armed forces, in 1954 the Japan Self-Defense Forces were established under a civilian director. Cold War realities and the hot war in nearby Korea also contributed significantly to the United States-influenced economic redevelopment, the suppression of communism, and the discouragement of organized labor in Japan during this period.

Continual fragmentation of parties and a succession of minority governments led conservative forces to merge the Liberal Party (Jiyûtô) with the Japan Democratic Party (Nihon Minshutô), an offshoot of the earlier Democratic Party, to form theLiberal Democratic Party (Jiyû-Minshutô; LDP) in November 1955, called 1955 System. This party continuously held power from 1955 through 1993, except for short when it was replaced by a new minority government. LDP leadership was drawn from the elite who had seen Japan through the defeat and occupation. It attracted former bureaucrats, local politicians, businessmen, journalists, other professionals, farmers, and university graduates.

In October 1955, socialist groups reunited under the Japan Socialist Party, which emerged as the second most powerful political force. It was followed closely in popularity by the Kômeitô, founded in 1964 as the political arm of the Soka Gakkai(Value Creation Society), until 1991, a lay organization affiliated with the Nichiren Shoshu Buddhist sect. The Komeito emphasized the traditional Japanese beliefs and attracted urban laborers, former rural residents, and women. Like theJapan Socialist Party, it favored the gradual modification and dissolution of the Japan-United States Mutual Security Assistance Pact.

Political developments since 1990

The LDP domination lasted until the Diet Lower House elections on 18 July 1993, in which LDP failed to win a majority. Acoalition of new parties and existing opposition parties formed a governing majority and elected a new prime minister,Morihiro Hosokawa, in August 1993. His government's major legislative objective was political reform, consisting of a package of new political financing restrictions and major changes in the electoral system. The coalition succeeded in passing landmark political reform legislation in January 1994.

In April 1994, Prime Minister Hosokawa resigned. Prime Minister Tsutomu Hata formed the successor coalition government, Japan's first minority government in almost 40 years. Prime Minister Hata resigned less than two months later. Prime MinisterTomiichi Murayama formed the next government in June 1994 with the coalition of Japan Socialist Party (JSP), the LDP, and the small New Party Sakigake. The advent of a coalition containing the JSP and LDP shocked many observers because of their previously fierce rivalry.

Prime Minister Murayama served from June 1994 to January 1996. He was succeeded by Prime Minister Ryutaro Hashimoto, who served from January 1996 to July 1998. Prime Minister Hashimoto headed a loose coalition of three parties until the July 1998 Upper House election, when the two smaller parties cut ties with the LDP. Hashimoto resigned due to a poor electoral performance by the LDP in the Upper House elections. He was succeeded as party president of the LDP and prime minister by Keizo Obuchi, who took office on

30 July 1998. The LDP formed a governing coalition with the Liberal Party in January 1999, and Keizo Obuchi remained prime minister. The LDP-Liberal coalition expanded to include the New Komeito Party in October 1999.

Political developments since 2000

Prime Minister Obuchi suffered a stroke in April 2000 and was replaced by Yoshiro Mori. After the Liberal Party left the coalition in April 2000, Prime Minister Mori welcomed a Liberal Party splinter group, the New Conservative Party, into the ruling coalition. The three-party coalition made up of the LDP, New Komeito, and the New Conservative Party maintained its majority in the Diet following the June 2000 Lower House elections.

After a turbulent year in office in which he saw his approval ratings plummet to the single digits, Prime Minister Mori agreed to hold early elections for the LDP presidency in order to improve his party's chances in crucial July 2001 Upper House elections. On 24 April 2001, riding a wave of grassroots desire for change, maverick politician Junichiro Koizumi defeated former Prime Minister Hashimoto and other party stalwarts on a platform of economic and political reform.

Koizumi was elected as Japan's 87th Prime Minister on 26 April 2001. On 11 October 2003, Prime Minister Koizumi dissolved the lower house and he was re-elected as the president of the LDP. Likewise, that year, the LDP won the election, even though it suffered setbacks from the new opposition party, the liberal and social-democratic Democratic Party (DPJ). A similar event occurred during the 2004 Upper House elections as well.

In a strong move, on 8 August 2005, Prime Minister Junichiro Koizumi called for a snap election to the lower house, as threatened, after LDP stalwarts and opposition DPJ parliamentarians defeated his proposal for a large-scale reform and privatization of Japan Post, which besides being Japan's state-owned postal monopoly is arguably the world's largest financial institution, with nearly 331 trillion yen of assets. The election was scheduled for 11 September 2005, LDP managed landslide victory by under the leadership of Junichiro Koizumi's.

The ruling LDP started losing hold since 2006. No prime minister except Koizumi had good public support. On 26 September 2006, new LDP President Shinzo Abe was elected by a special session of the Diet to succeed Junichiro Koizumi as Prime Minister. He was the Japan's youngest post-World War II prime minister and the first born after the war. On 12 September 2007, Prime Minister Shinzo Abe surprised Japan by announcing his resignation from office. He was eventually replaced byYasuo Fukuda, a veteran of LDP.

In the meantime, on 4 November 2007, leader of the main opposition party, Ichiro Ozawa announced his resignation from the post of party president, after controversy over an offer to the DPJ to join the ruling coalition in a grand coalition, but has since, with some embarrassment, rescinded his resignation.

On 11 January 2008, Prime Minister Yasuo Fukuda forced a bill allowing ships to continue a refueling mission in the Indian Ocean in support of US-led operations in Afghanistan. To do so, PM Fukuda used the LDP's overwhelming majority in the Lower House to ignore a previous 'no-vote' of the opposition-controlled Upper House. This was the first time in 50 years that the Lower House voted to ignore the opinion of the Upper House. Fukuda resigned suddenly on 1 September 2008, just a few weeks after reshuffling his cabinet. On 1 September 2008, Fukuda's resignation was designed so that the LDP did not suffer a "power vacuum." It thus caused a leadership election within the LDP, and the winner, Taro Aso was chosen as the new party president and on 24 September 2008, he was appointed as 92nd Prime Minister after the House of Representatives voted in his favor in the extraordinary session of Diet.

Later, on 21 July 2009, Prime Minister Aso dissolved the House of Representatives and elections were held on 30 August.The election results for the House of Representatives were announced on 30 and 31 August 2009. The opposition party DPJ led by Yukio Hatoyama, won a majority by gaining 308 seats (10 seats were won by its allies the Social Democratic Party and the People's New Party). On 16 September 2009, president of DPJ, Hatoyama was elected by the House of Representatives as the 93rd Prime Minister of Japan.

Political developments since 2010

On 2 June 2010, Hatoyama resigned due to lack of fulfillments of his policies, both domestically and internationally and soon after, on 8 June, Akihito, Emperor of Japan ceremonially swore in the newly elected DPJ's president, Naoto Kan as prime minister. Kan suffered an early setback in the Japanese House of Councillors election, 2010. In a routine political change in Japan, DPJ's new president and former finance minister of Naoto Kan's cabinet, Yoshihiko Noda was cleared and elected by the Diet as 95th prime minister on 30 August 2011. He was officially appointed as prime minister in the attestation ceremony at imperial palace on 2 September 2011.

In an undesired move, Noda dissolved the lower house on 16 November 2012 (as he fails to get support outside the Diet on various domestic issues i.e. tax, nuclear energy) and elections were held on 16 December. The results were in the favor of LDP, which won absolute majority in the leadership of former Prime Minister Shinzô Abe. He was appointed as the 96th Prime Minister of Japan on 26 December 2012. With the changing political situation, earlier in November 2014, Prime Minister Abe called for fresh mandate for the Lower House. In an opinion poll the government failed to win the public trust due to bad economic achievements in the two consecutive quarters and on the tax reforms.

The election was held on 14 December 2014, and the results were in the favor of LDP and its ally New Komeito. Together they managed to secure a huge majority by winning 325 seats for the Lower House. The opposition, DPJ, could not manage to provide the alternatives to the voters with its policies and programs. "Abenomics", the ambitious self-titled fiscal policy of the current prime minister, managed to attract more voters in this election, many Japanese voters supported the policies. Shinzô Abe was sworn as the 97th prime minister on 24 December 2014 and would like go ahead with his agenda of economic revitalization and structural reforms in Japan.

Foreign relations

Japan is a member state of the United Nations and pursues a permanent membership of the Security Council - Japan is one of the "G4 nations" seeking permanent membership. Japan plays an important role in East Asia. The Japanese Constitution prohibits the use of military forces to wage war against other countries. The government maintains a "Self-Defense Force", which include air, land and sea components. Japan's deployment of non-combat troops to Iraq marked the first overseas use of its military since World War II.

As an economic power, Japan is a member of the G8 and Asia-Pacific Economic Cooperation (APEC), and has developed relations with ASEAN as a member of "ASEAN plus three" and the East Asia Summit. Japan is a major donor in international aid and development efforts, donating 0.19% of its Gross National Income in 2004.

Japan has territorial disputes with Russia over the Kuril Islands (Northern Territories), with South Korea over Liancourt Rocks (known as "Dokdo" in Korea, "Takeshima" in Japan), with China and Taiwan over the Senkaku Islands and with China over the status of Okinotorishima.

These disputes are in part about the control of marine and natural resources, such as possible reserves of crude oil and natural gas. Japan has an ongoing dispute with North Korea over its abduction of Japanese citizens and nuclear weapons program.

5

Foreign Relations and Policy

FOREIGN RELATIONS OF JAPAN

The Foreign relations of Japan (*Nihon no kokusai kankei*)is handled by the Ministry of Foreign Affairs of Japan. Japanese foreign relations had to begin askew in 1945, when it was defeated in war and stripped of all of its foreign conquests and possessions.

History of Japanese foreign relations. The United States, acting for the Allied powers, occupied Japan 1945-51. Since gaining full independence with theTreaty of San Francisco, Japanese diplomatic policy has been based on close partnership with the United States and the emphasis on the international cooperation such as the United Nations.

In the Cold War, Japan took a part in the Western world's confrontation of the Soviet Union in East Asia. In the rapid economic developments in the 1960s and 1970s, Japan recovered its influences and became regarded as one of the major powers in the world. However, Japanese influences are regarded as negative by two particular countries: China and South Korea.

During the Cold War, Japanese foreign policy was not self-assertive, relatively focused on their economic growth. However, the end of the Cold War and bitter lessons from the Gulf War changed the policy slowly. Japanese government decided to participate in the Peacekeeping operations by the UN, and sent their troops to Cambodia, Mozambique, Golan Heights and the East Timor in the 1990s and 2000s. After the September 11 attacks in 2001, Japanese naval vessels have been assigned to resupply duties in the Indian Ocean to the present date. The Ground Self-Defense Force also dispatched their troops to Southern Iraq for the restoration of basic infrastructures.

Beyond its immediate neighbors, Japan has pursued a more active foreign policy in recent years, recognizing the responsibility which accompanies its economic strength.

Prime Minister Yasuo Fukuda stressed a changing direction in a policy speech to the National Diet: "Japan aspires to become a hub of human resource development as well as for research and intellectual contribution to further promote cooperation in the field of peace-building."This follows the modest success of a Japanese-conceived peace plan which became the foundation for nationwide elections in Cambodia in 1998.

History

Links

- Foreign relations of Meiji Japan
- International relations of the Great Powers (1814–1919)
- Diplomatic history of World War I
- International relations (1919–1939)
- Causes of World War II
- Diplomatic history of World War II
- Cold War
- History of Sino-Japanese relations, China
- France–Japan relations
- Germany–Japan relations
- Greater East Asia Co-Prosperity Sphere, 1930-1945
- History of Japan–Korea relations
- Japan–North Korea relations
- Japan–South Korea relations
- Japanese foreign policy on Southeast Asia
- Japan–Russia relations
- Japan–Soviet Union relations
- Japan–United Kingdom relations
- Japan–United States relations

ASIA

Southeast Asia

By 1990 Japan's interaction with the vast majority of Asia-Pacific countries, especially its burgeoning economic exchanges, was multifaceted and increasingly important to the recipient countries. The developing countries of the Association of Southeast Asian Nations (ASEAN) regarded Japan as critical to their development. Japan's aid to the ASEAN countries totaled US $1.9 billion in Japanese fiscal year (FY) 1988 versus about US $333 million for the United States during U.S. FY 1988. Japan was the number one foreign investor in the ASEAN countries, with cumulative investment as of March 1989 of about US $14.5 billion, more than twice that of the United States. Japan's share of total foreign investment in ASEAN countries in the same period ranged from 70 to 80 percent in Thailand to 20 percent in Indonesia.

In the late 1980s, the Japanese government was making a concerted effort to enhance its diplomatic stature, especially in Asia. Toshiki Kaifu's much publicized spring 1991 tour of five Southeast Asian nations — Malaysia, Brunei, Thailand,Singapore, and the Philippines — culminated in a 3 May major foreign policy address in Singapore, in which he called for a new partnership with the ASEAN and pledged that Japan would go beyond the purely economic sphere to seek an "appropriate role in the political sphere as a nation of peace." As evidence of this new role, Japan took an active part in promoting negotiations to resolve the Cambodian conflict.

In 1997, the ASEAN member nations and the People's Republic of China, South Korea and Japan agreed to hold yearly talks to further strengthen regional cooperation, the ASEAN Plus Three meetings. In 2005 the ASEAN plus Three countries together with India, Australia and New Zealand held the inaugural East Asia Summit (EAS).

South Asia

In South Asia, Japan's role is mainly that of an aid donor. Japan's aid to seven South Asian countries totaled US$1.1 billion in 1988 and 1989, dropping to just under US$900 million in 1990. Except for Pakistan, which received heavy inputs of aid from the United States, all other South Asian countries receive most of their aid from Japan. Four South Asian nations — India, Pakistan, Bangladesh, and Sri Lanka — are in the top ten list of Tokyo's aid recipients worldwide. A point to note is that Indian Government has a no receive aid policy since the tsunami that struck India but Indian registerred NGOs look to Japan for much investment in their projects

Prime Minister Toshiki Kaifu signaled a broadening of Japan's interest in South Asia with his swing through the region in April 1990. In an address to the Indian parliament, Kaifu stressed the role of free markets and democracy in bringing about "a new international order," and he emphasized the need for a settlement of the Kashmir territorial dispute between India and Pakistan and for economic liberalization to attract foreign investment and promote dynamic growth. To India, which was very short of hard currency, Kaifu pledged a new concessional loan of ¥100 billion (about US$650 million) for the coming year.

INDIA–JAPAN RELATIONS

India–Japan relations have traditionally been strong. the people of India andJapan have engaged in cultural exchanges, primarily as a result of Buddhism, which spread indirectly from India to Japan, via China and Korea. The people of India and Japan are guided by common cultural traditions including the heritage of Buddhism, and share commitment to the ideals of democracy, tolerance, pluralism and open society.

India and Japan, two of the largest and oldest democracies in Asia, having a high degree of congruence of political, economic and strategic interests, view each other as partners that have responsibility for and are capable of responding to global and regional challenges. India is the largest recipient of Japanese official development assistance (ODA). As of 2013, bilateral trade between India and Japan stood at US$16.31 billion and is expected to reach US$50 billion by 2019-20.

India, under British colonial rule, and Japan were enemies in World War II, but political relations between the two nations have remained warm since India's independence. Japanese companies, such as Sony, Toyota, and Honda, have manufacturing facilities in India, and with the growth of the Indian economy, India is a big market for Japanese firms. Japanese firms in fact, were some of the first firms to invest in India. The most prominent Japanese company to have an investment in India is automobiles multinational Suzuki, which is in partnership with Indian automobiles company Maruti Suzuki, the largest car manufacturer in the Indian market, and a subsidiary of the Japanese company.

In December 2006, Indian Prime Minister Manmohan Singh's visit to Japan culminated in the signing of the "Joint Statement Towards Japan-India Strategic and Global Partnership". Japan has helped finance many infrastructure projects in India, most notably the Delhi Metro system. Indian applicants were welcomed in 2006 to the JET Programme, starting with just one slot available in 2006 and 41 in 2007. Also, in the year 2007, the Japanese Self-Defence Forces and the Indian Navy took part in a joint naval exercise in the Indian Ocean, known as Malabar 2007, which also involved the naval forces of Australia, Singapore and theUnited States. The year 2007 was declared "India-Japan Friendship Year."

According to a 2013 BBC World Service Poll, 42% of Japanese people think India's international impact is mainly positive, with 4% considering it negative.

Historical relations

In my opinion, if all our rich and educated men once go and see Japan, their eyes will be opened. —
Swami Vivekananda, The Complete Works of Swami Vivekananda/Volume 5/Conversations and Dialogues/VI - X Shri Priya Nath Sinha

Though Hinduism is a little-practiced religion in Japan, it has still had a significant, but indirect role in the formation of Japanese culture. This is mostly because many Buddhist beliefs and traditions (which share a common Dharmic root with Hinduism) spread to Japan from China via Korean peninsula in the 6th Century. One indication of this is the Japanese "Seven Gods of Fortune", of which four originated as Hindu deities: Benzaitensama (Sarasvati), Bishamon (VaiœravaGa or Kubera), Daikokuten (Mahâkâla/Shiva), and Kichijôten (Lakshmi). Along with Benzaitennyo/Sarasvati andKisshoutennyo/Laxmi and completing the nipponization of the three Hindu Tridevi goddesses, the Hindu goddess Mahakali isnipponized as the Japanese goddess Daikokutennyo , though she is only counted among Japan's Seven Luck Deities when she is regarded as the feminine manifestation of her male counterpart Daikokuten . Benzaiten arrived in Japan during the 6th through 8th centuries, mainly via the Chinese translations of the *Sutra of Golden Light* , which has a section devoted to her. She is also mentioned in the Lotus Sutra. In Japan, the lokapâlas take the Buddhist form of the Four Heavenly Kings . The Sutra of Golden Light became one of the most important sutras inJapan because of its fundamental message, which teaches that the Four Heavenly Kings protect the ruler who governs his country in the proper manner. The Hindu god of death, Yama, is known in his Buddhist form as Enma. Garuda, the mount (vahana) of Vishnu, is known as the Karura , an enormous, fire-breathing creature in Japan. It has the body of a human and the face or beak of an eagle. Tennin originated from the apsaras. The Hindu Ganesha is displayed more than Buddha in a temple in Futako Tamagawa, Tokyo. Other examples of Hindu influence on Japan include the belief of "six schools" or "six doctrines" as well as use of Yoga and pagodas. Many of the facets of Hindu culture which have influenced Japan have also influenced Chinese culture.People have written books on the worship of Hindu gods in Japan. Even today, it is claimed Japan encourages a deeper study of Hindu gods.

Buddhism

Buddhism has been practiced in Japan since its official introduction in 552 CE according to the *Nihon Shoki* from Baekje,Korea by Buddhist monks. Although some Chinese sources place the first spreading of the religion earlier during theKofun period (250 to 538). Buddhism has had a major influence on the development of Japanese society and remains an influential aspect of the culture to this day.

Cultural exchanges between India and Japan began early in the 6th century with the introduction of Buddhism to Japan from India. The Indian monk Bodhisena arrived in Japan in 736 to spread Buddhism and performed eye-opening of the Great Buddha built inTôdai-ji, and would remain in Japan until his death in 760. Buddhism and the intrinsically linked Indian culture had a great impact on Japanese culture, still felt today, and resulted in a natural sense of amiability between the two nations.

As a result of the link of Buddhism between India and Japan, monks and scholars often embarked on voyages between the two nations. Ancient records from the now-destroyed library atNalanda University in India describe scholars and pupils who attended the school from Japan. One of the most famous Japanese travellers to the Indian subcontinent was Tenjiku Tokubei (1612–1692), named after *Tenjiku*("Heavenly Abode"), the Japanese name for India.

The cultural exchanges between the two countries created many parallels in their folklore. Modern popular culture based upon this folklore, such as works of fantasy fiction in manga and anime, sometimes bear references to common deities (deva), demons (asura) and philosophical concepts. The Indian goddess Saraswati for example, is known as Benzaiten in Japan.Brahma, known as 'Bonten', and Yama, known as 'Enma', are also part of the traditional Japanese Buddhist pantheon. In addition to the common Buddhist influence on the two societies, Shintoism, being an animist religion, is similar to the animist strands of Hinduism, in contrast to the religions present in the rest of the world, which are monotheistic. Sanskrit, a classical language used in Buddhism and Hinduism, is still used by some ancient Chinese priests who immigrated to Japan, and the SiddhaC script is still written to this day, despite having passed out of usage in India. It is also thought that the distinctive torii gateways at temples in Japan, may be related to the torana gateways used in Indian temples.

In the 16th century, Japan established political contact with Portuguese colonies in India. The Japanese initially assumed that the Portuguese were from India and that Christianity was a new "Indian faith". These mistaken assumptions were due to the Indian city of Goa being a central base for the Portuguese East India Company and also due to a significant portion of the crew on Portuguese ships being Indian Christians. Throughout the 16th and 17th centuries, Indian *lascar* seamen frequently visited Japan as crew members aboard Portuguese ships, and later aboard British ships in the 18th and 19th centuries.

During the anti-Christian persecutions in 1596, many Japanese Christians fled to the Portuguese colony of Goa in India. By the early 17th century, there was a community of Japanese traders in Goa in addition to Japanese slaves brought by Portuguese ships from Japan.

Relations between the two nations have continued since then, but direct political exchange began only in the Meiji era(1868–1912), when Japan embarked on the process of modernisation. Japan-India Association was founded in 1903.Further cultural exchange occurred during the mid-late 20th century through Asian cinema, with Indian cinema andJapanese cinema both experiencing a "golden age" during the 1950s and 1960s. Indian films by Satyajit Ray, Guru Duttwere influential in Japan, while Japanese films by Akira Kurosawa, Yasujirô Ozu and Takashi Shimizu have likewise been influential in India.

Indian Independence Movement

Japan's emergence as a power in the early 20th century was positively viewed in India and symbolised what was seen as the beginning of an Asian resurgence. In India, there was great admiration for Japan's post-war economic reconstruction and subsequent rapid growth. Sureshchandra Bandopadhyay, Manmatha Nath Ghosh and Hariprova Takeda were among the earliest Indians who visited Japan and had written on their experiences there.Correspondences between distinguished individuals from both nations had a noticeable increase at the time; historical documents show a friendship between Japanese thinker Okakura Tenshin and Indian writer Rabindranath Tagore,Okakura Tenshin and Bengali poet Priyamvada Banerjee.

As part of theBritish Empire, many Indians resented the British rule. The Anglo-Japanese Alliance was ended on 17 August 1923. As a result, during the two World Wars, the INA adopted the "an enemy of our enemy is our friend" attitude, legacy that is still controversial today given the war crimes committed by Imperial Japan and its allies.

Many Indian independence movement activists escaped from British rule and stayed in Japan.

The leader of the Indian Independence Movement, Rash Behari Bose created India–Japan relations. Future prime minister Tsuyoshi Inukai, pan-Asianist Mitsuru Tôyama and other Japanese supported the Indian Independence movement. A. M. Nair, a student from India, became an Independence Movement activist. Nair supported Netaji Subhas Chandra Bose during the war and JusticeRadha Binod Pal after the war.

In 1899 Tokyo Imperial University set up a chair in Sanskrit and Pali, with a further chair in Comparative religion being set up in 1903. In this environment, a number of Indian students came to Japan in the early twentieth century, founding the Oriental Youngmen's Association in 1900. Their anti-British political activity caused consternation to the Indian Government, following a report in the London Spectator.

During World War II

Since India was under British rule when World War II broke out, it was deemed to have entered the war on the side of the Allies. Over 2 million Indians participated in the war; many served in combat against the Japanese who conquered Burma and reached the Indian border. Some 67,000 Indian soldiers were captured by the Japanese when Singapore surrendered in 1942, many of whom later became part of the Indian National Army . In 1944-45, the combined British and Indian forces defeated the Japanese in a series of battles in Burma and the INA disintegrated.

Indian National Army

Subhas Chandra Bose, who led the Azad Hind, a nationalist movement which aimed to end the British raj through military means, used Japanese sponsorship to form the Azad Hind Fauj or *Indian National Army* (INA). The INA was composed mainly of former prisoners of war from the British Indian Army who had been captured by the Japanese after the fall of Singapore. They joined primarily because of the very harsh, often fatal conditions in POW camps. The INA also recruited volunteers from Indian expatriates in Southeast Asia. Bose was eager for the INA to participate in any invasion of India, and persuaded several Japanese that a victory such as Mutaguchi anticipated would lead to the collapse of British rule in India. The idea that their western boundary would be controlled by a more friendly government was attractive. Japan never expected India to be part of its Greater East Asia Co-Prosperity Sphere.

The Japanese Government built, supported and controlled the Indian National Army and the Indian Independence League.. Japanese forces included INA units in many battles, most notably at the U Go Offensive at Manipur. The offensive culminated in Battles of Imphal and Kohima where the Japanese forces were pushed back and the INA lost cohesion.

Modern relations

At the International Military Tribunal for the Far East, Indian Justice Radhabinod Palbecame famous for his dissenting judgement in favour of Japan. The judgement of Justice Radhabinod Pal is remembered even today in Japan. This became a symbol of the close ties between India and Japan.

A relatively well-known result of the two nations' was in 1949, when India sent theTokyo Zoo two elephants to cheer the spirits of the defeated Japanese empire.

India refused to attend the San Francisco Peace Conference in 1951 due to its concerns over limitations imposed upon Japanese sovereignty and national independence. After the restoration of Japan's sovereignty, Japan and India signed a peace treaty, establishing official diplomatic relations on 28 April 1952, in which India waived all reparation claims against Japan. This treaty was one of the first treaties Japan signed after World War II. Diplomatic, trade, economic, and technical relations between India and Japan were well established. India's iron ore helped Japan's recovery from World War II devastation, and following Japanese Prime Minister Nobusuke Kishi's visit to India in 1957, Japan started providing yen loans to India in 1958, as the first yen loan aid extended by Japanese government. Relations between the two nations were constrained, however, by Cold War politics. Japan, as a result of World War II reconstruction, was a U.S. ally, whereas India pursued a non-aligned foreign policy, often leaning towards the Soviet Union. Since the 1980s, however, efforts were made to strengthen bilateral ties. India's 'Look East' policy posited Japan as a key partner. Since 1986, Japan has become India's largest aid donor, and remains so.

Relations between the two nations reached a brief low in 1998 as a result ofPokhran-II, an Indian nuclear weapons test that year. Japan imposed sanctions on India following the test, which included the suspension of all political exchanges and the cutting off of economic assistance. These sanctions were lifted three years later. Relations improved exponentially following this period, as bilateral ties between the two nations improved once again, to the point where the Japanese prime minister, Shinzo Abe was to be the chief guest at India's 2014 Republic Day parade.

In 2014, the Indian PM Narendra Modi visited Japan. During his tenure as theChief Minister of Gujarat, Modi had maintained good ties with the Japanese PM Shinzo Abe. His 2014 visit further strengthened the ties between the two countries, and resulted in several key agreements, including the establishment of a "Special Strategic Global Partnership".

Modi visited Japan for the second time as Prime Minister in November 2016. During the meeting, India and Japan signed the "Agreement for Cooperation in Peaceful Uses of Nuclear Energy", a landmark civil nuclear agreement, under which Japan will supply nuclear reactors, fuel and technology to India. India is not a signatory to the non-Proliferation Treaty (NPT), and is the only non-signatory to receive an exemption from Japan. The two sides also signed agreements on manufacturing skill development in India, cooperation in space, earth sciences, agriculture, forestry and fisheries, transport and urban development.

Economic

In August 2000, the Japanese Prime Minister visited India. At this meeting, Japan and India agreed to establish "Japan-India Global Partnership in the 21st Century." Indian Prime Minister Vajpayee visited Japan in December, 2001, where both Prime Ministers issued "Japan-India Joint Declaration." In April, 2005, Japanese Prime Minister Koizumi visited India and signed Joint Statement "Japan-India Partnership in the New Asian Era: Strategic Orientation of Japan-India Global Partnership."

Japan is currently India's fourth largest source of foreign direct investment.

In October 2008, Japan signed an agreement with India under which it would provide the latter a low-interest loan worth US$4.5 billion to construct a railway project between Delhi and Mumbai. This is the single largest overseas project being financed by Japan and reflected growing economic partnership between the two nations. India is also one of the only three countries in the world with whom Japan has security pact.As of March 2006, Japan was the third largest investor in India.

Kenichi Yoshida, a director of Softbridge Solutions Japan, stated in late 2009 that Indian engineers were becoming the backbone of Japan's IT industry and that "it is important for Japanese industry to work together with India". Under the memorandum, any Japanese coming to India for business or work will be straightway granted a three-year visa and similar procedures will be followed by Japan. Other highlights of this visit includes abolition of customs duties on 94 per cent of trade between the two nations over the next decade. As per the Agreement, tariffs will be removed on almost 90 per cent of Japan's exports to India and 97 per cent of India's exports to Japan Trade between the two nations has also steadily been growing.

India and Japan signed an agreement in December 2015 to build a bullet train line between Mumbai and Ahmedabad using Japan's Shinkansen technology.. The agreement between India and Japan and the Indian Bullet Train that will be built will cost Japan £12bn and a 0.1% interest rate loan. With the help from Japan, both countries hope this will strengthen their economic ties and suspend China's influence in Asia.

Military

India and Japan also have close military ties. They have shared interests in maintaining the security of sea-lanes in the Asia-Pacific and Indian Ocean, and in co-operation for fighting international crime, terrorism, piracy and proliferation of weapons of mass destruction. The two nations have frequently held joint military exercises and co-operate on technology. India and Japan concluded a security pact on 22 October 2008. Japanese Prime Minister Shinzo Abe is seen by some to be an "Indophile" and, with rising tensions in territorial disputes with Japan's neighbors, has advocated closer security cooperation with India. In July 2014, the Indian Navy participated in Exercise Malabar with the Japanese and US navies, reflecting shared perspectives on Indo-Pacific maritime security. India is also negotiating to purchase US-2 amphibious aircraft for the Indian Navy.

Cultural

Japan and India have strong cultural ties, based mainly on Japanese Buddhism, which remains widely practiced through Japan Today. The two nations announced 2007, the 50th anniversary year of Indo-Japan Cultural Agreement, as the Indo-Japan Friendship and Tourism-Promotion Year, holding cultural events in both the countries. One such cultural event is the annual Namaste India Festival, which started in Japan over twenty years ago and is now the largest festival of its kind in the world. At the 2016 festival, representatives from Onagawa Town performed as a sign of appreciation for the support the town received from the Indian Government during the Great East Japan Earthquake. Onagawa is the town where the Indian National Disaster Response Force (NDRF) team was dispatched as its very first overseas mission and conducted search and rescue operations for missing persons.

Osamu Tezuka wrote biographical manga *Buddha* from 1972 to 1983. Recently, Japan has also supported the reconstruction of Nalanda University, an ancient Buddhist centre of learning and has agreed to provide financial assistance, and recently approached the Indian government with a proposal.

Tamil movies are very popular in Japan and Rajnikanth is the most popular Indian star in the country. Bollywood has become more popular among the Japanese people in recent decades, and the Indian yogi and pacifist Dhalsim is one of the most popular characters in the Japanese video game series *Street Fighter*....

Starting from July 3, 2014 Japan issues multiple entry visas for the short term stay of Indian nationals.

2016 nuclear deal

In November 2016, Indian Prime Minister Narendra Modi on a three-day visit to Japan signed a deal with his counterpart Shinzo Abe on nuclear energy. The deal took six years to negotiate, delayed in part by the 2011 Fukushima nuclear disaster. This is the first time that Japan signed such deal with a non-signatory of Non-Proliferation Treaty. The deal gives Japan the right to supply nuclear reactors, fuel and technology, to India. This deal aimed to help India build the six nuclear reactors planned in Delhi, to be completed by 2032.

JAPAN'S FOREIGN RELATIONS AND ROLE IN THE WORLD TODAY

Until the Meiji period (1868-1912) Japan's relationship with the rest of the world was defined mostly in terms of an East Asian world order traditionally dominated by China. Japan was part of trade routes that included much of Southeast and East Asia, and this trade resulted in much cultural exchange as well as material exchange. In the sixteenth century Japan began trading with Western countries, but soon found it disruptive both because of the connections with Christianity and because of the demand it created for precious metals. The government therefore officially limited foreign trade to that with Dutch and Chinese traders.

In the 19th century, Asia became more and more attractive to expansionist Europeans and many countries were colonized. China itself was greatly weakened and the old East Asia world order no longer functioned. Western countries aggressively demanded that Japan begin to participate in trade with them, and eventually Japan had no choice but to agree.

In the 1850s and 60s Japan signed various treaties with Western nations. At the time, imperialism and colonization were the main institutions that defined international relations and Japan soon became a colonizing power of its own, governing both Taiwan and Korea. At the beginning of the 20th century, Japan was recognized by Western powers as a force to be reckoned with, and Japan became a member of the League of Nations.

In the years leading to World War II, Japan created a puppet state in Manchuria, and became interested in gaining colonial power in other Asian countries being vacated by European powers. The bombing of Pearl Harbor and Japan's aggression in Asia led to war with the United States.

In the years following the defeat of Japan and the subsequent occupation by American forces, Japan has been heavily influenced by the United States in the political, economic and cultural arenas. Japan's constitution, written during the occupation, with its prohibition against militarization, and the U.S.-Japan Security Treaty, which allows for extensive American military presence in Japan, exemplify the post war relationship between these two countries.

But with the collapse of the Soviet Union, this relationship has been questioned. Many have asked whether Japan, particularly as a country with great economic strength, should be responsible for its own military. Japan gives much in foreign aid, but complaints continue that it is not yet a responsible member of the First World bloc. These complaints come mostly from Western countries, while another type of complaint comes from many Asian countries. These complaints are mostly a result of Japan's reluctance to accept the responsibility of accurately accounting for its actions during World War II.

These complaints are symptomatic of the great changes in the world order in the past decades, and Japan's difficulty in defining its position in this new order.

The United States

Since World War II, Japan's most important tie has been with the United States. Japan's mutual defense treaty with the United States is central to its security. The United States is committed to defend Japan and maintains military bases in Japan partially for that purpose. Despite Japan's defeat and subsequent occupation by Americans, relations with the United States have been friendly and close except for intermittent bouts of trade friction beginning in the 1970s. The United States sponsored Japan's membership in various international organizations, including the United Nations, the Organization for Economic Cooperation and Development (OECD), and the General Agreement on Tariffs and Trade (GATT). Trade between the United States and Japan is very important to both countries. The United States is a major market for Japanese exports as well as a primary source of imports (including a large percentage of Japan's food imports).

Southeast Asia

In World War II Japan went to war partly to gain control of this region's resources. The harsh occupation of many Southeast Asian countries left resentment and bitterness, and the Japanese government is today making efforts to improve the relationship with those countries. Taken as a whole, the countries of Southeast Asia make up Japan's second largest export market (after the United States), and they provide important food, oil, metal ore, lumber and rubber imports.

Korea

While Korea and Japan have traditionally shared many cultural aspects— including the Chinese writing system and Chinese philosophical and religious influences, Japan's harsh colonization of Korea in the early twentieth century has left relations strained between the two countries.

European Economic Community (EEC)

The countries that make up the EEC are highly developed economically and have an important voice in world affairs. Many of these countries share membership with Japan and the United States in important international economic organizations such as the OECD, GATT, and World Bank. Their alliance with the United States through the North Atlantic Treaty Organization (NATO) provides an indirect military link with Japan. The EEC is Japan's third largest market and supplies much of Japan's imports of industrial goods.

Persian Gulf Nations

Japan's relations with these nations have developed relatively recently, as oil imports from the Persian Gulf region have grown rapidly. Almost all of Japan's imports from these countries consist of petroleum and petroleum products, which total one-third of all Japanese imports. These nations make up Japan's fourth largest market, but because they import relatively little from Japan, Japan has a trade deficit with these nations. How to secure its economic interests in the face of political and military unrest in the region is one of Japan's most pressing problems.

China

Japan's long history of close cultural contact with China has left a special interest and friendliness toward the Chinese. Japan's writing system and many religious, literary, and artistic traditions originally came from China. During World War II, however, Japan colonized parts of Manchuria and invaded many major cities of China. Under

U.S. pressure, Japan did not establish relations with the People's Republic of China until after President Nixon surprised the world (and Japan) by establishing relations in 1972. Japan quickly followed suit and is now involved in assisting the Chinese in their efforts to develop their economy. Japan has been the largest source of official development assistance (ODA) to China.

Japan is also China's largest export market: in 1997 mainland China's exports to Japan were 18.7 percent of its total exports, in comparison, for example, with 15.1 percent of total exports from mainland China to the United States.

Russia.

Japan's relations with Russia have been strained throughout the postwar period. In the last days of World War II, the Soviets occupied South Sakhalin Islands and the Kurile islands, including a few islands close to Hokkaidô that the Japanese claim as part of their native land. The issue of these islands is under negotiation between the two countries. They have set a goal to resolve the conflict and sign a peace treaty by the year 2000.

HISTORY OF JAPANESE FOREIGN RELATIONS

History of Japanese foreign relations Covers the international relations in terms of diplomacy, economics and political affairs from about 1850 to 2000.

Meiji Restoration

Beginning with the Meiji Restoration of 1868, which established a new, centralized regime, Japan set out to "gather wisdom from all over the world" and embarked on an ambitious program of military, social, political, and economic reforms that transformed it within a generation into a modern nation-state and major world power. The Meiji oligarchy was aware of Western progress, and "learning missions" were sent abroad to absorb as much of it as possible. The Iwakura Mission, the most important one, was led by Iwakura Tomomi, Kido Takayoshi and Ôkubo Toshimichi, contained forty-eight members in total and spent two years (1871–73) touring the United States and Europe, studying every aspect of modern nations, such as government institutions, courts, prison systems, schools, the import-export business, factories, shipyards, glass plants, mines, and other enterprises. Upon returning, mission members called for domestic reforms that would help Japan catch up with the West.

European powers imposed a series of "unequal treaties" in the 1850s and 1860s that gave privileged roles to their nationals in specially designated treaty ports. Representative was the 1858 Treaty with the United States, called the "Harris Treaty." It opened the ports of Kanagawa and four other Japanese cities to trade, And provided for the exchange of diplomats. It granted extraterritoriality to foreigners, So that they govern themselves and were not under the control of Japanese courts or authorities. There were numerous trading stipulations favorable to the Americans. The Dutch, British and Russians quickly followed suit with their own treaties, backed up by their own powerful naval forces. The unequal treaties were part of the series imposed on non-Western countries, such as Persia 1857, Turkey 1861, Siam 1855, and China 1858. The inequality was not quite as severe as suffered by these other countries, but it rankled so much that ending the inequality became a priority that was finally achieved in the 1890s. The humiliation was not as bad as China suffered, but it energized anti-foreign forces inside Japan. On the other hand, the new treaties, provided for tariffs on imports from Europe; imports multiplied by a factor of nine between 1860 and 1864, and the tariff revenue provided major financial backing for the Meiji regime. Exports of tea, silk and other Japanese products multiplied by a factor of four in four years, dramatically stimulating the local economy while causing galloping inflation that drove up the price of rice. The Meiji leaders sketched a new vision for a modernized Japan's leadership role in Asia, but they realized that this role required that Japan develop its national strength, cultivate Japanese nationalism among the population, and carefully craft policies toward potential enemies. The skills and tricks of negotiation had to be learned, so they could compete on an equal basis with experienced Western diplomats. No longer could Westerners be seen as "barbarians"; In time, Japan formed a corps of professional diplomats and negotiators.

Japan becomes a power

Starting in the 1860s Japan rapidly modernized along Western lines, adding industry, bureaucracy, institutions and military capabilities that provided the base for imperial expansion into Korea, China, Taiwan and islands to the south. It saw itself vulnerable to aggressive Western imperialism unless it took control of neighboring areas. It took control of Okinawa and Formosa. Japan's desire to control Taiwan, Korea and Manchuria, led to the first Sino-Japanese War with China in 1894–1895 and the Russo-Japanese War with Russia in 1904–1905. The war with China made Japan the world's first Eastern, modern imperial power, and the war with Russia proved that a Western power could be defeated by an Eastern state. The aftermath of these two wars left Japan the dominant power in the Far East with a sphere of influence extending over southern Manchuria and Korea, which was formally annexed as part of the Japanese Empire in 1910.

Okinawa

Okinawa island is the largest of the Ryukyu Islands, and paid tribute to China from the late 14th century. Japan took control of the entire Ryukyu island chain in 1609 and formally incorporated it into Japan in 1879.

War with China

Friction between China and Japan arose from the 1870s from Japan's control over the Ryukyu Islands, rivalry for political influence in Korea and trade issues. Japan, having built up a stable political and economic system with a small but well-trained army and navy, easily defeated China in the First Sino-Japanese War of 1894. Japanese soldiers massacred the Chinese after capturing Port Arthur on the Liaotung Peninsula. In the harsh Treaty of Shimonoseki of April 1895, China recognize the independence of Korea, and ceded to Japan Formosa, the Pescatores Islands and the Liaotung Peninsula. China further paid an indemnity of 200 million silver taels, opened five new ports to international trade, and allowed Japan (and other Western powers) to set up and operate factories in these cities. However, Russia, France, and Germany saw themselves disadvantaged by the treaty and in the Triple Intervention forced Japan to return the Liaotung Peninsula in return for a larger indemnity. The only positive result for China came when those factories led the industrialization of urban China, spinning off a local class of entrepreneurs and skilled mechanics.

Taiwan

The island of Formosa (Taiwan) had an indigenous population when Dutch traders in need of an Asian base to trade with Japan and China arrived in 1623. The Dutch East India Company (VOC) built Fort Zeelandia. They soon began to rule the natives. China took control in the 1660s, and sent in settlers. By the 1890s there were about 2.3 million Han Chinese and 200,000 members of indigenous tribes. After its victory in the First Sino-Japanese War in 1894–95, the peace treaty ceded the island to Japan. It was Japan's first colony.

Japan expected far more benefits from the occupation of Taiwan than the limited benefits it actually received. Japan realized that its home islands could only support a limited resource base, and it hoped that Taiwan, with its fertile farmlands, would make up the shortage. By 1905, Taiwan was producing rice and sugar and paying for itself with a small surplus. Perhaps more important, Japan gained Asia-wide prestige by being the first non-European country to operate a modern colony. It learned how to adjust its German-based bureaucratic standards to actual conditions, and how to deal with frequent insurrections. The ultimate goal was to promote Japanese language and culture, but the administrators realized they first had to adjust to the Chinese culture of the people. Japan had a civilizing mission, and it opened schools so that the peasants could become productive and patriotic manual workers. Medical facilities were modernized, and the death rate plunged. To maintain order, Japan installed a police state that closely monitored everyone. In 1945, Japan was stripped of its empire and Taiwan was returned to China.

Korea

Further information: History of Japan–Korea relations and Korea under Japanese rule

In 1905, the Empire of Japan and the Korean Empire signed the Eulsa Treaty, which brought Korea into the Japanese sphere of influence as a protectorate. The Treaty was a result of the Japanese victory in the Russo-Japanese War and Japan wanting to increase its hold over the Korean Peninsula. The Eulsa Treaty led to the signing of the 1907 Treaty two years later. The 1907 Treaty ensured that Korea would act under the guidance of a Japanese resident general and Korean internal affairs would be under Japanese control. Korean Emperor Gojong was forced to abdicate in favour of his son,Sunjong, as he protested Japanese actions in the Hague Conference. Finally in 1910, the Annexation Treaty was signed, formally annexing Korea to Japan.

POLITICAL LEADERS

Prime Minister Ito

Prince Itô Hirobumi (1841-1909) was prime minister for most of the period 1885-1901 and dominated foreign policy. He strengthened diplomatic ties with Western powers including Germany, the United States and especially Great Britain through the Anglo-Japanese Alliance of 1905. In Asia he oversaw the short, victorious war against China 1894-95. He negotiated Chinese surrender on terms aggressively favourable to Japan, including the annexation of Taiwan and the release of Koreafrom the Chinese tribute system. He also gained control of the Liaodong Peninsula with Darien and Port Arthur, but was immediately forced by Russia, Germany and France acting together in the Triple Intervention to give that back to China. In the Anglo-Japanese Treaty of Commerce and Navigation of 1894, he succeeded in removing some of the onerous unequal treaty clauses that had plagued Japanese foreign relations since the start of the Meiji period. His major breakthrough was the Anglo-Japanese Alliance signed in 1902. It was a diplomatic milestone, it saw an end to Britain's splendid isolation. The alliance was renewed and expanded in scope twice, in 1905 and 1911, before its demise in 1921. It was officially terminated in 1923.

Itô sought to avoid a Russo-Japanese War through the policy of *Man-Kan kôkan* – surrendering Manchuria to the Russian sphere of influence in exchange for the acceptance of Japanese hegemony in Korea. A diplomatic tour of the United States and Europe brought him to Saint Petersburg in November 1901, where he was unable to find compromise on this matter with Russian authorities. Soon the government of Katsura Tarô elected to abandon the pursuit of *Man-Kan kôkan*, and tensions with Russia continued to escalate towards war.

Prime Minister Katsura Tarô

Prince Katsura Tarô (1848 – 1913) was an unpopular prime minister in his three terms stretching off and on from 1901 to 1911. During his first term (1901-1906) Japan emerged as a major imperialist power in East Asia. In terms of foreign affairs, it was marked by the Anglo-Japanese Alliance of 1902 and victory over Russia in the Russo-Japanese War of 1904-1905. During his tenure, the Taft–Katsura agreement with the U.S. acknowledged Japanese hegemony over Korea. His second term (1908-1911) was noteworthy for the Japan–Korea Annexation Treaty of 1910.

WORLD WAR I

Japan put heavy pressure on China in 1915, especially in the *Twenty-One Demands*. The U.S. helped China push back, thus moderating the pressure. As the Russian pro-Allied state collapsed into Bolshevik central control and multiple civil wars on the Russian periphery, United States sent 8000 troops to Siberia, and Japan, sent 80,000. Japan's goal was to take control of the trans-Siberian Railroad, and adjacent properties, giving it massive control over Manchuria. The Americans were originally sent to help check prisoners escape, but increasingly, their role was to watch and block Japanese expansion. Both nations remove their troops in 1920, as Lenin's Bolsheviks solidified their control over Russia. At the Paris Peace Conference in 1919, Japan was given the mandate over a number of smaller islands that had been part of the German Empire. Japan was disappointed when it's draft resolution condemning racism in international affairs, was dropped from the agenda. However, its main demand, which it pursued relentlessly, was to obtain permanent control of Germany's holdings in Shantung, China. which Japan had captured early in the war. China protested furiously, but have little leverage. TheShandong Problem appeared to be a Japan victory, but Tokyo soon had second thoughts as widespread protests inside China led to the May Fourth Movement led by angry radical students. Finally in 1922 with mediation by the U.S. and Britain Japan returned Shantung to China.

1920s

A sort of rapprochement took place between Washington and Tokyo, although there were still philosophical differences in their approaches. The Japanese operated in terms of traditional Power diplomacy, emphasizing control over distinct spheres of influence, while the United States adhered to Wilsonianism based on the "open door" and internationalist principles. Both sides compromised, and were successful in diplomatic endeavors such as the naval limitations at the Washington conference in 1922. The conference set a naval ratio for capital warships of 5:5:3 among the United States, Britain and Japan. The result was a de-escalation of the naval arms race for a decade. Japan was outraged at the racism inherent in the 1924 American immigration laws, which reduce the long-standing Japanese quota of 100 immigrants annually to zero.Japan was likewise annoyed at similar restrictions imposed by Canada and Australia. Britain, responding to anti—Japanese sentiment in its Commonwealth, and in the United States, did not renew its two deca e old treaty with Japan in 1923.

ARMY'S ROLE 1919-1941

The Army increasingly took control of the government, assassinated opposing leaders, suppressed the left, and promoted a highly aggressive foreign policy with respect to China. Japanese policy angered the United States, Britain, France, and the Netherlands. Japanese nationalism was the primary inspiration, coupled with a disdain for democracy. The extreme right became influential throughout the Japanese government and society, notably within the Kwantung Army, which was stationed in Manchuria along the Japanese-owned South Manchuria Railroad. During the Manchurian Incident of 1931, radical army officers conquered Manchuria from local officials and set up the puppet government of Manchukuo there without permission from the Japanese government. International criticism of Japan following the invasion led to Japan withdrawing from the League of Nations. Japan's expansionist vision grew increasingly bold. Many of Japan's political elite aspired to have Japan acquire new territory for resource extraction and settlement of surplus population. These ambitions led to the outbreak of the Second Sino-Japanese War in 1937. After their victory in the Chinese capital, the Japanese military committed the infamous Nanking Massacre. The Japanese military failed to destroy the Chinese government led by Chiang Kai-shek, which retreated to remote areas. The conflict was a stalemate that lasted until 1945. Japan's war aim was to establish the Greater East Asia Co-Prosperity Sphere, a vast pan-Asian union under Japanese domination. Hirohito's role in Japan's foreign wars remains a subject of controversy, with various historians portraying him as either a powerless figurehead or an enabler and supporter of Japanese militarism. The United States grew increasingly worried about the Philippines, an American colony, within easy range of Japan And started looking for ways to contain Japanese expansion.

WORLD WAR II

American public and elite opinion — including even the isolationists — strongly opposed Japan's invasion of China in 1937. President Roosevelt imposed increasingly stringent economic sanctions intended to deprive Japan of the oil and steel in needed to continue its war in China. Japan reacted by forging an alliance with Germany and Italy in 1940, known as the Tripartite Pact, which worsened its relations with the US. In July 1941, the United States, Great Britain, and the Netherlands froze all Japanese assets and cut off oil shipments—Japan had little oil of its own.

Japan had conquered all of Manchuria and most of coastal China by 1939, but the Allies refused to recognize the conquests and stepped up their commitment. President Franklin Roosevelt arranged for American pilots and ground crews to set up an aggressive Chinese Air Force nicknamed the Flying Tigers that would not only defend against Japanese air power but also start bombing the Japanese islands.Diplomacy provided very little space for the adjudication of the deep differences between Japan and the United States. The United States was firmly and almost unanimously committed to defending the integrity of China. The isolationism that characterized the strong opposition of many Americans toward war in Europe did not apply to Asia. Japan had no friends in the United States, nor in Great Britain, nor the Netherlands. The United States had not yet declared war on Germany, but was closely collaborating with Britain and the Netherlands regarding the Japanese threat. United States started to move its newest B-17 heavy bombers to bases in the Philippines, well within range of Japanese cities. The goal was deterrence of any Japanese attacks to the south. Furthermore, plans were well underway to ship American air forces to China, where American pilots in Chinese uniforms flying American warplanes, were preparing to bomb Japanese cities well before Pearl Harbor. Great Britain, although realizing it could not defend Hong Kong, was confident in its abilities to defend its major base in Singapore and the surrounding Malaya Peninsula. When the war did start in December 1941, Australian soldiers were rushed to Singapore, weeks before Singapore surrendered, and all the Australian and British forces were sent to prisoner of war camps. the Netherlands, with its homeland overrun by Germany, had a small Navy to defend the Dutch East Indies. Their role was to delay the Japanese invasion long enough to destroy the oil wells, drilling equipment, refineries and pipelines that were the main target of Japanese attacks.

Decisions in Tokyo were controlled by the Army, and then rubber-stamped by Emperor Hirohito; the Navy also had a voice. However, the civilian government and diplomats were largely ignored. The Army saw the conquest of China as its primary mission, but operations in Manchuria had created a long border with the Soviet Union. Informal, large-scale military confrontations with the Soviet forces at Nomonhan in summer 1939 demonstrated that the Soviets possessed a decisive military superiority. Even though it would help Germany's war against Russia after June 1941, the Japanese army refused to go north. The Japanese realized the urgent need for oil, over 90% of which was supplied by the United States, Britain and the Netherlands. From the Army's perspective, a secure fuel supply was essential for the warplanes, tanks and trucks— as well as the Navy's warships and warplanes of course. The solution was to send the Navy south, to seize the oilfields in the Dutch East Indies and nearby British colonies. Some admirals and many civilians, including Prime Minister Konoe Fumimaro, believed that a war with the U.S. would end in defeat. The alternative was loss of honor and power. While the admirals were also dubious about their long-term ability to confront the American and British navies, they hoped that a knockout blow destroying the American fleet at Pearl Harbor would bring the enemy to the negotiating table for a favorable outcome. Japanese diplomats were sent to Washington in summer 1941 to engage in high-level negotiations. However, they did not speak for the Army leadership that made the decisions. By early October both sides realized that no compromises were possible between the Japan's commitment to conquer China, and America's commitment to defend China. Japan's civilian government fell and the Army took full control, bent on war.

Imperial conquests

Japan launched several quick wars in East Asia, and they all worked. In 1937, the Japanese Army invaded and captured most of the coastal Chinese cities such as Shanghai. Japan took over French Indochina (Vietnam, Laos, Cambodia) in 1940-41. After declaring war on the U.S., Britain and the Netherlands in December 1941, it quickly conquered British Malaya(Brunei, Malaysia, Singapore) as well as the Dutch East Indies (Indonesia). Thailand managed to stay independent by becoming a satellite state of Japan. In December 1941 to May 1942, Japan sank major elements of the American, British and Dutch fleets, captured Hong Kong, Singapore, the Philippines and the Dutch East Indies, and reached the borders of India and began bombing Australia. Japan suddenly had achieved its goal of ruling the Greater East Asia Co-Prosperity Sphere.

Imperial rule

The ideology of Japan's colonial empire, as it expanded dramatically during the war, contained two contradictory impulses.

On the one hand, it preached the unity of the Co-Prosperity Sphere, a coalition of Asian races, directed by Japan, against the imperialism of Britain, France, the Netherlands, United States, and Europe in general. This approach celebrated the spiritual values of the East in opposition to the crass materialism of the West. In practice, it was a euphemistic title for grabbing land and acquiring essential natural resources. The Japanese installed organizationally-minded bureaucrats and engineers to run their new empire, and they believed in ideals of efficiency, modernization, and engineering solutions to social problems. Economist Akamatsu Kaname (1896-1974) devised the "Flying geese paradigm" in the late 1930s that provided a model of imperialistic economic behavior. Japan (the lead goose) would specialize in high technology, high-value manufacturing. It would purchase food, cotton, and iron ore at artificially low prices from the trailing Co-Prosperity Sphere geese, and sell them high-priced final products such as chemicals, fertilizers, and machinery. These dealings were carried out by the powerful zaibatsu corporations and supervised by the Japanese government. The Flying geese paradigm was revived after 1950 and was given credit for the rapid economic growth of Japan's East Asia trading partners.

The Japanese Army operated ruthless governments in most of the conquered areas, but paid more favorable attention to the Dutch East Indies. The main goal was to obtain oil, but Japan sponsored an Indonesian nationalist movement under Sukarno. Sukarno finally came to power in the late 1940s after several years of battling the Dutch. The Dutch destroyed their oil wells but the Japanese reopened them. However most of the tankers taking oil to Japan were sunk by American submarines, so Japan's oil shortage became increasingly acute.

Puppet states in China

Manchuria, the historic homeland of the Manchu dynasty, had an ambiguous character after 1912. It was run by local warlords. The Japanese Army seized control in 1931, and set up a puppet state of Manchukuo in 1932 for the 34,000,000 inhabitants. Other areas were added, and over 800,000 Japanese moved in as administrators. The nominal ruler was Puyi, who as a small child had been the last Emperor of China. He was deposed during the revolution of 1911, and now the Japanese brought him back in a powerless role. Only Axis countries recognized Manchukuo. The United States in 1932 announced the Stimson Doctrine stating that it would never recognize Japanese sovereignty. Japan modernized the economy and operated it as a satellite to the Japanese economy. It was out of range of American bombers, so its factories were expanded and continued their output to the end. Manchukuo was returned to China in 1945. When Japan seized control of China proper in 1937–38, the Japanese Central China Expeditionary Army set up the Reorganized National Government of China, a puppet state, under the nominal leadership of Wang Ching-wei (1883–1944). It was based in Nanjing. The Japanese were in full control; the puppet state declared war on the Allies in 1943. Wang was allowed to administer the International Settlement in Shanghai. The puppet state had an army of 900,000 soldiers, and was positioned against the Nationalist army under Chiang Kai-shek. It did little fighting.

1945-1990S

American Occupation

The Americans under General Douglas MacArthur were in ultimate command of Japanese affairs 1945-51. The other allies and former colonial possessions of Japan demanded revenge, but MacArthur operated a highly favorable system in which harsh measures were limited to war criminals, who were tried and executed. Japan lacked sovereignty and had no diplomatic relations—its people were not allowed to travel abroad. MacArthur worked to democratize Japan along the lines of the American New Deal, with the destruction of militarism and monopolistic corporations, and the inculcation of democratic values and electoral practices. MacArthur worked well with Emperor Hirohito, who was kept on the throne as a symbolic constitutional ruler. In practice, the actual administration of national and government was handled by the Japanese themselves under Prime Minister Yoshida Shigeru. His policy, known as the Yoshida Doctrine was to focus Japanese energies on rebuilding the economy, while relying entirely on the United States to handle defense and foreign policy generally. Yoshida shared and implemented MacArthur's goals was to democratize Japanese political, social and economic institutions, while completely de-militarizing the nation and renouncing its militaristic heritage.

MacArthur ordered a limited rearmament of Japan the week after the war broke out in June 1950, calling for a national police reserve of 75,000 men, which would be organized separately from the 125,000 police force that already existed. The Coast Guard grew from 10,000 to 18,000. The argument that these were police forces for domestic internal use carried the day over the objections of the anti-militarists. However, Washington envisioned a quasi-military force that would use military equipment on loan from the United States. Japan now had a small army of its own. Japan became the logistical base for the American and allied forces fighting in Korea, with a surge in orders for goods and services that jump-started the economy.

The occupation culminated in the Peace Treaty of 1951, signed by Japan, the United States, and 47 other involved nations, not including the Soviet Union or either Chinese government. The occupation officially ended in April 1952. American diplomat John Foster Dulles was in charge of drafting the peace treaty. He had been deeply involved in 1919, when severe reparations and the guilt clause was imposed against Germany at the Paris Peace Conference. Dulles thought that was a terrible mistake that energized the far right and the Nazis in Germany, and he made sure it never happened again. Japan was therefore not obligated to pay reparations to anyone.

"Economic Miracle" of 1950s

From 1950 onward, Japan rebuilt itself politically and economically. The U.S. and its allies used Japan as their logistics base during the Korean War (1950-53), which poured money into the economy. Historian Yone Sugita finds that "the 1950s was a decade during which Japan formulated a unique corporate capitalist system in which government, business, and labor implemented close and intricate cooperation".

Japan's newfound economic power soon gave it far more dominance than it ever had militarily. The Yoshida Doctrine and the Japanese government's economic intervention, spurred on an economic miracle on par with that of West Germany a few years earlier. The Japanese government strove to spur industrial development through a mix of protectionism and trade expansion. The establishment of the Ministry of International Trade and Industry (MITI) was instrumental in the Japanese post-war economic recovery. By 1954, the MITI system was in full effect. It coordinated industry and government action and fostered cooperative arrangements, and sponsored research to develop promising exports as well as imports for which substitutes would be sought (especially dyestuffs, iron and steel, and soda ash). Yoshida's successor, Hayato Ikeda, began implementing economic policies which removed much of Japan's anti-monopoly laws. Foreign companies were locked out of the Japanese market and strict protectionist laws were enacted.

Meanwhile, the United States under President Eisenhower saw Japan as the economic anchor for Western Cold War policy in Asia. Japan was completely demilitarized and did not contribute to military power, but did provide the economic power. The US and UN forces used Japan as their forward logistics base during the Korean War (1950–53), and orders for supplies flooded Japan. The close economic relationship strengthened the political and diplomatic ties, so that the two nations survived a political crisis in 1960 involving left-wing opposition to the U.S.-Japan Security Treaty. The left failed to force the removal of large American military bases in Japan, especially on Okinawa. Shimizu argues that the American policy of creating "people of plenty" was a success in Japan and reached its goal of defusing anti-capitalist protest on the left.

By the 1980s Japan's economy was the second-largest in the world after the United States. It kept this position until 2011, when the economy of China surpassed it.

FOREIGN POLICY OF JAPAN

The primary responsibility for the Japanese foreign policy, as determined by the 1947 constitution, is exercised by the cabinet and subject to the overall supervision of the National Diet. The prime minister is required to make periodic reports on foreign relations to the Diet, whose upper and lower houseseach have a foreign affairs committee. Each committee reports on its deliberations to plenary sessions of the chamber to which it belongs. Idlmm committees are formed occasionally to consider special questions. Diet members have the right to raise pertinent policy questions—officially termed interpellations—to the minister of foreign affairs and the prime minister. Treaties with foreign countries require ratification by the Diet. As head of state, the emperor performs the ceremonial function of receiving foreign envoys and attesting to foreign treaties ratified by the Diet.

Constitutionally the dominant figure in the political system, the prime minister has the final word in major foreign policy decisions. The minister of foreign affairs, a senior member of the cabinet, acts as the prime minister's chief adviser in matters of planning and implementation. The minister is assisted by two vice ministers: one in charge of administration, who was at the apex of theMinistry of Foreign Affairs structure as its senior career official, and the other in charge of political liaison with the Diet. Other key positions in the ministry include members of the ministry's Secretariat, which has divisions handling consular, emigration, communications, and cultural exchange functions, and the directors of the various regional and functional bureaus in the ministry.

Postwar period

Throughout the post–World War II period, Japan concentrated on economic growth. It accommodated itself flexibly to the regional and global policies of the United States while avoiding major initiatives of its own; adhered to pacifist principles embodied in the 1947 constitution, referred to as the "peace constitution"; and generally took a passive, low-profile role in world affairs. Relations with other countries were governed by what the leadership called "omnidirectional diplomacy," which was essentially a policy of maintaining political neutrality in foreign affairs while expanding economic relations wherever possible. This policy was highly successful and allowed Japan to prosper and grow as an economic power, but it was feasible only while the country enjoyed the security and economic stability provided by its ally, the United States.

Post-occupation Japan

When Japan regained its sovereignty in 1952 and reentered the international community as an independent nation, it found itself in a world preoccupied by the Cold War between East and West, in which the Soviet Union and the United States headed opposing camps. By virtue of the Treaty of Peace with Japan signed in San Francisco on September 8, 1951 (effective April 28, 1952), ending the state of war between Japan and most of the Allied powers except the Soviet Union and the People's Republic of China, and the Mutual Security Assistance Pact between Japan and the United States, signed in San Francisco the same day, Japan essentially became a dependent ally of the United States, which continued to maintainbases and troops on Japanese soil.

Japan's foreign policy goals during most of the early postwar period were essentially to regain economic viability and establish its credibility as a peaceful member of the world community. National security was entrusted to the protective shield and nuclear umbrella of the United States, which was permitted under the security pact that came into effect in April 1952 to deploy its forces in and about Japan. The pact provided a framework governing the use of United States forces against military threats — internal or external — in the region. A special diplomatic task was to assuage the suspicions and alleviate the resentments of Asian neighbors who had suffered from Japanese colonial rule and imperialist aggression in the past. Japan's diplomacy toward its Asian neighbors, therefore, tended to be extremely low-key, conciliatory, and nonassertive. With respect to the world at large, the nation avoided political issues and concentrated on economic goals. Under its omnidirectional diplomacy, it sought to cultivate friendly ties with all nations, proclaimed a policy of "separation of politics and economics," and adhered to a neutral position on some East-West issues.

During the 1950s and 1960s, foreign policy actions were guided by three basic principles: close cooperation with the United States for both security and economic reasons; promotion of a free-trade system congenial to Japan's own economic needs; and international cooperation through the United Nations (UN) — to which it was admitted in 1956 — and other multilateral bodies. Adherence to these principles worked well and contributed to phenomenal economic recovery and growth during the first two decades after the end of the occupation.

1970s

In the 1970s, the basic postwar principles remained unchanged but were approached from a new perspective, owing to the pressure of practical politics at home and abroad. There was growing domestic pressure on the government to exercise more foreign policy initiatives independent of the United States, without, however, compromising vital security and economic ties. The so-called Nixon "shock," involving the surprise visit to China by Richard Nixon and the sudden reconciliation inSino-American relations, also argued for a more independent Japanese foreign policy. A similar move in Sino-Japanese relations followed.

The nation's phenomenal economic growth had made it a ranking world economic power by the early 1970s and had generated a sense of pride and self-esteem, especially among the younger generation. The demand for a more independent foreign policy reflected this enhanced self-image. On the other hand, Japan's burgeoning economic growth and expansion into overseas markets had given rise to foreign charges of "economic aggression" and demands that it adopt more balanced trade policies. Changes in the power relationships in the Asia-Pacific quadrilateral—made up of Japan, thePeople's Republic of China, the United States, and the Soviet Union—also called for reexamination of policies. The deepening Sino-Soviet split and confrontation, the dramatic rapprochement between the United States and China, the rapid reduction of the United States military presence in Asia following the Vietnam War (Second Indochina War, 1954–75), and the 1970s expansion of Soviet military power in the western Pacific all required a reevaluation of Japan's security positionand overall role in Asia.

The move toward a more autonomous foreign policy was accelerated in the 1970s by the United States decision to withdraw troops from Indochina. Japanese public opinion had earlier favored some distance between Japan and the United States involvement in war in Vietnam. The collapse of the war effort in Vietnam was seen as the end of United States military and economic dominance in Asia and brought to the fore a marked shift in Japan's attitudes about the United States. This shift, which had been developing since the early 1970s, took the form of questioning the credibility of the United States nuclear umbrella, as well as its ability to underwrite a stable international currency system, guarantee Japan's access to energy and raw materials, and secure Japan's interests in a stable political order. The shift therefore required a reassessment of omnidirectional diplomacy.

Changes in world economic relations during the 1970s also encouraged a more independent stance. Japan had become less dependent on the Western powers for resources. Oil, for example, was obtained directly from the producing countries in the Middle East and not from the Western-controlled multinational companies. Other important materials also came increasingly from sources other than the United States and its allies, while trade with the United States as a share of total trade dropped significantly during the decade of the 1970s. But the oil crises of the 1970s sharpened Japanese awareness of the country's vulnerability to cutoffs of raw material and energy supplies, underscoring the need for a less passive, more independent foreign policy. Thus, political leaders began to argue that in the interests of economic self-preservation, more attention should be paid to the financial and development needs of other countries, especially those that provided Japan with vital energy and raw material supplies.

Soon after, in the troublesome year of 1979, Japan's leaders welcomed the reassertion of United States military power in Asian and world affairs following the Islamic revolution in Iran, the Teheran hostage crisis, and the Soviet military invasion of Afghanistan. Japanese leaders played a strong supporting role in curbing economic and other interaction with the Soviet Union and its allies in order to help check the expansion of Soviet power in sensitive areas among the developing world countries.

1980s

Japanese thinking on foreign policy was also influenced by the rise of a new postwar generation to leadership and policy-making positions. The differences in outlook between the older leaders still in positions of power and influence and the younger generation that was replacing them complicated formulation of foreign policy. Under Prime Minister Yasuhiro Nakasone, a more hawkish stance on foreign policy was introduced. Japan built up a close political-military relationship with the United States as part of a de facto international front of a number of developed and developing countries intent on checking Soviet expansion. Japan's defense spending continued to grow steadily despite overall budgetary restraint. Japan became increasingly active in granting foreign assistance to countries of strategic importance in East-West competition.

The realignment of United States and Japanese currencies in the mid-1980s increased the growth of Japanese trade, aid, and investment, especially in Asia. It also accelerated the reversal of the United States fiscal position, from one of the world's largest creditors in the early 1980s to the world's largest debtor at the end of the decade. Japan became the world's largest creditor, an increasingly active investor in the United States, and a major contributor to international debt relief, financial institutions, and other assistance efforts. Japan had also become the second largest donor of foreign aid.

1990s

By 1990 Japan's foreign policy choices often challenged the leadership's tendency to avoid radical shifts and to rely on incremental adjustments. Although still generally supportive of close ties, including the alliance relationship with the United States, Japanese leaders were well aware of strong American frustrations with Japanese economic practices and Japan's growing economic power relative to the United States in world affairs. Senior United States leaders were calling upon

Japanese officials to work with them in crafting "a new conceptual framework" for Japan-United States relations that would take account of altered strategic and economic realities and changes in Japanese and United States views about the bilateral relationship. The results of this effort were far from clear. Some optimistically predicted "a new global partnership" in which the United States and Japan would work together as truly equal partners in dealing with global problems. Pessimists predicted that negative feelings generated by the realignment in United States and Japanese economic power and persistent trade frictions would prompt Japan to strike out more on its own, without the "guidance" of the United States. Given the growing economic dominance of Japan in Asia, Tokyo was seen as most likely to strike out independently there first, translating its economic power into political and perhaps, eventually, military influence.

Still, the image of Japan as a "military dwarf" was in a sense ironic, as Japan had one of the biggest defense budgets in the world throughout the 1980s and 1990s and defense expenditure is one of the most frequently used indicators of military power. It also had very advanced naval and air self-defense capabilities.

The collapse of the Soviet Union and the growing preoccupation of its former republics and the East European nations with internal political and economic problems increased the importance of economic competition, rather than military power, to Japan. These formerly communist countries were anxiously seeking aid, trade, and technical benefits from the developed countries, such as Japan. The power of Japan's ally, the United States, was also seen by many as waning. The United States was forced to look increasingly to Japan and others to shoulder the financial burdens entailed in the transformation of former communist economies in Eastern Europe and other urgent international requirements that fall upon the shoulders of world leaders.

Japanese industries and enterprises were among the most capable in the world. High savings and investment rates and high-quality education solidified the international leadership of these enterprises during the mid- to late 1990s. Its economic power gave Japan a steadily growing role in the World Bank, the International Monetary Fund, and other international financial institutions. Investment and trade flows give Japan by far the dominant economic role in Asia, and Japanese aid and investment were widely sought after in other parts of the world. It appears to be only a matter of time before such economic power would be translated into greater political power. The crucial issue for the United States and many other world governments centers on how Japan will employ this growing economic power.

Inside Japan, both elite and popular opinion expressed growing support for a more prominent international role, proportionate to the nation's economic power, foreign assistance, trade, and investment. But the traditional post–World War II reluctance to take a greater military role in the world remained. A firm consensus continued to support the 1960 Treaty of Mutual Cooperation and Security and other bilateral agreements with the United States as the keystones of Japan's security policy. However, Japanese officials were increasingly active in using their economic and financial resources in seeking a greater voice in international financial and political organizations and in shaping the policies of the developed countries toward international trouble spots, especially in Asia.

ROLE OF DOMESTIC POLITICS

General satisfaction in Japan with the peace and prosperity that had been brought to the country made it hard for opposition parties to garner much support for a radical move to the left in Japan's foreign policy. The collapse of communism in Eastern Europe and the widely publicized brutalities of communist regimes in Asia in the late 1980s further dampened popular Japanese interest in shifting foreign policy to the left.

Meanwhile, the ruling LDP modified its base of political power. By the 1980s, it had markedly shifted the social composition of LDP support away from the traditional conservative reliance on business and rural groups to include every category of the electorate. This shift resulted from efforts by LDP politicians to align various local interests in mutually advantageous arrangements in support of LDP candidates. The LDP had brought together various candidates and their supporting interest groups and had reached a policy consensus to pursue economic development while depending strongly on the United States security umbrella.

Domestic political challenges to LDP dominance waxed and waned later in the 1980s as the party faced major influence-peddling scandals with weak and divided leadership, such as the Lockheed bribery scandals and the Recruit scandal. In 1989 the opposition Japan Socialist Party won control of the Diet's House of Councillors. But the Japan Socialist Party's past ideological positions on foreign policy appeared to be more of a liability than an asset going into the House of

Representatives elections in 1990, and the party attempted to modify a number of positions that called for pushing foreign policy to the left. In contrast, the LDP standard bearer, Prime Minister Kaifu Toshiki, used identification with the United States and the West to his advantage in the successful LDP effort to sustain control of the House of Representatives in February 1990.

In 1993 the coalition government of Prime Minister Hosokawa Morihiro pledged to continue the LDP policy of economic and security ties with the United States; of responding to domestic and international expectations of greater Japanese political and economic contributions; and of international cooperation through the UN and other international organizations in the cause of world peace, disarmament, aid to developing countries, and educational and technical cooperation. Foreign policy speeches by the prime minister and the minister of foreign affairs were widely disseminated, and pamphlets and booklets on major foreign policy questions were issued frequently.

Political groups opposing the government's foreign policy presented their views freely through political parties and the mass media, which took vocal and independent positions on wide-ranging external issues. Some of the opposing elements included were leftists who sought to exert influence through their representatives in the Diet, through mass organizations, and sometimes through rallies and street demonstrations. In contrast, special interest groups supporting the government — including the business community and agricultural interests — brought pressure to bear on the prime minister, cabinetmembers, and members of the Diet, usually through behind-the-scenes negotiations and compromises.

Partisan political activities of all ideological tendencies were undertaken freely and openly, but the difference in foreign policy perspectives appeared increasingly in the 1980s to derive less from ideology than from more pragmatic considerations. Broadly stated, the partisan disagreement among the various groups competing for power had centered on the question of Japan's safety from external threat or attack. The dominant view was that although the Japanese should be responsible for defending their homeland, they should also continue their security ties with the United States, at least until they could gain sufficient confidence in their own self-defense power, which has been interpreted as not being proscribed by Article 9 of the constitution. Proponents of this view agreed that this self-defense capability should be based on conventional arms and that any nuclear shield should be provided by the United States under the 1960 security treaty.

The Sino-United States rapprochement of the 1970s and the stiffening of Japan-Soviet relations in the 1980s caused the opposition parties to be less insistent on the need to terminate the security treaty. The Democratic Socialist Party and theKômeitô indicated their readiness to support the treaty, while the Japan Socialist Party dropped its demand for immediate abrogation. Only the Japan Communist Party remained adamant. Despite partisan differences, all political parties and groups were nearly unanimous during the 1970s and 1980s that Japan should exercise more independence and initiative in foreign affairs and not appear so ready to follow the United States on matters affecting Japan's interests. They also agreed that Japan should continue to prohibit the introduction of nuclear weapons into the country. These shared views stemmed from the resurgence of nationalism during the post–World War II era and from the pride of the Japanese people in their own heritage and in the economic achievements of the postwar decades. Although there were indications that the "nuclear allergy" produced by Japan's traumatic experience with theatomic bombings of Hiroshima and Nagasaki in August 1945 was beginning to moderate, nuclear weapons remains a sensitive political issue.

Except for security-related matters, most foreign affairs issues involved economic interests and mainly attracted the attention of the specific groups affected. The role of interest groups in formulating foreign policy varied with the issue at hand. Because trade and capital investment issues were involved, for example, in relations with the People's Republic of Chinaand with South Korea, the business community increasingly became an interested party in the conduct of foreign affairs. Similarly, when fishing rights or agricultural imports were being negotiated, representatives of the industries affected worked with political leaders and the foreign affairs bureaucracies in shaping policy.

Because of the continuous control of the government enjoyed by the LDP since its formation in 1955, the policy-making bodies of the LDP had become the centers of government policy formulation. Because the unified will of the majority party almost invariably prevailed in the Diet, some observers believed that the Diet had been reduced to a mere sounding board for government policy pronouncements and a rubber-stamp ratifier of decisions made by the prime minister and his cabinet. This situation meant that significant debate and deliberations on foreign policy matters generally took place not in the Diet but in closed-door meetings of the governing LDP. Deliberations took place, for example, between representatives of the Foreign Affairs Section of the LDP's Policy Research Council and officials of the Ministry of Foreign Affairs, MITI, or leaders of major LDP support groups, such as the Federation of Economic Organizations (Keizai Dantai Rengokai—better known asKeidanren). The loss of the LDP majority in the July 1993 election for the House of Representatives was bound to affect this situation, but it remained to be seen how it would affect it.

The role of public opinion in the formulation of foreign policy throughout the postwar period has been difficult to determine. Japan continued to be extremely concerned with public opinion, and opinion polling became a conspicuous feature of national life. The large number of polls on public policy issues, including foreign policy matters, conducted by the Office of the Prime Minister, the Ministry of Foreign Affairs, other government organizations, and the media led to the presumption by analysts that the collective opinions of voters do exert significant influence on policymakers. The public attitudes toward foreign policy that had held throughout much of the postwar period appeared to have shifted in the 1980s. Opinion polls reflected a marked increase in national pride and self-esteem. Moreover, public discussion of security matters by government officials, political party leaders, press commentators, and academics had become markedly less volatile and doctrinaire and more open and pragmatic, suggesting indirectly that public attitudes on this subject had evolved as well.

The mass media, and particularly the press, as the champion of the public interest and critic of the government, continues to mold public attitudes strongly. The media is the chief source of demands that the government exercise a more independent and less "weak-kneed" diplomacy in view of the changing world situation and Japan's increased stature in the world. An example of this attitude has been the continued support for whaling through the International Whaling Commission that has brought increasing opposition from several important trading partner countries such as the US, the UK, New Zealand and Australia .

ANTI-TERRORISM AS A PART OF JAPANESE FOREIGN POLICY

Japan, since the end of the WWII has operated via a policy of pacifism and passivism. This began to change in the late eighties and early nineties, in tandem with a shift in national identity, as understood via a change in its conception of its international role as a great economic power. Among the major catalysts were a shift in Japan's national security objectives, and widespread criticism of its "checkbook diplomacy" policy during the first Gulf War. This shift, ultimately, moved Japan from the realm of pacifism into a more activist assertive power. It was characterized by increased participation in international and regional organizations (monetarily) and by increased participation in global Peace-Keeping operations and in conflict resolution more broadly, under the umbrella of the UN. Japan's anti-terrorism policy can be seen as a part of this broader foreign policy platform, as it stems from these large objectives. Its anti-terrorism policy is an integral part of its larger foreign policy objectives, which are 1) the maintenance of the US/Japanese security alliance 2) continued international peace and security 3) a moderate defense buildup. This last objective is new, and ends up being very connected to its anti-terrorism policies. This represents some concern for the US as it signals the beginning of a more independent Japan in the future, but for the time being it hasn't resulted in any significant increase in Japanese independence from the US in terms of foreign policy formation, especially as it relates to anti-terrorism.

6

Military and Defence

JAPAN SELF-DEFENSE FORCES

History

Early development

Deprived of any military capability after being defeated by the United States in World War II and signing a surrender agreement presented byGeneral Douglas MacArthur in 1945, Japan had only the U.S. occupation forces and a minor domestic police force on which to rely for security. Rising Cold War tensions in Europe and Asia, coupled with leftist-inspired strikes and demonstrations in Japan, prompted some conservative leaders to question the unilateral renunciation of all military capabilities. These sentiments were intensified in 1950 as occupation troops began to be moved to the Korean War (1950–53) theater. This left Japan virtually defenseless, vulnerable, and very much aware of the need to enter into a mutual defense relationship with the United States to guarantee the nation's external security. Encouraged by the American occupation authorities, the Japanese government in July 1950 authorized the establishment of a National Police Reserve, consisting of 75,000 men equipped with light infantry weapons.

Under the terms of the Treaty of Mutual Cooperation and Security between the United States and Japan, United States forces stationed in Japan were to deal with external aggression against Japan while Japanese ground and maritime forces would deal with internal threats and natural disasters. Accordingly, in mid-1952, the National Police Reserve was expanded to 110,000 men and named the National Safety Forces. The Coastal Safety Force, which had been organized in 1950 as a waterborne counterpart to the National Police Reserve, was transferred with it to the National Safety Agency to constitute an embryonic navy.

On July 1, 1954, the National Security Board was reorganized as the Defense Agency, and the National Security Force was reorganized afterwards as the Japan Ground Self-Defense Force (*de facto* post-war Japanese Army), the Japan Maritime Self-Defense Force (*de facto* post-war JapaneseNavy) and the Japan Air Self-Defense Force(*de facto* post-war Japanese Air Force), with General Keizô Hayashi appointed as the first Chairman of Joint Staff Council—professional head of the three branches. The enabling legislation for this was the 1954 Self-Defense Forces Act (Act No. 165 of 1954).

The Far East Air Force, U.S. Air Force, announced on 6 January 1955, that 85 aircraft would be turned over to the fledgling Japanese air force on about 15 January, the first equipment of the new force.

Although possession of nuclear weapons is not explicitly forbidden in the constitution, Japan, as the only nation to have experienced the devastation of nuclear attacks, expressed early its abhorrence of nuclear arms and its determination never to acquire them. The Atomic Energy Basic Law of 1956 limits research, development, and use of nuclear power to peaceful uses only. Beginning in 1956, national policy embodied "three non-nuclear principles"—forbidding the nation to possess or manufacture nuclear weapons or to allow them to be introduced into its territories. In 1976 Japan ratified the Treaty on the Non-Proliferation of Nuclear Weapons (adopted by the United Nations Security Council in 1968) and reiterated its intention never to "develop, use, or allow the transportation of nuclear weapons through its territory". Nonetheless, because of its generally high technology level and large number of operating nuclear power plants, Japan is generally considered to be "nuclear capable", i.e., it could develop a usable weapon in a short period if the political situation changed significantly.

On June 8, 2006, the Cabinet of Japan endorsed a bill elevating the Defense Agency under the Cabinet Office to full-fledged cabinet-level Ministry of Defense . This was passed by the Diet in December 2006 and has been enforced since January 9, 2007.

(1) Aspiring sincerely to an international peace based on justice and order, the Japanese people forever renounce war as a sovereign

right of the nation and the threat or use of force as means of settling international disputes.

(2) In order to accomplish the aim of the preceding paragraph, land, sea, and air forces, as well as other war potential, will never be maintained. The right of belligerency of the state will not be recognized.

The trauma of the last war had produced strong pacifist sentiments among the nation. In addition, under Article 9 of the United States–written 1947 constitution, Japan forever renounces war as an instrument for settling international disputes and declares that Japan will never again maintain "land, sea, or air forces or other war potential." Later cabinets interpreted these provisions as not denying the nation the inherent right to self-defense and, with the encouragement of the United States, developed the JSDF step by step.

Recent developments

According to an article in Pravda, the Russian political publication, on May 30, 2013, the Council of National Defense of the ruling Liberal Democratic Party (LDP), approved a draft proposal for the "full-scale rearmament of the country." This was said to include the renaming of the Japan Self-Defense Forces into that of a full army for national defense. Ex-ministers of the LDP, Shigeru Ishiba andGen Nakatani were identified as the prime movers behind the proposed large scale rearmament of Japan. They presented a draft reform of the rearmament that was approved and sent to the Government for consideration. Shigeru Ishiba called the current restrictions imposed after the Second World War on the size of the Japanese armed forces as long out of date.

In the same article, Valery Kistanov, director of the Center for the Japanese Studies at the Institute of the Far East, was quoted as saying he believes that Japanese offensive weapons could be deployed in any direction. "Of course, first of all Japanese weapons would be directed against North Korea (the DPRK), and then China (the PRC).

Japanese missile defense system is ramping up its power due to the increasing missile and nuclear forces in China.

Either way the country will continue to spend billions of dollars on the military industry. According to Japanese political analysts and politicians, it is primarily due to the situation on the Korean peninsula and growth of China's military. These two factors are considered a threat by Japan, and therefore the country will actively rearm."

In September 2015, the Japanese Diet enacted the 2015 Japanese military legislation, a series of laws that allows them todefend other allies in case of war being declared upon them, including that the Self-Defense Forces may provide material support to allies engaged in combat internationally. The justification is that by not defending/supporting an ally, it would weaken alliances and endanger Japan.

In May 2017, Japanese Prime Minister Abe set a 2020 deadline for revising the Article 9 of the Japanese Constitution, a clause in the national Constitution of Japan outlawing war as a means to settle international disputes involving the state.

STRUCTURE

The Prime Minister is the commander-in-chief of the Japan Self Defense Forces. Military authority runs from the Prime Minister to the cabinet-level Minister of Defense of the Japanese Ministry of Defense.

The Prime Minister and Minister of Defense are advised by the Chief of Staff, Joint Staff (currently Katsutoshi Kawano), who heads the Joint Staff . The Joint Staff includes a Senior Enlisted Advisor to the *Chief of Staff, Joint Staff*, the Vice Chief of Staff, Joint Staff (currently Kôichi Isobe), an Administrative Vice Chief of Staff, as well as numerous departments and special staffs. Each service branch is headed by their respective Chiefs of Staff; the Chief of Staff of the Japan Ground Self-Defense Force (JGSDF) (currently Kiyofumi Iwata), the Japan Maritime Self-Defense Force(JMSDF) (currently Tomohisa Takei), and the Japan Air Self-Defense Force(JASDF) (currently Haruhiko Kataoka).

The *Chief of Staff, Joint Staff*, a four star Admiral or General, is the highest-ranking military officer in the Japan Self Defense Forces, and is the head of the Operational Authority over the Japan Self Defense Forces, executing orders of the Minister of Defense with directions from the Prime Minister. The *Chief of Staff, Joint Staff*supervises the service branches operations, and would assume command in the event of a war, but his or her powers are limited to policy formation and defense coordination during peacetime.

The chain of Operational Authority runs from the *Chief of Staff, Joint Staff* to the Commanders of the several Operational Commands. Each service branches Chiefs of Staff (JGSDF, JMSDF, JASDF) have administrative control over their own services.

Service branches

- Japan Ground Self-Defense Force

- Japan Maritime Self-Defense Force
- Japan Air Self-Defense Force

Service units

- Five armies
- Five maritime districts
- Four air defense forces

DEFENSE POLICY

National Security Council

On December 4, 2013, the National Security Council was established, with the aim of establishing a forum which will undertake strategic discussions under the Prime Minister on a regular basis and as necessary on various national security issues and exercising a strong political leadership.

National Security Strategy

On December 17, 2013, National Security Strategy was adopted by Cabinet decision. NSS sets the basic orientation of diplomatic and defense policies related to national security. NSS presents the content of the policy of "Proactive Contribution to Peace" in a concrete manner and promotes better understanding of Japan's national security policy.

Budget

In 1976, then Prime Minister Miki Takeo announced defense spending should be maintained within 1% of Japan's gross domestic product (GDP), a ceiling that was observed until 1986. As of 2005, Japan's military budget was maintained at about 3% of the national budget; about half is spent on personnel costs, while the rest is for weapons programs, maintenance and operating costs. As of 2014, Japan is in the list of top ten largest defense budgets in the world by expenditure, spending about one percent of GDP.

ANTI-BALLISTIC MISSILE DEPLOYMENT

After the North Korean KwangmyOngsOng-1 satellite launching in August 1998, which some regarded as a ballistic missile test, the Japanese government decided to participate in the American anti-ballistic missile (ABM) defense program. In August 1999, Japan,

Germany and the US governments signed a Memorandum of Understanding of joint research and development on the Aegis Ballistic Missile Defense System. In 2003, the Japanese government decided to deploy three types of ABM system, air defense vehicles, sea-based Aegis and land-based PAC-3ABM.

The four Kongô class Aegis destroyers of the Japan Maritime Self-Defense Forcewere modified to accommodate the ABM operational capability. On December 17, 2007, JDS Kongô successfully shot down a mock ballistic missile by its SM-3 Block IA, off the coast of Hawaii. The first PAC-3 (upgraded version of the MIM-104 Patriot) firing test by the Japan Air Self-Defense Force was carried out in New Mexico on September 17, 2008. PAC-3 units are deployed in 6 bases near metropolises, including Tokyo, Osaka, Nagoya, Sapporo, Misawa and Okinawa.

Japan participates in the co-research and development of four Aegis components with the US: the nose cone, the infrared seeker, the kinetic warhead, and the second-stage rocket motor.

Unarmed combat system

JSDF soldiers are trained in the military self-defence art of toshu kakuto , developed in 1952 by Major Chiba Sansu from a synthesis of jujutsu, karate, aikijujutsu, boxing and wrestling. The techniques of *toshu kakuto* are simplified and direct, to allow for their application whilst in combat dress and carrying field kit. There is an emphasis on the rapid transmission of maximum force in strikes, and for this reason *toshu kakuto* eschews the fully rotated punches and instep kicks of most karate forms in favour of vertical thrust punches and straight heel kicks.

Missions and deployments

The outer outline specified quotas of personnel and equipment for each force that were deemed necessary to meet its tasks. Particular elements of each force's mission were also identified. The JGSDF was to defend against ground invasion and threats to internal security, be able to deploy to any part of the nation, and protect the bases of all three services of the Self-Defense Forces. The JMSDF was to meet invasion by sea, sweep mines, patrol and survey the surrounding waters, and guard and defend coastal waters, ports, bays, and major straits. The JASDF was to render aircraft and missile interceptor capability, provide support fighter units for maritime and ground operations, supply air reconnaissance and air transport for all forces, and maintain airborne and stationary early warning units.

The JSDF disaster relief role is defined in Article 83 of the Self-Defense Forces Law of 1954, requiring units to respond to calls for assistance from prefectural governors to aid in fire fighting, earthquake disasters, searches for missing persons, rescues, and reinforcement of embankments and levees in the event of flooding. The JSDF has not been used in police actions, nor is it likely to be assigned any internal security tasks in the future.

In late June/early July 2014, Prime Minister Shinzo Abe and his cabinet agreed to lift the long-term ban in engaging Japanese troops abroad, since the end of the Second World War, in a bid to strengthen the Japanese situation amid an ever-growing Chinese military aggression and North Korea's nuclear weapons programme. Japan had adhered to the "pacifist" article 9 of the constitution, but would revise and might reinterpret it in order for this to take effect.

Peacekeeping

In June 1992, the National Diet passed a UN Peacekeeping Cooperation Law which permitted the JSDF to participate in UN medical, refugee repatriation, logistical support, infrastructural reconstruction, election-monitoring, and policing operations under strictly limited conditions.

The non-combatant participation of the JSDF in the United Nations Transitional Authority in Cambodia (UNTAC) in conjunction with Japanese diplomatic efforts contributed to the successful implementation of the 1991 Paris Peace Accords for Cambodia.

In 2004, the Japanese government ordered a deployment of troops to Iraq at the behest of the United States: A contingent of the Japan Self-Defense Forces was sent in order to assist the U.S.-led Reconstruction of Iraq. This controversial deployment marked a significant turning point in Japan's history, as it is the first time since the end of World War II that Japan sent troops abroad except for a few minor UN peacekeeping deployments. Public opinion regarding this deployment was sharply divided, especially given that Japan's military is constitutionally structured as solely a self-defense force, and operating in Iraq seemed at best tenuously connected to that mission. The Koizumiadministration, however, decided to send troops to respond to a request from the US. Even though they deployed with their weapons, because of constitutional restraints, the troops were protected by Japanese Special Forces troops and Australian units. The Japanese soldiers were there purely for humanitarian and reconstruction work, and were prohibited from opening fire on Iraqi insurgents unless they were fired on first. Japanese forces withdrew from Iraq in 2006.

Japan provided logistics units for the United Nations Disengagement Observer Force Zone, which supervises the buffer zone in the Golan Heights, monitors Israeli and Syrian military activities, and assists local civilians.

In the aftermath of an earthquake in Haiti, Japan deployed a contingent of troops, including engineers with bulldozers and heavy machinery, to assist the United Nations Stabilization Mission in Haiti. Their duties were peacekeeping, removal of rubble, and the reconstruction of roads and buildings. Japanese forces are frequent among the international disaster relief teams, with deployments in Rwanda (1994), Honduras (1998), Turkey (1999), West Timor (1999-2000), India (2001),Afghanistan (2001), Iraq (2003), Iran (2003-2004), Thailand (2004-2005), Indonesia (2005), Russia (2005), Pakistan(2005), Indonesia (2006), Indonesia (2009), Haiti (2010), Pakistan (2010), New Zealand (2011).

Naval and air overseas deployments

The Japan Maritime Self-Defense Force deployed a force off the coast of Somalia to protect Japanese ships from Somali Pirates. The force consists of two destroyers (manned by approximately 400 sailors), patrol helicopters, speedboats, eight officers of the Japan Coast Guard to collect criminal evidence and handle piracy suspects, a force of commandos from the elite Special Boarding Unit, and P-3 Orion patrol aircraft in the Gulf of Aden. On 19 June 2009, the Japanese Parliament finally passed an anti-piracy bill, which allows their force to protect non Japanese vessels. In May 2010, Japan announced it intended to build a permanent naval base in Djibouti to provide security for Japanese ships against Somali pirates.Construction of the JSDF Counter-Piracy Facility in Djibouti commenced in July 2010, completed in June 2011 and opened on 1 July 2011. Initially, the base was to house approximately 170 JSDF personnel and include administrative, housing, medical, kitchen/dining, and recreational facilities as well as an aircraft maintenance hangar and parking apron. The base now houses approximately 200 personnel and two P-3C aircraft. In a recent press release, Chief Cabinet Secretary Nobutaka Machimura had stated that discussions with Defense MinisterShigeru Ishiba and Foreign Minister Masahiko Komura were taking place regarding the possibility of creating a permanent law for JSDF forces to be deployed in peacekeeping missions outside Japan. The adoption of a permanent peacekeeping law has been considered by the government, according to the Mainichi Daily News.

Amphibious force

In light of tensions over the Senkaku Islands, Japan is in the process of creating the Amphibious Rapid Deployment Brigade. This unit will be designed to conduct amphibious operations and to recover any Japanese islands taken by an adversary.

UNIFORMS, RANKS, AND INSIGNIA

The arm of service to which members of the ground force are attached is indicated by branch insignia and piping of distinctive colors: for infantry, red; artillery, yellow; armor, orange; engineers, violet; ordnance, light green; medical, green; army aviation, light blue; signals, blue; quartermaster, brown; transportation, dark violet; airborne, white; and others, dark blue. The cap badge insignia the JGSDF is a sakura cherry blossom bordered with two ivy branches underneath, and a single chevron centered on the bottom between the bases of the branches; the JMSDF cap badge insignia consists of a fouled anchor underneath a cherry blossom bordered on the sides and bottom by ivy vines; and the JASDF cap badge insignia features a heraldic eagle under which is a star and crescent, which is bordered underneath with stylized wings.

There are nine officer ranks in the active JSDF, along with a warrant officer rank, five NCO ranks, and three enlisted ranks. The highest NCO rank, first sergeant (senior chief petty officer in the JMSDF and senior master sergeant in the JASDF), was established in 1980 to provide more promotion opportunities and shorter terms of service as sergeant first class, chief petty officer, or master sergeant. Under the earlier system, the average NCO was promoted only twice in approximately thirty years of service and remained at the top rank for almost ten years.

RECRUITMENT AND CONDITIONS OF SERVICE

The total strength of the JSDF is 247,154 in 2016. In addition, the JSDF maintained a total of 47,900 reservists attached to the three services. Even when Japan's active and reserve components are combined, however, the country maintains a lower ratio of military personnel to its population than does any member nation of the North Atlantic Treaty Organization (NATO). Of the major Asian nations, only India, Indonesia, Malaysia and Thailand keep a lower ratio of personnel in arms, although because India and Indonesia have much larger populations, they have larger numbers of personnel.

The JSDF is an all-volunteer force. Conscription *per se* is not forbidden by law, but many citizens consider Article 18 of theconstitution, which prohibits involuntary servitude except as punishment for a crime, as a legal prohibition of any form of conscription. Even in the absence of so strict an interpretation, however, a military draft appears politically impossible.

JSDF uniformed personnel are recruited as private, E-1, seaman recruit, and airman basic for a fixed term. Ground forces recruits normally enlist for two years; those seeking training in technical specialties enlist for three. Naval and air recruits normally enlist for three years. Officer candidates, students in the National Defense Academy and National Defense Medical College, and candidate enlist students in technical schools are enrolled for an indefinite period. The National Defense Academy and enlisted technical schools usually require an enrollment of four years, and the National Defense Medical College require six years.

When the JSDF was originally formed, women were recruited exclusively for the nursing services. Opportunities were expanded somewhat when women were permitted to join the JGSDF communication service in 1967 and the JMSDF and JASDF communication services in 1974. By 1991, more than 6,000 women were in the JSDF, about 80% of service areas, except those requiring direct exposure to combat, were open to them. The National Defense Medical College graduated its first class with women in March 1991, and the National Defense Academy began admitting women in FY 1992.

In the face of some continued post–World War II public apathy or antipathy toward the armed services, the JSDF has difficulties in recruiting personnel. The JSDF has to compete for qualified personnel with well-paying industries, and most enlistees are "persuaded" volunteers who sign up after solicitation from recruiters. Predominantly rural prefectures supply military enlistees far beyond the proportions of their populations. In areas such as southern Kyushu and northern

Hokkaido, where employment opportunities are limited, recruiters are welcomed and supported by the citizens.

Because the forces are all volunteer and legally civilian, members can resign at any time, and retention is a problem. Many enlistees are lured away by the prospects of high paying civilian jobs, and Defense Agency officials complain of private industries luring away their personnel. The agency attempts to stop these practices by threats of sanctions for offending firms that hold defense contracts and by private agreements with major industrial firms. Given the nation's labor shortage, however, the problem is likely to continue.

Some older officers, although not old enough to have participated in the Second World War, consider the members of the modern forces unequal to personnel of the former Imperial Army and Imperial Navy. Literacy is universal, and school training is extensive. Personnel are trained in the martial arts, such as judo and kendo, and physical standards are strict. Graduates of the top universities rarely enter the armed forces, and applicants to the National Defense Academy are generally considered to be on the level of those who apply to second-rank local universities.

General conditions of military life are not such that a career in the JSDF seems an attractive alternative to one in private industry or the bureaucracy. The conditions of service provide less dignity, prestige, and comfort than they had before theSecond World War, when militarism was at a high point and military leaders were considered influential in not only military affairs but virtually all aspects of society. For most members of the defense establishment, military life offers less status than does a civilian occupation with a major corporation.

As special civil servants, JSDF personnel are paid according to civilian pay scales that do not always discriminate between ranks. At times, JSDF salaries are greater for subordinates than for commanding officers; senior non-commissioned officers(NCOs) with long service can earn more than newly promoted colonels. Pay raises are not included in Defense Agency budgets and cannot be established by military planners. Retirement ages for officers below general/flag rank range from fifty-three to fifty-five years, and from fifty to fifty-three for enlisted personnel. Limits are sometimes extended because of personnel shortages. In the late 1980s, the Defense Agency, concerned about the difficulty of finding appropriate post retirement employment for these early retirees, began providing vocational training for enlisted personnel about to retire and transferring them to units close to the place where they intend to retire. Beginning in October 1987, the Self-Defense Forces Job Placement Association provided free job placement and reemployment support for retired JSDF personnel. Retirees also receive pensions immediately upon retirement, some ten years earlier than most civil service personnel. Financing the retirement system promises to be a problem of increasing scope in the 1990s, with the aging of the population.

JSDF personnel benefits are not comparable to such benefits for active-duty military personnel in other major industrialized nations. Health care is provided at the JSDF Central Hospital, fourteen regional hospitals, and 165 clinics in military facilities and on board ship, but the health care only covers physical examinations and the treatment of illness and injury suffered in the course of duty.

There are no commissary or exchange privileges. Housing is often substandard, and military appropriations for facilities maintenance often focus on appeasing civilian communities near bases rather than on improving on-base facilities.

In 2010, Sapporo District Court fined the state after a female Air JSDF member was sexually assaulted by a colleague then forced to retire, while the perpetrator was suspended for 60 days.

Overseas dispatch

The Self-Defense Forces sent six small-scale squadrons to the Persian Gulf on April 26, 1991, and approved the June 1994 UN Peacekeeping Activity (Parliamentary Peacekeeping) Cooperation bill in the House of Representatives in Japan.

From September 11, Self-Defense Forces have started overseas activities such as dispatching UN peacekeepers to Cambodia.In 2003, Japan created a law to deal with armed attacks, amend the Self-Defense Forceslaw. In 2004, Japan dispatched for two and a half years to the Samawa district of southern Iraq under the Special Measures for Iraqi Recovery Support Act. in 2005

Role in Japanese society

Appreciation of the JSDF continued to grow in the 1980s, with over half of the respondents in a 1988 survey voicing an interest in the JSDF and over 76% indicating that they were favourably impressed. Although the majority (63.5%) of respondents were aware that the primary purpose of the JSDF was maintenance of national security, an even greater number (77%) saw disaster relief as the most useful JSDF function.

The JSDF therefore continued to devote much of its time and resources to disaster relief and other civic action. Between 1984 and 1988, at the request of prefectural governors, the JSDF assisted in approximately 3,100 disaster relief operations, involving about 138,000 personnel, 16,000 vehicles, 5,300 aircraft, and 120 ships and small craft. In addition, the JSDF participated in earthquake disaster prevention operations and disposed of a large quantity of World War II explosive ordnance, especially in Okinawa Prefecture.

The forces also participated in public works projects, cooperated in managing athletic events, took part in annual Antarctic expeditions, and conducted aerial surveys to report on ice conditions for fishermen and on geographic formations for construction projects. Especially sensitive to maintaining harmonious relations with communities close to defense bases, the JSDF built new roads, irrigation networks, and schools in those areas. Soundproofing was installed in homes and public buildings near airfields.

MILITARY HISTORY OF JAPAN

The military history of Japan is characterized by a period of clan warfare that lasted until the 12th century AD. This was followed by feudal wars that culminated in military governments known as the "Shogunate". Feudal militarism transitioned to imperial militarism in the 19th century after thelandings of Admiral Perry and the elevation of the Meiji Emperor. This led to rampant imperialism until Japan's defeat by the Allies in World War II. TheOccupation of Japan marks the inception of modern Japanese military history, with the drafting of a new Constitution prohibiting the ability to wage war against other nations.

Prehistory

Recent archaeological research has uncovered traces of wars as far back as the Jômon period (ca. 10,000–300 BC) between the various tribes existing on the Japanese Archipelago. Some theorists believe that shortly after the Yayoi period(ca. 300 BC – 250 AD) horse riders from the Korean Peninsula invaded southern Kyûshû, then spread to northern Honshû. At this time, horse-riding and iron tools were first introduced to the islands.

Jômon Period (ca. 10,000–300 BC)

Near the end of the Jômon period (ca. 300 BC), villages and towns became surrounded by moats and wooden fences due to increasing violence within or between communities. Battles were fought with weapons like the sword, sling, spear, and bowand arrow. Some human remains have been found with arrow wounds.

Yayoi period (300 BC – 250 AD)

Bronze goods and bronze-making techniques from the Asian mainland reached what is now Japan as early as the 3rd century BC. It is believed that bronze and, later, iron implements and weapons were introduced to Japan near the end of this time (and well into the early Yamato period). Archaeological findings suggest that bronze and iron weapons were not used for war until later, starting at the beginning of the Yamato period, as the metal weapons found with human remains do not show wear consistent with use as weapons. The transition from the Jômon to Yayoi, and later to the Yamato period, is likely to have been characterized by violent struggle as the natives were soon displaced by the invaders and their vastly superior military technology. Historian John Kuehn believes that a possible "partial genocide" of Japan's aboriginal people occurred during this period.

Around this time, San Guo Zhi first referred to the nation of "Wa (Japan)". According to this work, Wa was "divided into more than 100 tribes", and for some 70 or 80 years there were many disturbances and wars. About 30 communities had been united by a sorceress-queen named Himiko. She sent an emissary named Nashime (ja:ã–GSs|, Nashonmi in Chinese) with a tribute of slaves and cloth to Daifang in China, establishing diplomatic relations with Cao Wei (the Chinese kingdom of Wei).

ANCIENT AND CLASSICAL JAPAN

By the end of the 4th century, the Yamato clan was well established on the Nara plain with considerable control over the surrounding areas. The Five kings of Wa sent envoys to China to recognize their dominion of the Japanese Islands. The Nihon Shokistates that the Yamato were strong enough to have sent an army against the powerful state of Goguryeo. Yamato Japan had close relations with the southwestern Korean kingdom of Baekje. In 663, Japan, supporting Baekje, was defeated by the allied forces of Tang China and Silla, at the Battle of Hakusonko in the Korean peninsula. As a result, the Japanese were banished from the peninsula. To defend the Japanese archipelago, a military base was constructed in Dazaifu, Fukuoka, on Kyushu.

Yamato Period (250–710 AD)

Ancient Japan had close ties with the Gaya Confederacy in the Korean Peninsula, as well as with the Korean kingdom of Baekje. Gaya, where there was an abundance of naturally occurring iron, exported abundant quantities of iron armor and weapons to Wa, and there may have even been a Japanese military post there with Gaya and Baekje cooperation.

In 552, the ruler of Baekje appealed to Yamato for help against its enemies, the neighboring Silla. Along with his emissaries to the Yamato court, the Baekje king sent bronze images of Buddha, some Buddhist scriptures, and a letter praising Buddhism. These gifts triggered a powerful burst of interest in Buddhism.

In 663, near the end of the Korean Three Kingdoms period, the Battle of Baekgang took place. The Nihon shokirecords that Yamato sent 32,000 troops and 1,000 ships to support Baekje against the Silla-Tang force. However, these ships were intercepted and defeated by a Silla-Tang fleet. Baekje, without aid and surrounded by Silla and Tang forces on land, collapsed. Silla, now viewing Wa Japan as a hostile rival, prevented Japan from having any further meaningful contact with the Korean Peninsula until a far later time. The Japanese then turned directly to China.

Nara Period (710–794 AD)

In many ways, the Nara period was the beginning of Japanese culture as we know it today. It was in this period thatBuddhism, the Chinese writing system, and a codified system of laws made their appearance. The country was unified and centralized, with basic features of the later feudal system.

Much of the discipline, weapons, and armor of the samurai came to be during this period, as techniques of mounted archery, swordsmanship, and spear fighting were adopted and developed.

Succession disputes were prevalent during this period, just as in most of the later periods. The Nara period saw the appointment of the first Shogun, Ôtomo no Otomaro (731 – June 14, 809).

Heian Period (794–1185 AD)

The Heian Period marks a crucial shift, away from a state that was united in relative peace against outside threats to one that did not fear invasion and, instead, focused on internal division and clashes between ruling factions of samurai clans, over political power and control of the line of succession to theChrysanthemum Throne.

With the exception of the Mongol invasions of the 13th century, Japan did not face a considerable outside threat until the arrival of Europeans in the 16th century. Thus, pre-modern Japanese military history is largely defined not by wars with other states, but by internal conflicts. The tactics of the samurai of this period involved archery and swordsmanship. Nearly all duels and battles began with an exchange of arrow fire and then hand-to-hand combat with swords and daggers.

The Imperial family struggled against the control of the Fujiwara clan, which almost exclusively monopolized the post of regent (Sesshô and Kampaku). Feudal conflicts over land, political power, and influence eventually culminated in the Genpei War between the Taira and Minamoto clans, with a large number of smaller clans being allied with one side or the other. The later Heian period conflicts, particularly the Genpei War, and the establishment of the Kamakura shogunate that followed, mark the ascendancy of the samurai class over the court nobility (*kuge*). The shogunates, which were essentially military governments, dominated Japanese politics for nearly seven hundred years (1185–1868), subverting the power of the Emperor and that of the Imperial Court.

The end of the Genpei War brought about the end of the Heian period and the beginning of the Kamakura period.

FEUDAL JAPAN

This period is marked by the departure from relatively small or medium-sized clan-like battles, to massive clashes of clans for battle over the control of Japan. In the Kamakura period, Japan successfully repulsed the Mongol invasions, and this saw a large growth in the size of military forces, with samurai as an elite force and as commanders. Following roughly fifty years of bitter fighting over control of the Imperial succession, the Muromachi period, under the Ashikaga shogunate, saw a brief period of peace as the power of the traditional systems of administration by the Court gradually declined. Later, the position of the provincial governors and other officials under the shogunate slowly gave way into a new class of *daimyôs* (feudal lords), and thus brought the archipelago into a period of 150 years of fractious disunity and war.

Kamakura Period (1185–1333)

Having subdued their rivals, the Taira clan, the Minamoto clan established the Kamakura shogunate, which brought a period of peace. The battles fought during this period mainly consisted of agents of the Minamoto suppressing rebellions.

The Mongols, who controlled China at the time, under the Yuan Dynasty, attempted to invade Japan twice in the 13th century, marking the most important military event of the Kamakura period, two of the few attempts to invade Japan. In early October 1274, theBattle of Bun'ei began with a combined force of Mongols and Koreans seizing Tsushima, and then attacking Kyûshû, landing atHakata Bay. On October 19, the Mongols lost many warships due to a typhoon, and the remaining troops retreated. Anticipating a second assault, the shogunate organized the construction of walls and fortresses along the shore, and gathered forces to defend against further invasions. The second invasion took place in 1281. In what has come to be known as the Battle of Kôan, the Mongol-led forces retreated after losing many ships again due to a typhoon.

The equipment, tactics, and military attitudes of the samurai and their Mongol opponents differed greatly, and while both invasions failed miserably, their impact on developments and changes in samurai battle were quite significant. The samurai remained attached to ideas of single combat, that of honorable battle between individual warriors, and to certain ritual elements of battle, such as a series of archery exchanges conducted before entering into hand-to-hand fighting. The Mongols, of course, knew nothing of Japanese conventions, and were arguably much more organized in their strike tactics. They did not select individual opponents with whom to conduct honorable duels, but rode forth on horseback, with various forms of gunpowder weapons and the famous Mongol bow, charging into enemy lines and killing as many as they could without regard to Japanese conceptions of protocol. Though archery and mounted combat were central to Japanese warfare at this time as well, the Mongols remain famous even today for their prowess in these matters. The ways that samurai tactics and attitudes were affected by these experiences are difficult to ascertain, but they were certainly significant.

Muromachi Period (1336–1467)

The shogunate fell in the wake of the 1331 Genkô War, an uprising against the shogunate organized by the Emperor Go-Daigo. After a brief period under true Imperial rule, the Ashikaga shogunate was established in 1336, and a series of conflicts known as the Nanboku-chô Wars began. For over fifty years, the archipelago became embroiled in disputes over control of Imperial succession, and thus over the country.

Battles grew larger in this period, and were less ritualized. Though single combats and other elements of ritual and honorable battle remained, organized strategies and tactics under military commanders began to emerge, along with a greater degree of organization of formations and divisions within armies. It was in this period, as well, that weaponsmithing techniques emerged, creating so-called "Japanese steel" blades, flexible yet extremely hard and sharp. The katana, and myriad similar or related blade weapons, appeared at this time and would dominate Japanese arms, relatively unchanged, through the mid-20th century. As a result, it was also during this period that the shift of samurai from being archers to swordsmen began in a significant way.

Sengoku Period (1467–1603)

Less than a century after the end of the Nanboku-chô Wars, peace under the relatively weak Ashikaga shogunate was destroyed by the outbreak of the Ônin War, a roughly ten-year struggle that converted the capital of Kyoto into a battlefield and a heavily fortified city that suffered severe destruction.

The authority of both the shogunate and the Imperial Court had weakened, and provincial Governors (*shugo*) and other local samurai leaders emerged as the *daimyôs*, who battled each other, religious factions (e.g. the Ikkô-ikki), and others for land and power for the next 150 years or so. The period has come to be called Sengoku , after the Warring Statesperiod in ancient Chinese history. Over one hundred domains clashed and warred throughout the archipelago, as clans rose and fell, boundaries shifted, and some of the largest battles in all of global pre-modern history were fought.

A great many developments and significant events took place during this period, ranging from advances in castle design to the advent of the cavalry charge, the further development of campaign strategies on a grand scale, and the significant changes brought on by the introduction of firearms. The composition of the army changed, with masses of *ashigaru*, footsoldiers armed with long lances (*yari*), archers, and, later, gunners serving alongside mounted samurai. Naval battles likewise consisted of little more than using boats to move troops within range of bow or arquebus, and then into hand-to-hand fighting.

The Hôjô clan, in and around the Kantô area, were among the first to establish networks of satellite castles, and the complex use of these castles both for mutual defense and coordinated attacks. The Takeda, under Takeda Shingen, developed the Japanese equivalent of the cavalry charge. Though debate continues today as to the force of his charges, and the appropriateness of comparing them to Western cavalry charges, it is evident from contemporary sources that it was a revolutionary development, and powerful against defenders unused to it. Battles of particular interest or significance are too numerous to list here, but suffice it to say that this period saw a myriad of strategic and tactical developments, and some of the longest sieges and largest battles in the history of the pre-modern world.

Azuchi–Momoyama Period (1568–1600)

This period, named for the increasingly important castle-cities, is marked by the introduction of firearms, after contact with the Portuguese, and a further push towards all-out battle, away from individual combats and concepts of personal honor and bravery.

The arquebus was introduced to Japan in 1543, by Portuguese on board a Chinese ship that crashed upon the tiny island of Tanegashima in the southernmost parts of the Japanese archipelago. Though the weapon's introduction was not seen to have particularly dramatic effects for several decades, by the 1560s thousands of gunpowder weapons were in use in Japan, and began to have revolutionary effects upon Japanese tactics, strategy, army compositions, and castle architecture.

The 1575 Battle of Nagashino, in which about 3,000 arquebusiers led by Oda Nobunaga cut down charging ranks of thousands of samurai, remains one of the chief examples of the effect of these weapons. Highly inaccurate, and taking a long time to reload, arquebusses, or *hinawa-jû* as they are called in Japanese, did not win battles on their own. Oda Nobunaga, Toyotomi Hideyoshi, and other commanders developed tactics that honed arquebus use to the greatest advantage. At Nagashino, Nobunaga's gunners hid behind wooden barricades, embedded with large wooden spikes to ward off cavalry, and took turns firing volleys and reloading.

As in Europe, the debilitating effects of wet (and therefore largely useless) gunpowder were decisive in a number of battles. But, one of the key advantages of the weapon was that unlike bows, which required years of training largely available only to the samurai class, guns could be used by relatively untrained footmen. Samurai stuck to their swords and their bows, engaging in cavalry or infantry tactics, while the *ashigaru* wielded the guns. Some militant Buddhist factions began to produce firearms in foundries normally employed to make bronze temple bells. In this manner, the Ikkô-ikki, a group of monks and lay religious zealots, turned their Ishiyama Honganji cathedral-fortress into some of the most well-defended fortresses in the country. The *ikki* and a handful of other militant religious factions thus became powers unto themselves, and fought fierce battles against some of the chief generals and samurai clans of the archipelago.

Though civil strife continued to rage as it had for the previous century, the battles growing larger and more tactically complex, it was at this time that the many "warring states" began to be united, first under Oda Nobunaga, then underToyotomi Hideyoshi, and finally by Tokugawa Ieyasu.

Between 1592 and 1598, Toyotomi Hideyoshi organized an army of 150,000 soldiersfor the conquest of China's Ming Dynasty by way of Korea. After the latter's refusal to allow Japanese forces to march through, Japan completed the occupation of the Korean peninsula in three months. However, a Chinese army was sent to Korea at the behest of the Korean king. Eventually, the supply lines of the Japanese army became overstretched until it became impossible for the Japanese army to maintain the occupation of the Korean peninsula. After Hideyoshi's death, the Council of Five Eldersordered the remaining Japanese forces in Korea to retreat.

Tokugawa Ieyasu, one of the regents, took control of most of the former leader's forces. In 1600, he won the battle of Sekigahara and solidified his rule. In 1603, he received the title of shogun, making him the nominal ruler of the entire country.

Edo period (1603–1867)

This period was one of relative peace under the authority of the Tokugawa shogunate, a forced peace that was maintained through a variety of measures that weakened the *daimyôs* and ensured their loyalty to the shogunate. The Tokugawa peace was ruptured only rarely and briefly prior to the violence that surrounded theMeiji Restoration of the 1860s.

The Siege of Osaka, which took place in 1614–1615, was essentially the last gasp for Toyotomi Hideyori, heir to Hideyoshi, and an alliance of clans and other elements who opposed the shogunate. A samurai battle on a grand scale, in terms of strategy, scale, methods employed, and the political causes behind it, this is widely considered the final conflict of the Sengoku period.

Outside of the siege of Osaka, and the later conflicts of the 1850s to 1860s, violence in the Edo period was restricted to small skirmishes in the streets, peasant rebellions, and the enforcement of maritime restrictions. Social tension in the Edo period brought a number of rebellions and uprisings, the largest of which was the 1638 Shimabara Rebellion. In the far north of the country, the island of Hokkaido was inhabited by Ainu villagers and Japanese settlers. In 1669, an Ainu leader led a revolt against the Matsumae clan who controlled the region, and it was the last major uprising against Japanese control of the region. It was put down in 1672. In 1789, another Ainu revolt, the Menashi-Kunashir Rebellion, was crushed.

The appearance of gunboat diplomacy in Japan in the 1850s, and the forced so-called "opening of Japan" by Western forces, underscored the weakness of the shogunate and led to its collapse. Though the actual end of the shogunate and establishment of an Imperial Western-style government was handled peacefully, through political petitions and other methods, the years surrounding the event were not entirely bloodless. Following the formal termination of the shogunate, the Boshin War (b° • &b‰ N *Boshin Sensô*, "War of the Fifth Year of Year of the Yang Earth Dragon") was fought in 1868–1869 between the Tokugawa army and a number of factions of nominally pro-Imperial forces.

MODERN PERIOD

After a long period of peace, Japan rearmed by importing, then manufacturing, Western weapons, and finally by manufacturing weapons of Japanese design. During the Russo-Japanese War (1904–1905), Japan became the first modern Asian nation to win a war against a European nation. In 1902, it became the first Asian nation to sign a mutual defense pact with a European nation, Britain.

Japan was the last major power to enter the race for global colonization. Severely hampered by its still-developing industries, Japan started a war against the United States during World War II with less than one-tenth of the industrial capabilities of the US.

Even though Japan maintains a powerful defense force today, its Constitution, originally drawn under the guidelines of General Douglas MacArthur in 1945, formally renounces war and the use of military force in aggressive ways. Japan also maintains a policy against the exporting of military hardware.

In September 2015, the Liberal Democratic Party under the leadership of Prime Minister Shinzo Abe, reinterpreted the Constitution, allowing Japan to use military force in assistance of its allies. The legality of these changes has been questioned by many academics and citizens.

Meiji Period

Modern army established

From 1867, Japan requested various Western military missions in order to help Japan to modernize its armed forces. The first foreign military mission in Japan was held by France in 1867. Captain Jules Brunet, initially a French artillery advisor of the Japanese central government, eventually took up arms alongside the Shogun's army against the Imperial troops during the Boshin War.

In 1873, the Imperial government enacted a conscription law and established the Imperial Japanese Army. As class distinctions were all but eliminated in attempts to modernize and create a representative democracy, the samurai lost their status as the only class with military privileges.

Sino-Japanese War (1894–1895)

The Sino-Japanese War was fought against the forces of the Qing Dynasty of China in theKorean peninsula, Manchuria, and the coast of China. It was the first major conflict between Japan and an overseas military power in modern times.

The Treaty of Shimonoseki signed between Japan and China ended the war. Through this treaty, Japan forced China to open ports for international trade and cede the southern portion of China's Liaoning province as well as the island ofTaiwan to Japan. China also had to pay a war indemnity of 200 million Kuping taels. As a result of this war, Korea ceased to be a tributary state of China, but fell into Japan's sphere of influence. However, many of the material gains from this war were lost by Japan due to theTriple Intervention.

Japanese invasion of Taiwan (1895)

The Japanese occupation of Taiwan was strongly resisted by various interests on the island, and was only completed after a full-scale military campaign requiring the commitment of the Imperial Guards Division and most of the 2nd and 4th Provincial Divisions. The campaign began in late May 1895 with a Japanese landing at Keelung, on the northern coast of Taiwan, and ended in October 1895 with the Japanese capture of Tainan, the capital of the self-styled Republic of Formosa. The Japanese defeated regular Chinese and Formosan formations relatively easily but their marching columns were often harassed by guerillas. The Japanese responded with brutal reprisals, and sporadic resistance to their occupation of Taiwan continued until 1902.

The Boxer Rebellion

The Eight-Nation Alliance was an international military coalition set up in response to the Boxer Rebellion in the Qing Empire of China. The eight nations were the Empire of Japan, the Russian Empire, the British Empire, the French Third Republic, the United States, the German Empire, the Kingdom of Italy and the Austro-Hungarian Empire. In the summer of 1900, when the extra-jurisdictional international legations in Beijing came under attack by Boxer rebels supported by the Qing government, the coalition dispatched their armed forces, in the name of "humanitarian intervention", to defend their respective nations' citizens, as well as a number of Chinese Christians who had taken shelter in the legations. The incident ended with a coalition victory and the signing of the Boxer Protocol.

Russo-Japanese War

The Japanese victory in the Russo-Japanese War of 1904–1905 marks the emergence of Japan as a major military power. Japan demonstrated that it could apply Western technology, discipline, strategy, and tactics effectively.

Taisho Period and World War I

In 1914, Japan was a member of the Allies during World War I and was rewarded with control of German colonies in the Pacific. A

70,000-strong Japanese force also intervened in Russiaduring the Russian Civil War, supporting the anti-Communist factions, but failed to achieve its objective and was forced to withdraw. A small group of Japanese cruisers and destroyers also participated in various missions in the Indian Ocean and Mediterranean Sea.

Showa Period and World War II

Already controlling the area along the South Manchuria Railroad, Japan's Kwantung Armyfurther invaded Manchuria (Northeast China) in 1931, following the Mukden Incident, in where Japan claimed to have had territory attacked by the Chinese. By 1937, Japan had annexed territory north of Beijing and, following the Marco Polo Bridge Incident, a full-scale invasion of China began. Japanese military superiority over a weak and demoralized Chinese Republican army allowed for swift advances down the eastern coast, leading to the fall of Shanghai and Nanjing (Nanking, then capital of the Republic of China) the same year. The Chinese suffered greatly in both military and civilian casualties. An estimated 300,000 civilians were killed during the first weeks of Japanese occupation of Nanjing, during theNanking Massacre.

In September 1940, Germany, Italy, and Japan became allies under the Tripartite Pact. Germany, which had previously trained and supplied the Chinese army, halted all Sino-German cooperation, and recalled its military advisor (Alexander von Falkenhausen). In July 1940, the U.S. banned the shipment of aviation gasoline to Japan, while Imperial Japanese Army invaded French Indochina and occupied its naval and air bases in September 1940.

In April 1941, the Empire of Japan and the Soviet Union signed a neutrality pact and Japan increased pressure on the Vichy French and Dutch colonies in Southeast Asia to cooperate in economic matters. Following Japan's refusal to withdraw from China (with the exclusion of Manchukuo) and Indochina, United States, Great Britain, and the Netherlands imposed, on July 22, 1941, an embargo on gasoline, while shipments ofscrap metal, steel, and other materials had virtually ceased. Meanwhile, American economic support to China began to increase.

Following the Japanese attack on Pearl Harbor and against several other countries on December 7–8, 1941, the United States, United Kingdom, and other Allies declared war. The Second Sino-Japanese War became part of the global conflict ofWorld War II. Japanese forces initially experienced great success against Allied forces in the Pacific and Southeast Asia, capturing Thailand, Hong Kong, Malaya,

Singapore, the Dutch East Indies, the Philippines, and many Pacific Islands. They also undertook major offensives in Burma and launched air and naval attacks against Australia. The Allies turned the tide of war at sea in mid-1942, at the Battle of Midway. Japanese land forces continued to advance in the New Guinea and Solomon Islands campaigns but suffered significant defeats or were forced to retreat at the battles of Milne Bay, the Kokoda Track, and Guadalcanal. The Burma campaign turned, as the Japanese forces suffered catastrophic losses at Imphal and Kohima, leading to the greatest defeat in Japanese history up to that point.

From 1943 onwards, hard-fought campaigns at the battles of Buna-Gona, the Tarawa, the Philippine Sea, Leyte Gulf, Iwo Jima, Okinawa, and others resulted in horrific casualties, mostly on the Japanese side, and produced further Japanese retreats. Very few Japanese ended up in POW camps. This may have been due to Japanese soldiers' reluctance to surrender. The brutality of the conflict is exemplified by US troops taking body parts from dead Japanese soldiers as "war trophies" or "war souvenirs" and Japanese cannibalism.

Throughout the Pacific War, the Japanese military engaged in war crimes, in particular the mistreatment of prisoners of warand civilians. Some estimate that around 6 million people, primarily Chinese civilians, were killed by Japanese forces. These numbers are disputed, given that, between 1939 and 1945, more than 16 million civilians were injured in China alone. This was the largest civilian casualty count in any country. Mistreatment of Allied prisoners of war through forced labour and brutality received extensive coverage in the west. It is widely perceived that the Japanese government has failed to acknowledge the suffering caused by its forces and in particular the teaching of history in its schools has caused international protest.

On August 6 and August 9, 1945, the U.S. dropped two atomic bombs on Hiroshima and Nagasaki. An estimated 150,000–246,000 people died as a direct result of these two bombings, during which the Soviet Union entered the war against Japan.

Japan surrendered on August 15, 1945, and a formal Instrument of Surrender was signed on September 2, 1945, on the battleship USS *Missouri* in Tokyo Bay. The surrender was accepted, from a Japanese delegation led by Mamoru Shigemitsu, by General Douglas MacArthur, as Supreme Allied Commander, along with representatives of each Allied nation. A separate surrender ceremony between Japan and

China was held in Nanking on September 9, 1945. Following this period, MacArthur established bases in Japan to oversee the postwar development of the country. This period in Japanese history is known as the Occupation. U.S. President Harry Truman officially proclaimed an end to hostilities on December 31, 1946.

Over the course of the war, Japan displayed many significant advances in military technology, strategy, and tactics. Among them were the *Yamato*-class battleship, the Sen-Toku submarine bomber carriers, the Mitsubishi Zero fighters, and Kamikaze bombers.

Post–World War II

Article 9 of the Japanese Constitution:

(1) Aspiring sincerely to an international peace based on justice and order, the Japanese people forever renounce war as a sovereign right of the nation and the threat or use of force as means of settling international disputes.

(2) In order to accomplish the aim of the preceding paragraph, land, sea, and air forces, as well as other war potential, will never be maintained. The right of belligerency of the state will not be recognized.

After a period of occupation (15 August 1945 – 28 April 1952), Japan regained its independence. Japan is forbidden to have a military and to wage war by Article 9 of its Constitution, although in 1954, the Japan Self-Defense Forces(JSDF) was created with standing armies, modern weapons and material.

As Japan perceived a growing external threat without adequate forces to counter it, the National Safety Forces underwent further development that entailed difficult political problems. The war renunciation clause of the constitution was the basis for strong political objections to any sort of armed force other than conventional police force. In 1954, however, separate land, sea, and air forces for purely defensive purposes were created, subject to the command of thePrime Minister.

The armed forces consist of the Japan Ground Self-Defense Force (JGSDF), theJapan Maritime Self-Defense Force (JMSDF), and the Japan Air Self-Defense Force (JASDF).

The JSDF is one of the most technologically advanced armed forces in the world and Japanese military expenditures are the seventh highest in the world. Though the Treaty of Mutual Cooperation and

Security, signed in 1960, allows for the continued presence of American military bases in Japan, most of them on Okinawa Prefecture, no formal agreement was ever set by which Japan officially relies on the United States, United Nations, or anybody else for its defense.

In the aftermath of the Occupation, attempts were made by some administrations in Japan, particularly at the urging of the United States, to amend the Constitution to rearm. This was prevented by intense popular sentiment against this action, and against war in general, along with the attitudes and agendas of significant elements within the government. In 1967, Prime Minister Eisaku Satô outlined the Three Non-Nuclear Principles by which Japan stands against the production or possession of nuclear weaponry. Similar ideas were expressed several years later against the production and export of conventional arms.

Japan has deployed the JSDF to aid in a number of non-combat missions, especially those involving humanitarian aid, such as aiding the victims of the 1995 Kobe earthquake, providing administrative support to the United Nations Interim Force In Lebanon (UNIFIL) Norwegian Battalion (NORBATT) in the 1990s, and helping rebuild Iraq.

Some Japanese people have stated a desire to have their own military due to fear of the growing power of China and the hostility of North Korea. They claim that the U.S. has failed to properly address these issues, and Japan must grant itself the means to adequately defend itself.

In 2004, then-United Nations Secretary General Kofi Annan announced a plan to expand the number of permanent seats on the United Nations Security Council, and Japan seeks to gain one of those seats. Despite Japan's economic power and political influence, some debate whether or not a country with no "official" standing military can be considered a "world power" that should have a permanent seat on the Council. Recent disputes with neighboring countries over territories—such as over the Senkaku Islands (against China and Taiwan), Liancourt Rocks (against South Korea), and the Kuril Islands(against Russia), as well as accusations of Japanese whitewashing of history in various textbook controversies—have also complicated this process.

7

Economy

The economy of Japan is the third-largest in the world by nominal GDP and the fourth-largest by purchasing power parity (PPP).and is the world's second largest developed economy. Japan is a member of the G7. According to the International Monetary Fund, the country's per capita GDP (PPP) was at $37,519, the 28th highest in 2014, down from the 22nd position in 2012. Due to a volatile currency exchange rate, Japan's GDP as measured in dollars fluctuates widely. Accounting for these fluctuations through use of theAtlas method, Japan is estimated to have a GDP per capita of around $38,490.

Japan is the world's third largest automobile manufacturing country,has the largest electronics goods industry, and is often ranked among the world's most innovative countries leading several measures of global patent filings. Facing increasing competition from China and South Korea, manufacturing in Japan today now focuses primarily on high-tech and precision goods, such as optical instruments, hybrid vehicles, and robotics. Besides the Kantô region, theKansai region is one of the leading industrial clusters and manufacturing centers for the Japanese economy. The size and industrial structure of cities in Japan have maintained tight regularities despite substantial churning of population and industries across cities overtime. Japan is the world's largest creditor nation. Japan generally runs an annual trade surplus and has a considerable net international investment surplus. As of 2010, Japan possesses 13.7% of the world's private financial assets (the third largest in the world) at an estimated $13.5 trillion. As of 2015, 54 of the Fortune Global 500companies are based in Japan, down from 62 in 2013.

Japan has the highest ratio of public debt to GDP of any developed nation. However, the national debt is predominantly owned by Japanese nationals. The Japanese economy faces considerable challenges posed by a declining population. Statistics showed an official decline for the first time in 2015, while projections suggest that it will continue to fall from 127 million down to below 100 million by the middle of the 21st century. The Japanese economy is forecasted by the Quarterly Tankan survey of business sentiment conducted by theBank of Japan. The Nikkei 225 presents the monthly report of topBlue chip (stock market) equities on Japan Exchange Group.

OVERVIEW OF ECONOMY

In the three decades of economic development following 1960, Japan ignored defense spending in favor of economic growth, thus allowing for a rapid economic growth referred to as the Japanese post-war economic miracle. By the guidance of Ministry of Economy, Trade and Industry, with average growth rates of 10% in the 1960s, 5% in the 1970s, and 4% in the 1980s, Japan was able to establish and maintain itself as the world's second largest economy from 1978 until 2010, when it was surpassed by the People's Republic of China. By 1990, income per capita in Japan equalled or surpassed that in most countries in the West.

However, in the second half of the 1980s, rising stock and real estate prices caused the economic bubble to the Japanese economy by Bank of Japan. The economic bubble came to an abrupt end as the Tokyo Stock Exchange crashed in 1990–92 and real estate prices peaked in 1991. Growth in Japan throughout the 1990s at 1.5% was slower than growth in other major developed economies, giving rise to the term Lost Decade. After another decade of low growth rate, the term became the Lost 20 Years. Nonetheless, GDP per capita growth from 2001 to 2010 has still managed to outpace Europe and the United States.

Although 1.0% annual GDP growth is considered an aberration, Theodore Breton shows that this is the expected growth rate for a country with a shrinking work force and rates of investment in physical and human capital that have not increased since the 1970s. His analysis indicates that Japan has converged on its steady-state growth rate.

With this low growth rate, national debt of Japan is difficult for the government to manage due to its considerable social welfare spending related to an aging society. The scenario of "Abandoned homes" continues to spread from rural areas to urban areas in Japan. The Japanese economy rebounded under Junichirô Koizumi by acting against bad debts with commercial banks and privatizing the postal savings system. Abenomics has thus far given the economy of Japan a low and unsteady growth rate.

The ICT industry has generated the major outputs to the Japanese economy. Japan is the second largest music market in the world. Manga cafe business expands to 2000 stores nationwide in Japan in 2002. With fewer children in the aging Japan, Japanese anime industry is facing growing Chinese competition in the targeted Chinese market. Japanese manga industry (from the Japanese manga (and anime) profession) enjoys popularity in most of the Asian markets. And anime industry share in Japan GDP has exceeded 10 percent. Local gourmets of 47 Prefectures of Japan are guided and promoted by Ministry of Agriculture, Forestry and Fisheries (Japan). Japan Cup in the Tokyo Racecourse is one of the richest horse racing in the world.

A mountainous, volcanic island country, Japan has inadequate natural resources to support its growing economy and large population, and therefore exports goods in which it has a comparative advantage such as engineering-oriented, research and development-led industrial products in exchange for the import of raw materials and petroleum. Japan is among the top-three importers for agricultural products in the world next to the European Union and United States in total volume for covering of its own domestic agricultural consumption. Japan is the world's largest single national importer of fish and fishery products. Tokyo Metropolitan Central Wholesale Market is the largest wholesale market for primary products in Japan, including the renowned Tsukiji fish market. Japanese whaling, ostensibly for research purposes, has been sued as illegal under international law.

Although many kinds of minerals were extracted throughout the country, most mineral resources had to be imported in the postwar era. Local deposits of metal-bearing ores were difficult to process because they were low grade. The nation's large and varied forest resources, which covered 70 percent of the country in the late 1980s, were not utilized extensively. Because of political decisions on local, prefectural, and national levels, Japan decided not to exploit its forest resources for economic gain. Domestic sources only supplied between 25 and 30 percent of the nation's timber needs. Agriculture and fishing were the best developed resources, but only through years of painstaking investment and toil. The nation therefore built up the manufacturing and processing industries to convert raw materials imported from abroad. This strategy of economic development necessitated the establishment of a strong economic infrastructure to provide the needed energy, transportation, communications, and technological know-how.

Deposits of gold, magnesium, and silver meet current industrial demands, but Japan is dependent on foreign sources for many of the minerals essential to modern industry. Iron ore, copper, bauxite, and alumina must be imported, as well as many forest products.

ECONOMIC HISTORY

The economic history of Japan is one of the most studied economies for its spectacular growth in three different periods. First was the foundation of Edo (in 1603) to whole inland economical developments, second was the Meiji Restoration(in 1868) to be the first non-European power, third was after the defeat of World War II (in 1945) when the island nation rose to become the world's second largest economy.

First contacts with Europe (16th century)

Japan was considered as a country rich in precious metals, mainly owing to Marco Polo's accounts of gilded temples and palaces, but also due to the relative abundance of surface ores characteristic of a massive huge volcanic country, before large-scale deep-mining became possible in Industrial times. Japan was to become a major exporter of silver, copper, and gold during the period until exports for those minerals were banned.

Renaissance Japan was also perceived as a sophisticated feudal society with a high culture and a strong pre-industrial technology. It was densely populated and urbanized. Prominent European observers of the time seemed to agree that the Japanese *"excel not only all the other Oriental peoples, they surpass the Europeans as well"* (Alessandro Valignano, 1584, "Historia del Principo y Progresso de la Compania de Jesus en las Indias Orientales).

Early European visitors were amazed by the quality of Japanese craftsmanship and metalsmithing. This stems from the fact that Japan itself is rather rich in natural resources found commonly in Europe, especially iron.

The cargo of the first Portuguese ships (usually about 4 smaller-sized ships every year) arriving in Japan almost entirely consisted of Chinese goods (silk, porcelain). The Japanese were very much looking forward to acquiring such goods, but had been prohibited from any contacts with the Emperor of China, as a punishment for Wakô pirate raids. The Portuguese (who were called *Nanban*, lit. Southern Barbarians) therefore found the opportunity to act as intermediaries in Asian trade.

Edo period (1603–1868)

The beginning of the Edo period coincides with the last decades of the Nanban trade period, during which intense interaction with European powers, on the economic and religious plane, took place. It is at the beginning of the Edo period that Japan built her first ocean-going Western-style warships, such as the *San Juan Bautista*, a 500-ton galleon-type ship that transported a Japanese embassy headed by Hasekura Tsunenaga to the Americas, which then continued to Europe. Also during that period, the *bakufu* commissioned around 350 Red Seal Ships, three-masted and armed trade ships, for intra-Asian commerce. Japanese adventurers, such as Yamada Nagamasa, were active throughout Asia.

In order to eradicate the influence of Christianization, Japan entered in a period of isolation called sakoku, during which its economy enjoyed stability and mild progress.

Economic development during the Edo period included urbanization, increased shipping of commodities, a significant expansion of domestic and, initially, foreign commerce, and a diffusion of trade and handicraft industries. The constructiontrades flourished, along with banking facilities and merchant associations. Increasingly, *han* authorities oversaw the risingagricultural production and the spread of rural handicrafts.

By the mid-eighteenth century, Edo had a population of more than 1 million and Osaka and Kyoto each had more than 400,000 inhabitants. Many other castle towns grew as well. Osaka and Kyoto became busy trading and handicraft production centers, while Edo was the center for the supply of food and essential urban consumer goods.

Rice was the base of the economy, as the daimyo collected the taxes from the peasants in the form of rice. Taxes were high, about 40% of the harvest. The rice was sold at the *fudasashi* market in Edo. To raise money, the daimyo used forward contracts to sell rice that was not even harvested yet. These contracts were similar to modern futures trading. During the period, Japan progressively studied Western sciences and techniques (called *rangaku*, literally "Dutch studies") through the information and books received through the Dutch traders in Dejima. The main areas that were studied included geography, medicine, natural sciences, astronomy, art, languages, physical sciences such as the study of electrical phenomena, and mechanical sciences as exemplified by the development of Japanese clockwatches, or wadokei, inspired from Western techniques.

Pre-war period (1868–1945)

Since the mid-19th century, after the Meiji Restoration, the country was opened up to Western commerce and influence and Japan has gone through two periods of economic development. The first began in earnest in 1868 and extended through to World War II; the second began in 1945 and continued into the mid-1980s.

Economic developments of the prewar period began with the "Rich State and Strong Army Policy" by the Meiji government. During the Meiji period (1868–1912), leaders inaugurated a new Western-based education system for all young people, sent thousands of students to the United States and Europe, and hired more than 3,000 Westerners to teach modern science, mathematics, technology, and foreign languages in Japan (Oyatoi gaikokujin). The government also built railroads, improved road, and inaugurated a land reform program to prepare the country for further development.

To promote industrialization, the government decided that, while it should help private business to allocate resources and to plan, the public sector was best equipped to stimulate economic growth. The greatest role of government was to help provide good economic conditions for business. In short, government was to be the guide and business the producer. In the early Meiji period, the government built factories and shipyards that were sold to entrepreneurs at a fraction of their value. Many of these businesses grew rapidly into the larger conglomerates. Government emerged as chief promoter of private enterprise, enacting a series of probusiness policies. In the mid-1930s, the Japanese nominal wage rates were "10 times less" than the one of the U.S (based on mid-1930s exchange rates), while the price level is estimated to have been about 44% the one of the U.S.

Postwar period (1945–present)

From the 1960s to the 1980s, overall real economic growth was extremely large: a 10% average in the 1960s, a 5% average in the 1970s and a 4% average in the 1980s. By the end of said period, Japan had moved into being a high-wage economy.

Growth slowed markedly in the late 1990s also termed the Lost Decadeafter the collapse of the Japanese asset price bubble. As a consequence Japan ran massive budget deficits (added trillions in Yen to Japanese financial system) to finance large public works programs.

Japan Export Treemap by Product (2014) from Harvard Atlas of Economic Complexity By 1998, Japan's public works projects still could not stimulate demand enough to end the economy's stagnation. In desperation, the Japanese government undertook "structural reform" policies intended to wring speculative excesses from the stock and real estate markets. Unfortunately, these policies led Japan into deflation on numerous occasions between 1999 and 2004. In his 1998 paper, Japan's Trap, Princeton economics professor Paul Krugman argued that based on a number of models, Japan had a new option. Krugman's plan called for a rise in inflation expectations to, in effect, cut long-term interest rates and promote spending.

Japan used another technique, somewhat based on Krugman's, called Quantitative easing. As opposed to flooding the money supply with newly printed money, the Bank of Japan expanded the money supply internally to raise expectations of inflation. Initially, the policy failed to induce any growth, but it eventually began to affect inflationary expectations. By late 2005, the economy finally began what seems to be a sustained recovery. GDP growth for that year was 2.8%, with an annualized fourth quarter expansion of 5.5%, surpassing the growth rates of the US and European Union during the same period. Unlike previous recovery trends, domestic consumption has been the dominant factor of growth.

Despite having interest rates down near zero for a long period of time, the Quantitative easing strategy did not succeed in stopping price deflation. This led some economists, such as Paul Krugman, and some Japanese politicians, to advocate the generation of higher inflation expectations. In July 2006, the zero-rate policy was ended. In 2008, the Japanese Central Bank still had the lowest interest rates in the developed world, but deflation had still not been eliminated and the Nikkei 225 has fallen over approximately 50% (between June 2007 and December 2008). However, on 5 April 2013, theBank of Japan announced that it would be purchasing 60–70 trillion yen in bonds and securities in an attempt to eliminate deflation by doubling the money supply in

Japan over the course of two years. Markets around the world have responded positively to the government's current proactive policies, with the Nikkei 225 adding more than 42% since November 2012.The Economist has suggested that improvements to bankruptcy law, land transfer law, and tax laws will aid Japan's economy. In recent years, Japan has been the top export market for almost 15 trading nations worldwide.

INFRASTRUCTURE

In 2005, one half of Japan's energy was produced from petroleum, a fifth from coal, and 14% from natural gas. Nuclear power in Japan made a quarter of electricity production but due to the Fukushima Daiichi nuclear disaster there has been a large desire to end Japan's nuclear power program. In September 2013, Japan closed its last 50 nuclear power plants nationwide, causing the nation to be nuclear free.

Japan's spendings on roads has been considered large. The 1.2 million kilometers of paved road are one of the major means of transportation. Japan has left-hand traffic. A single network of speed, divided, limited-access toll roads connects major cities and are operated by toll-collecting enterprises. New and used cars are inexpensive, and the Japanese government has encouraged people to buy hybrid vehicles. Car ownership fees and fuel levies are used to promote energy-efficiency.

Rail transport is a major means of transport in Japan. Dozens of Japanese railway companies compete in regional and local passenger transportation markets; for instance, 6 passenger JR enterprises, Kintetsu Railway, Seibu Railway, and Keio Corporation. Often, strategies of these enterprises contain real estate or department stores next to stations, and many major stations have major department stores near them. The Japanese cities of Fukuoka, Kobe, Kyoto, Nagoya, Osaka,Sapporo, Sendai, Tokyo and Yokohama all have subway systems. Some 250 high-speed Shinkansen trains connect major cities. All trains are known for punctuality, and a delay of 90 seconds can be considered late for some train services.

There are 98 passenger and 175 total airports in Japan, and flying is a popular way to travel. The largest domestic airport, Tokyo International Airport, is Asia's second busiest airport. The largest international gateways are Narita International Airport (Tokyo area), Kansai International Airport (Osaka/Kobe/Kyoto area), and Chûbu

Centrair International Airport (Nagoya area). The largest ports in Japan include Nagoya Port, the Port of Yokohama, the Port of Tokyo and thePort of Kobe.

About 84% of Japan's energy is imported from other countries. Japan is the world's largest liquefied natural gas importer, second largest coal importer, and third largest net oil importer. Given its heavy dependence on imported energy, Japan has aimed to diversify its sources. Since the oil shocks of the 1970s, Japan has reduced dependence on petroleum as a source of energy from 77.4% in 1973 to about 43.7% in 2010 and increased dependence on natural gas and nuclear power. Other important energy source includes coal, and hydroelectricity is Japan's biggest renewable energy source. Japan's solar market is also currently booming. Kerosene is also used extensively for home heating in portable heaters, especially farther north. Many taxi companies run their fleets on liquefied natural gas. A recent success towards greater fuel economy was the introduction of mass-produced Hybrid vehicles. Prime MinisterShinzô Abe, who was working on Japan's economic revival, signed a treaty with Saudi Arabia and UAE about the rising prices of oil, ensuring Japan's stable deliveries from that region.

MACRO-ECONOMIC TREND

Sectors of the economy: Agriculture

The Japanese agricultural sector accounts for about 1.4% of the total country's GDP. Only 12% of Japan's land is suitable for cultivation. Due to this lack of arable land, a system of terraces is used to farm in small areas. This results in one of the world's highest levels of crop yields per unit area, with an overall agricultural self-sufficiency rate of about 50% on fewer than 56,000 km² (14 million acres) cultivated.

Japan's small agricultural sector, however, is also highly subsidized and protected, with government regulations that favor small-scale cultivation instead of large-scale agriculture as practiced in North America. There has been a growing concern about farming as the current farmers are aging with a difficult time finding successors.

Rice accounts for almost all of Japan's cereal production. Japan is the second-largest agricultural product importer in the world. Rice, the most protected crop, is subject to tariffs of 777.7%.

Although Japan is usually self-sufficient in rice (except for its use in making rice crackers and processed foods) and wheat, the country must import about 50% of its requirements of other grain and fodder crops and relies on imports for half of its supply of meat. Japan imports large quantities of wheat and soybeans. Japan is the 5th largest market for EU agricultural exports. Over 90% of mandarin oranges in Japan are grown in Japan. Apples are also grown due to restrictions on apple imports.

Fishery

Japan ranked fourth in the world in 1996 in tonnage of fish caught. Japan captured 4,074,580 metric tons of fish in 2005, down from 4,987,703 tons in 2000, 9,558,615 tons in 1990, 9,864,422 tons in 1980, 8,520,397 tons in 1970, 5,583,796 tons in 1960 and 2,881,855 tons in 1950. In 2003, the total aquaculture production was predicted at 1,301,437 tonnes. In 2010, Japan's total fisheries production was 4,762,469 fish. Offshore fisheries accounted for an average of 50% of the nation's total fish catches in the late 1980s although they experienced repeated ups and downs during that period.

Coastal fishing by small boats, set nets, or breeding techniques accounts for about one third of the industry's total production, while offshore fishing by medium-sized boats makes up for more than half the total production. Deep-sea fishing from larger vessels makes up the rest. Among the many species of seafood caught are sardines, skipjack tuna, crab, shrimp, salmon, pollock, squid, clams, mackerel, sea bream, sauries, tuna and Japanese amberjack. Freshwater fishing, including salmon, trout and eel hatcheries and fish farms, takes up about 30% of Japan's fishing industry. Among the nearly 300 fish species in the rivers of Japan are native varieties of catfish, chub, herring and goby, as well as such freshwater crustaceans as crabs and crayfish. Marine and freshwater aquaculture is conducted in all 47 prefectures in Japan.

Japan maintains one of the world's largest fishing fleets and accounts for nearly 15% of the global catch, prompting some claims that Japan's fishing is leading to depletion in fish stocks such as tuna. Japan has also sparked controversy by supporting quasi-commercial whaling.

Industry

Japanese manufacturing and industry is very diversified, with a variety of advanced industries that are highly successful. Industry accounts for 24% of the nation's GDP.

Industry is concentrated in several regions, with the Kantô region surrounding Tokyo, (the Keihin industrial region) as well as the Kansai region surrounding Osaka (the Hanshin industrial region) and the Tôkai region surrounding Nagoya (theChûkyô–Tôkai industrial region) the main industrial centers. Other industrial centers include the southwestern part of Honshû and northern Shikoku around the Seto Inland Sea (the Setouchi industrial region); and the northern part of Kyûshû (Kitakyûshû). In addition, a long narrow belt of industrial centers called the Taiheiyô Belt is found between Tokyo and Fukuoka, established by particular industries, that have developed as mill towns.

Japan enjoys high technological development in many fields, including consumer electronics, automobile manufacturing,semiconductor manufacturing, optical fibers, optoelectronics, optical media, facsimile and copy machines, and fermentation processes in food and biochemistry. However, many Japanese companies are facing emerging rivals from the United States, South Korea, and China.

Automobile manufacturing

Japan is the third biggest producer of automobiles in the world. Toyota is currently the world largest car maker, and the Japanese car makers Nissan,Honda, Suzuki, and Mazda also count for some of the largest car makers in the world.

Mining and petroleum exploration

Japan's mining production has been minimal, and Japan has very little mining deposits. However, massive deposits of rare earths have been found off the coast of Japan. In the 2011 fiscal year, the domestic yield of crude oil was 820 thousand kiloliters, which was 0.4% of Japan's total crude processing volume.

Services

Japan's service sector accounts for about three-quarters of its total economic output. Banking, insurance, real estate, retailing, transportation, and telecommunications are all major industries such as Mitsubishi UFJ, Mizuho, NTT,TEPCO, Nomura, Mitsubishi Estate, ÆON, Mitsui Sumitomo, Softbank, JR East,Seven & I, KDDI and Japan Airlines counting as one of the largest companies in the world.

Four of the five most circulated newspapers in the world are Japanese newspapers. The Koizumi government set Japan Post, one of the country's largest providers of savings and insurance services for privatization by 2015.The six major keiretsus are the Mitsubishi, Sumitomo, Fuyo, Mitsui, Dai-Ichi Kangyoand Sanwa Groups. Japan is home to 251 companies from the Forbes Global 2000 or 12.55% (as of 2013).

Tourism

In 2012, Japan was the fifth most visited country in Asia and the Pacific, with over 8.3 million tourists. In 2013, due to the weaker yen and easier visa requirements for southwest Asian countries, Japan received a record 11.25 million visitors, which was higher than the government's projected goal of 10 million visitors. The government hopes to attract 20 million visitors a year by the 2020 Summer Olympicsin Tokyo. Some of the most popular visited places include the Shinjuku, Ginza,Shibuya and Asakusa areas in Tokyo, and the cities of Osaka, Kobe and Kyoto, as well as Himeji Castle. Hokkaido is also a popular winter destination for visitors with several ski resorts and luxury hotels being built there.

FINANCE

The Tokyo Stock Exchange is the fourth largest stock exchange in the world bymarket capitalization, as well as the 2nd largest stock market in Asia, with 2,292 listed companies. The Nikkei 225 and the TOPIX are the two importantstock market indexes of the Tokyo Stock Exchange. The Tokyo Stock Exchange and the Osaka Stock Exchange, another major stock exchange in Japan, merged on 1 January 2013, creating one of the world's largest stock exchanges.Other stock exchanges in Japan include the Nagoya Stock Exchange, Fukuoka Stock Exchange and Sapporo Securities Exchange.

LABOR FORCE

The unemployment rate in December 2013 was 3.7%, down 1.5 percentage points from the claimed unemployment rate of 5.2% in June 2009 due to the strong economic recovery.

In 2008 Japan's labor force consisted of some 66 million workers — 40% of whom were women — and was rapidly shrinking. One major long-term concern for the Japanese labor force is its low birthrate. In the first half of 2005, the number of deaths in Japan exceeded the number of births, indicating that the decline in population, initially predicted to start in 2007, had already started. While one countermeasure for a declining birthrate would be to remove barriers to immigration, despite taking new steps towards it, the Japanese government has been reluctant to do so, since foreign immigration to Japan has been unpopular among citizens.

In 1989, the predominantly public sector union confederation, SOHYO (General Council of Trade Unions of Japan), merged with RENGO (Japanese Private Sector Trade Union Confederation) to form the Japanese Trade Union Confederation. Labor union membership is about 12 million.

LAW AND GOVERNMENT

Japan ranks 27th of 185 countries in the ease of doing business index 2013.

Japan has one of the smallest tax rates in the developed world. After deductions, the majority of workers are free frompersonal income taxes. Consumption tax rate is only 8%, while corporate tax rates are high, second highest corporate tax rate in the world, at 36.8%. However, the House of Representatives has passed a bill which will increase the consumption tax to 10% in October 2015. The government has also decided to reduce corporate tax and to phase out automobile tax.

In 2016, the IMF encouraged Japan to adopt an income policy that pushes firms to raise employee wages in combination with reforms to tackle the labor market dual tiered employment system to drive higher wages, on top of monetary and fiscal stimulus. Shinzo Abe has encouraged firms to raise wages by at least three percent annually (the inflation target plus average productivity growth).

Shareholder activism is rare despite the fact that the corporate law gives shareholders strong powers over managers.Under Prime Minister Shinzô Abe, corporate governance reform has been a key initiative to encourage economic growth. In 2012 around 40% of leading Japanese companies had any independent directors while in 2016 most all have begun to appoint independent directors.

The government's liabilities include the second largest public debt of any nation with debt of over one quadrillion yen, or $8,535,340,000,000 in USD. Former Prime Minister Naoto Kan has called the situation 'urgent'.

Japan's central bank has the second largest foreign-exchange reserves after the People's Republic of China, with over one trillion US Dollars in foreign reserves.

Culture

Nemawashi , or "consensus building", in Japanese culture is an informal process of quietly laying the foundation for some proposed change or project, by talking to the people concerned, gathering support and feedback, and so forth. It is considered an important element in any major change, before any formal steps are taken, and successful *nemawashi*enables changes to be carried out with the consent of all sides.

Japanese companies are known for management methods such as "The Toyota Way". Kaizen is a Japanese philosophy that focuses on continuous improvement throughout all aspects of life. When applied to the workplace, Kaizen activities continually improve all functions of a business, from manufacturing to management and from the CEO to the assembly line workers. By improving standardized activities and processes, Kaizen aims to eliminate waste. Kaizen was first implemented in several Japanese businesses during the country's recovery after World War II, including Toyota, and has since spread to businesses throughout the world. Within certain value systems, it is ironic that Japanese workers labor amongst the most hours per day, even though kaizen is supposed to improve all aspects of life.

Some companies have powerful enterprise unions and *shuntô*. The Nenko System or Nenko Joretsu, as it is called in Japan, is the Japanese system of promoting an employee based on his or her proximity to retirement. The advantage of the system is that it allows older employees to achieve a higher salary level before retirement and it usually brings more experience to the executive ranks. The disadvantage of the system is that it does not allow new talent to be combined with experience and those with specialized skills cannot be promoted to the already crowded executive ranks. It also does not guarantee or even attempt to bring the "right person for the right job".

Relationships between government bureaucrats and companies are often close. Amakudari *amakudari*, "descent from heaven") is the institutionalised practice where Japanese senior bureaucrats retire to high-profile positions in the private and public sectors. The practice is increasingly viewed as corrupt and a limitation on efforts to reduce ties between the private sector and the state that prevent economic and political reforms. Lifetime employment and seniority-based career advancement have been common in the Japanese work environment. Japan has begun to gradually move away from some of these norms.

Salaryman refers to someone whose income is salary based; particularly those working for corporations. Its frequent use by Japanese corporations, and its prevalence in Japanese manga and anime has gradually led to its acceptance in English-speaking countries as a noun for a Japanese white-collar businessman. The word can be found in many books and articles pertaining to Japanese culture. Immediately following World War II, becoming a salaryman was viewed as a gateway to a stable, middle-class lifestyle. In modern use, the term carries associations of long working hours, low prestige in the corporate hierarchy, absence of significant sources of income other than salary, wage slavery, and karôshi. The term salaryman refers almost exclusively to males.

An office lady, often abbreviated OL, is a female office worker in Japan who performs generallypink collar tasks such as serving tea and secretarial or clerical work. Like many unmarried Japanese, OLs often live with their parents well into early adulthood. Office ladies are usually full-time permanent staff, although the jobs they do usually have little opportunity for promotion, and there is usually the tacit expectation that they leave their jobs once they get married.

Freeter (other spellings below) is a Japanese expression for people between the age of 15 and 34 who lack full-time employment or are unemployed, excluding homemakers and students. They may also be described as *underemployed* or freelance workers. These people do not start a career after high school or university but instead usually live as parasite singles with their parents and earn some money with low skilled and low paid jobs. The low income makes it difficult for freeters to start a family, and the lack of qualifications makes it difficult to start a career at a later point in life.

Karôshi , which can be translated quite literally from Japanese as "death from overwork", is occupational sudden death. The major medical causes of karôshi deaths are heart attack and stroke due to stress.

Sôkaiya (sometimes also translated as *corporate bouncers, meeting-men*, or *corporate blackmailers*) are a form of specialized racketeer unique to Japan, and often associated with the yakuza that extort money from or blackmail companies by threatening to publicly humiliate companies and their management, usually in their annual meeting . Sarakin is a Japanese term for moneylender, or loan shark. It is a contraction of the Japanese words forsalaryman and cash. Around 14 million people, or 10% of the Japanese population, have borrowed from a *sarakin*. In total, there are about 10,000 firms (down from 30,000 a decade ago); however, the top seven firms make up 70% of the market. The value of outstanding loans totals $100 billion. The biggest *sarakin* are publicly traded and often allied with big banks.

The first "Western-style" department store in Japan was Mitsukoshi, founded in 1904, which has its root as a kimono store called Echigoya from 1673. When the roots are considered, however, Matsuzakaya has an even longer history, dated from 1611. The kimono store changed to a department store in 1910. In 1924, Matsuzakaya store in Ginza allowed street shoes to be worn indoors, something innovative at the time. These former kimono shop department stores dominated the market in its earlier history. They sold, or rather displayed, luxurious products, which contributed for their sophisticated atmospheres. Another origin of Japanese department store is that from railway company. There have been many private railway operators in the nation, and from the 1920s, they started to build department stores directly linked to their lines'termini. Seibu and Hankyu are the typical examples of this type. From the 1980s onwards, Japanese department stores face fierce competition from supermarkets and convenience stores, gradually losing their presences. Still, *depâto* are bastions of several aspects of cultural conservatism in the country. Gift certificates for prestigious department stores are frequently given as formal presents in Japan. Department stores in Japan generally offer a wide range of services and can includeforeign exchange, travel reservations, ticket sales for local concerts and other events.

Keiretsu

A keiretsu is a set of companies with interlocking business relationships and shareholdings. It is a type of business group. The prototypical *keiretsu* appeared in Japan during the "economic miracle" following World War II. Before Japan's surrender, Japanese industry was controlled by large family-controlled vertical monopolies called *zaibatsu*. The Allies dismantled the *zaibatsu* in the late 1940s, but the companies formed from the dismantling of the *zaibatsu* were reintegrated. The dispersed corporations were re-interlinked through share purchases to form horizontally integrated alliances across many industries. Where possible, *keiretsu* companies would also supply one another, making the alliances vertically integrated as well. In this period, official government policy promoted the creation of robust trade corporations that could withstand pressures from intensified world trade competition. The major *keiretsu* were each centered on one bank, which lent money to the *keiretsu's* member companies and held equity positions in the companies. Each central bank had great control over the companies in the *keiretsu* and acted as a monitoring entity and as an emergency bail-out entity. One effect of this structure was to minimize the presence of hostile takeovers in Japan, because no entities could challenge the power of the banks.

There are two types of *keiretsu*: vertical and horizontal. Vertical *keiretsu* illustrates the organization and relationships within a company (for example all factors of production of a certain product are connected), while a horizontal *keiretsu* shows relationships between entities and industries, normally centered on a bank and trading company. Both are complexly woven together and sustain each other.

The Japanese recession in the 1990s had profound effects on the keiretsu. Many of the largest banks were hit hard by bad loan portfolios and forced to merge or go out of business. This had the effect of blurring the lines between the keiretsu:Sumitomo Bank and Mitsui Bank, for instance, became Sumitomo Mitsui Banking Corporation in 2001, while Sanwa Bank(the banker for the Hankyu-Toho Group) became part of Bank of Tokyo-Mitsubishi UFJ. Additionally, many companies from outside the keiretsu system, such as Sony, began outperforming their counterparts within the system.

Generally, these causes gave rise to a strong notion in the business community that the old keiretsu system was not an effective business model, and led to an overall loosening of keiretsu alliances. While the keiretsu still exist, they are not as centralized or integrated as they were before the 1990s. This, in turn, has led to a growing corporate acquisition industry in Japan, as companies are no longer able to be easily "bailed out" by their banks, as well as rising derivative litigation by more independent shareholders.

8

Demographics

DEMOGRAPHY OF JAPAN

The demographic features of the population ofJapan include population density, ethnicity, education level, health of the populace, economic status, religious affiliations and other aspects regarding the population.

History

For information on historical demographic data in Japan prior to 1945 refer to:

- Demographic history of Japan before the Meiji Restoration
- Demography of Imperial Japan

Population

Historical population

Year	Pop.	±%
1910	50,984,840	—
1915	54,935,755	+7.7%
1920	55,963,053	+1.9%
1925	59,736,822	+6.7%
1930	64,450,005	+7.9%
1935	69,254,148	+7.5%
1940	73,075,071	+5.5%
1945	71,998,104	-1.5%

1950	83,199,637	+15.6%
1955	89,275,529	+7.3%
1960	93,418,501	+4.6%
1965	98,274,961	+5.2%
1970	103,720,060	+5.5%
1975	111,939,643	+7.9%
1980	117,060,396	+4.6%
1985	121,048,923	+3.4%
1990	123,611,167	+2.1%
1995	125,570,246	+1.6%
2000	126,925,843	+1.1%
2005	127,767,994	+0.7%
2010	128,057,352	+0.2%
2015	127,094,745	−0.8%
2017	126,672,000	−0.3%
2017 estimate		

Based on the census from October 2010, Japan's population was at its peak at 128,057,352. As of October 1, 2015, the population was 127,094,745 making it the world's tenth-most populous country at the time. It had declined by 0.8 percent from the time of the census five years ago, the first time it had declined since the 1945 census.Mexico's population was slightly less than Japan's in 2015, with projections suggesting Mexico will soon pass Japan. Current statistics do not indicate much difference in population numbers. Japan's population size can be attributed to high growth rates experienced during the late 19th and early 20th centuries.

Since 2010, Japan has experienced net population loss due to falling birth rates and almost no immigration, despite having one of the highest life expectancies in the world, at 85.00 years as of 2016 (it was 81.25 as of 2006). Using the annual estimate for October of each year, the population peaked in 2008 at 128,083,960 and had fallen 285,256 by October 2011. Japan's population density was 336 people per square kilometer.

Based on 2012 data from the National Institute of Population and Social Security Research, Japan's population will keep declining by about one million people every year in the coming decades, which will leave Japan with a population of 42 million in 2110. More than 40%

of the population is expected to be over age 65 in 2060. In 2012, the population had for six consecutive years declined by 212,000, the largest drop on record since 1947 and also a record low of 1.03 million births. In 2014, a new record of population drop happened with 268,000 people. In 2013, more than 20 percent of the population are age 65 and over.

The population ranking of Japan dropped from 7th to 8th in 1990, to 9th in 1998, and to 10th in the early 21st century. In 2015 it dropped further to 11th place, according to both the UN and PRB. Over the period of 2010–2015, the population shrank by almost a million.

Census

Japan collects census information every five years. The exercise is conducted by the Statistics Bureau of the Ministry of Internal Affairs.

Population density

Japan's population density was 336 people per square kilometer (874 people per square mile) according to the UN World Populations Prospects as of July 2005. It ranks 37th in a list of countries by population density, ranking directly aboveIndia (336 per km) and directly below Belgium (341 per km). Between 1955 and 1989, land prices in the six largest cities increased 15,000% (+12% a year). Urban land prices generally increased 40% from 1980 to 1987; in the six largest cities, the price of land doubled over that period. For many families, this trend put housing in central cities out of reach.

The result was lengthy commutes for many workers in the big cities, especially in Tokyo area where daily commutes of two hours each way are common. In 1991, as the bubble economy started to collapse, land prices began a steep decline, and within a few years fell 60% below their peak. After a decade of declining land prices, residents began moving back into central city areas (especially Tokyo's 23 wards), as evidenced by 2005 census figures. Despite nearly 70% of Japan being covered by forests, parks in many major cities — especially Tokyo and Osaka — are smaller and scarcer than in major West European or North American cities. As of 2014, parkland per inhabitant in Tokyo is 5.78 square meters, which is roughly half of the 11.5 square meters of Madrid.

National and regional governments devote resources to making regional cities and rural areas more attractive by developing transportation networks, social services, industry, and educational institutions in attempts to decentralize settlement and improve the quality of life. Nevertheless, major cities, especially Tokyo, Yokohama, and Chiba, and to a lesser extent Kyoto,Osaka and Kobe, remain attractive to young people seeking education and jobs.

Urban distribution

Japan has a high population concentration in urban areas on the plains since 75% of Japan's land area is made up of mountains, and also Japan has a forest cover rate of 68.5% (the only other developed countries with such a high forest cover percentage are Finland and Sweden). The 2010 census shows 90.7% of the total Japanese population live in cities.

Japan is an urban society with about only 5% of the labor force working in agriculture. Many farmers supplement their income with part-time jobs in nearby towns and cities. About 80 million of the urban population is heavily concentrated on the Pacific shore of Honshu.

Metropolitan Tokyo-Yokohama, with its population of 35 million residents, is the world's most populous city. Japan faces the same problems that confront urban industrialized societies throughout the world: overcrowded cities and congestedhighways.

Aging of Japan

Japan's population is aging faster than any other nation. The population of those 65 years or older roughly doubled in 24 years, from 7.1% of the population in 1970 to 14.1% in 1994. The same increase took 61 years in Italy, 85 years in Sweden, and 115 years in France. In 2014, 26% of Japan's population was estimated to be 65 years or older, and the Health and Welfare Ministry has estimated that over-65s will account for 40% of the population by 2060. The demographic shift in Japan's age profile has triggered concerns about the nation's economic future and the viability of its welfare state.

Overview of the changing age distribution 1935–2010

Year	Total population (census; in thousands)	Population by age (%)		
		0–14	15–64	65+
1935	69,254	36.9	58.5	4.7
1940	73,075	36.1	59.2	5.7
1945	71,998	36.8	58.1	5.1

1950	84,115	35.4	59.6	4.9
1955	90,077	33.4	61.2	5.3
1960	94,302	30.2	64.1	5.7
1965	99,209	25.7	68.0	6.3
1970	104,665	24.0	68.9	7.1
1975	111,940	24.3	67.7	7.9
1980	117,060	23.5	67.3	9.1
1985	121,049	21.5	68.2	10.3
1990	123,611	18.2	69.5	12.0
1995	125,570	15.9	69.4	14.5
2000	126,962	14.6	67.9	17.3
2005	127,768	13.7	65.8	20.1
2010	128,058	13.2	63.7	23.1
2017	126,830	12.4	60.2	27.4

DEMOGRAPHIC STATISTICS FROM THE CIA WORLD FACTBOOK

Population

Population in 5 households, 78.7% in urban areas (July 2000). High population density; 329.5 people per square kilometer for total area; 1,523 persons per square kilometer for habitable land. More than 50% of the population lives on 2% of the land. (July 1993)

Sex ratio

(2006 est.)

at birth: 1.05 male(s)/female

under 15 years: 1.05 male(s)/female

15–64 years: 1.01 male(s)/female

65 years and over: 0.73 male(s)/female

total population: 0.95 male(s)/female

(2010 est.)

at birth: 1.056 male(s)/female

under 15 years: 1.06 male(s)/female

15-64 years: 1.02 male(s)/female

65 years and over: 0.74 male(s)/female

total population: 0.95 male(s)/female

HIV/AIDS

Adult prevalence rate

less than 0.1% (2009 est.)

People living with HIV/AIDS

12,000 (2003 est.)

9,600 (2007 est.)

Deaths

500 (2003 est.)

fewer than 100 (2009 est.)

Ethnic groups

To measure ethnicity, the Japanese census asks respondents their nationality, rather than asking them to identify by ethnic group as other countries do. For example, the United Kingdom census asks for ethnic or racial background, regardless of nationality. Naturalized Japanese citizens and native-born Japanese nationals with multi-ethnic background are considered to be ethnically Japanese in the population census of Japan. Consequently, census data does not provide much information on ethnicity in Japan.

Marital status

Over 15: Never married Male 61.8%, Female 58.2%.

16–24: Never married Male 31.8%, Female 23.7%.

25–29: Never married Male 69.3%, Female 54.0%.

30–34: Never married Male 42.9%, Female 26.6% (July 2000).

MIGRATION

Internal migration

Between 6 million and 7 million people moved their residences each year during the 1980s. About 50% of these moves were within the same prefecture; the others were relocations from one prefecture to another. During Japan's economic development in the twentieth century, and especially during the 1950s and 1960s, migration was characterized by urbanization as people from rural areas in increasing numbers moved to the larger metropolitan areas in search of better jobs and education. Out-migration from rural prefectures continued in the late 1980s, but more slowly than in previous decades. In the 1980s, government policy provided support for new urban development away from the large cities, particularly Tokyo, and assisted regional cities to attract young people to live and work there. Regional cities offered familiarity to those from nearby areas, lower costs of living, shorter commutes, and, in general, a more relaxed lifestyle than could be had in larger cities. Young people continued to move to large cities, however, to attend universities and find work, but some returned to regional cities (a pattern known as U-turn) or to their prefecture of origin (a pattern referred to as "J-turn").

Government statistics show that in the 1980s significant numbers of people left the largest central cities (Tokyo and Osaka) to move to suburbs within their metropolitan areas. In 1988 more than 500,000 people left Tokyo, which experienced a net loss through migration of nearly 73,000 for the year. Osaka had a net loss of nearly 36,000 in the same year.

The prefectures showing the highest net growth are located near the major urban centers, such as Saitama, Chiba, Ibaraki, and Kanagawa around Tokyo, and Hyogo, Nara, and Shiga near Osaka and Kyoto. This pattern suggests a process ofsuburbanization, people moving away from the cities for affordable housing but still commuting there for work and recreation, rather than a true decentralization. More people in Japan like to live near coastal areas because they are easier to travel around in than the mountainous interior.

Emigration

About 663,300 Japanese were living abroad, approximately 75,000 of whom had permanent foreign residency, more than six times the number who had that status in 1975. More than 200,000 Japanese went abroad in 1990 for extended periods of study, research, or business assignments. As the government and private corporations have stressed internationalization, greater numbers of individuals have been directly affected, decreasing Japan's historical insularity. By the late 1980s, these problems, particularly the bullying of returnee children in schools, had become a major public issue both in Japan and in Japanese communities abroad.

Immigration

According to the Japanese immigration centre, the number of foreign residents in Japan has steadily increased, and the number of foreign residents (excluding a small number of illegal immigrants and short-term visitors, such as foreign nationals staying less than 90 days in Japan), exceeded 2.2 million people in 2008.

In 2010, the number of foreigners in Japan was 2,134,151. This includes 209,373 Filipinos, many of whom are married to Japanese nationals, 210,032 Brazilians, the majority possessing some degree of Japanese ancestry, 687,156 Chinese and 565,989 Koreans. Chinese, Filipinos, Koreans, and Brazilians account for about 69.5% of foreign residents in Japan.

The current issue of the shrinking workforce in Japan alongside its aging population have resulted in a recent need to attract foreign labour to the country. Reforms which took effect in 2015 relax visa requirements for "Highly Skilled Foreign Professionals" and create a new type of residence status with an unlimited period of stay.

The number of naturalizations peaked in 2008 at 16,000, declining to over 9,000 in the most recent year for which data are available. Most of the decline is accounted for by a steep reduction in the number of Japan-born Koreans taking Japanese citizenship. Historically the bulk of those taking Japanese citizenship have not been foreign-born immigrants but rather Japanese-born descendants of Koreans and Taiwanese who lost their citizenship in the Japanese Empire in 1947 as part of the American Occupation policy for Japan.

Japanese statistical authorities do not collect information on ethnicity, only nationality. As a result, both native and naturalized Japanese citizens are counted in a single group. Although official statistics show near homogeneity, one analysis describe the population as "multi-ethnic", although unofficial statistics still show that ethnic minorities are small compared with many other countries.

In 2015 the Japanese government under prime minister Shinzô Abe announced that its policy of restricting immigration would not change despite the current declining population. In the long term, its plan is to improve technology to address the labour shortage, while increasing Japanese fertility rates from the current level of 1.4 to 1.8, eventually stabilizing the population at 100,000,000.

LANGUAGES

The Japanese society of Yamato people is linguistically homogeneous with small populations of Koreans (0.9 million),Chinese/ Taiwanese (0.65 million), Filipino (306,000 some being Japanese Filipino;

children of Japanese and Filipino parentage). Brazilians (300,000, many of whom are ethnically Japanese) as well as Peruvians and Argentineans of both Latin American and Japanese descent. Japan has indigenous minority groups such as the Ainu and Ryukyuans, who generally speak Japanese.

Japanese citizenship is conferred *jus sanguinis*, and monolingual Japanese-speaking minorities often reside in Japan for generations under permanent residency status without acquiring citizenship in their country of birth, although legally they are allowed to do so. This is because Japanese law does not recognise dual citizenship after the age of adulthood, and so people becoming naturalised Japanese citizens must relinquish citizenship of other countries when they reach the age of 20. Some ethnic Koreans and Chinese and their descendants (who may speak only Japanese and may never have even visited the country whose nationality they hold) do not wish to abandon this other citizenship.

In addition, people taking Japanese citizenship must take a name using the Japanese character sets hiragana, katakana, and/or kanji. Names using Western alphabet, Korean alphabet, Arabic characters, etc. are not acceptable as legal names. Chinese characters are usually legally acceptable as nearly all Chinese characters are recognized as valid by the Japanese government. Transliterations of non-Japanese names using katakana (e.g. ¹0ß0¹00"Sumisu" for "Smith") are also legally acceptable.

However, some naturalizing foreigners feel that becoming a Japanese citizen should mean that they have a Japanese name and that they should abandon their foreign name, and some foreign residents do not wish to do this—although most Special Permanent Resident Koreans and Chinese already use Japanese names. Nonetheless, some 10,000 Zainichi Koreansnaturalize every year. Approximately 98.6% of the population are Japanese citizens, and 99% of the population speakJapanese as their first language. Non-ethnic Japanese in the past, and to an extent in the present, also live in small numbers in the Japanese archipelago.

SOCIETY

Lifestyle

Japanese people enjoy a high standard of living, and nearly 90% of the population consider themselves part of the middle class.

However, many studies on happiness and satisfaction with life tend to find that Japanese people average relatively low levels of life satisfaction and happiness when compared with most of the highly developed world; the levels have remained consistent if not declining slightly over the last half century. Japanese have been surveyed to be relatively lacking in financial satisfaction.

The suicide rates per 100,000 in Japan in 2009 were 29.2 for men and 10.5 for women. In 2010, 32,000 Japanese committed suicide, which translates to an average of 88 Japanese suicides a day in 2010.

MINORITIES

Discrimination against ethnic minorities

Three native Japanese minority groups can be identified. The largest are the *hisabetsu buraku* or "discriminated communities", also known as the *burakumin*. These descendants of premodern outcast hereditary occupational groups, such as butchers, leatherworkers, funeral directors, and certain entertainers, may be considered a Japanese analog of India's Dalits. Discrimination against these occupational groups arose historically because of Buddhist prohibitions against killing and Shinto notions of pollution, as well as governmental attempts at social control.

During the Tokugawa period, such people were required to live in special *buraku* and, like the rest of the population, were bound by sumptuary laws based on the inheritance of social class. The Meiji government abolished most derogatory names applied to these discriminated communities in 1871, but the new laws had little effect on the social discrimination faced by the former outcasts and their descendants. The laws, however, did eliminate the economic monopoly they had over certain occupations. The *buraku* continued to be treated as social outcasts and some casual interactions with the majority caste were perceived taboo until the era after World War II.

Estimates of their number range from 2 to 4 million (about 2% to 3% of the national population). Although members of these discriminated communities are physically indistinguishable from other Japanese, they often live in urban ghettoes or in the traditional special hamlets in rural areas, and membership can be surmised from the location of the family home, occupation, dialect, or mannerisms. Checks on family background designed to ferret out *buraku* were commonly performed as part of marriage arrangements and employment applications, but have been illegal since 1985 in Osaka. Past and current discrimination has resulted in lower educational attainment and socioeconomic status among *hisabetsu buraku* than among the majority of Japanese. Movements with objectives ranging from "liberation" to encouraging integration have tried to change this situation, with some success. Nadamoto Masahisa of the Buraku History Institute estimates that as of 1998, between 60 and 80% of burakumin marry a non-burakumin.

Ryukyuans

The second largest minority group among Japanese citizens is the Ryukyuan people. They are primarily distinguished from their use of several distinct Ryukyuan languages though use of Ryukyuan is dying out. The Ryukyuan people and language originated in the Ryukyu Islands, which are in Okinawa prefecture.

Ainu

The third largest minority group among Japanese citizens is the Ainu, whose language is an isolate. Historically, the Ainu were an indigenous hunting and gathering population who occupied most of northern Honshû as late as the Nara period (A.D. 710–94). As Japanese settlement expanded, the Ainu were pushed northward, by the Tokugawa shogunate, the Ainu were pushed into the island of Hokkaido.

Characterized as remnants of a primitive circumpolar culture, the fewer than 20,000 Ainu in 1990 were considered racially distinct and thus not fully Japanese. Disease and a low birth rate had severely diminished their numbers over the past two centuries, and intermarriage had brought about an almost completely mixed population.

Although no longer in daily use, the Ainu language is preserved in epics, songs, and stories transmitted orally over succeeding generations. Distinctive rhythmic music and dances and some Ainu festivals and crafts are preserved, but mainly in order to take advantage of tourism.

Foreign residents

In 2005, there were 1,555,505 foreign residents in Japan, representing 1.22% of the Japanese population. Foreign Army personnel, of which there were up to 430,000 from theSCAP (post-occupation, United States Forces Japan) and 40,000 BCOF in the immediate post-war years, have not been at any time included in Japanese foreign resident statistics.

A number of long-term resident Koreans in Japan today retain familial links with the descendants of Koreans, that either immigrated voluntarily or were forcibly relocated during theJapanese Occupation of the Korea. Within this group, a number holdSpecial Permanent Resident status, granted under the terms of the Normalisation Treaty (22. June 1965) between South Korea and Japan. In many cases special residents, despite being born in Japan and speaking Japanese, have chosen not to take advantage of the mostly automatic granting of citizenship to special resident applicants.

Beginning in 1947 the Japanese government started to repatriate Korean nationals, who had nominally been granted Japanese citizenship during the years of military occupation. When the Treaty of San Francisco came into force many ethnic Koreans lost their Japanese citizenship from April 28, 1952 and with it the right to welfare grants, to hold a government job of any kind or to attend Japanese schools. In the following year the government contrived, with the help of the Red Cross, a scheme to "repatriate" Korean residents, who mainly were from the Southern Provinces, to their "home" of North Korea. Between 1959 and 1984 93,430 people used this route. 6,737 were Japanese or Chinese dependents. Most of these departures – 78,276 – occurred before 1962.

All non-Japanese without special residential status (people whose residential roots go back to before WWII) are required by law to register with the government and carry alien registration cards. From the early 1980s, a civil disobedience movement encouraged refusal of the fingerprinting that accompanied registration every five years.

Opponents of fingerprinting argued that it was discriminatory because the only Japanese who were fingerprinted were criminals. The courts upheld fingerprinting, but the law was changed so that fingerprinting was done once rather than with each renewal of the registration, which until a law reform in 1989 was usually required every six months for anybody from the age of 16. Those refusing fingerprinting were denied re-entry permits, thus depriving them of freedom of movement.

Of these foreign residents below, the new wave started 2014 comes to Japan as students or trainees. These foreigners are registered under student visa or trainee visa which gives them the student residency status, Most of these new foreigners are under this visa. Almost all of these foreign students and trainees will return to their home country after 3–4 years (one valid period), few students extend their visa. Vietnamese makes the largest increase, however Burmese, Cambodians,Filipinos and Chinese are also increasing.

Migrant wives of young Japanese farmers have also contributed to the foreign-born population in the country. Many young single Japanese male farmers choose foreign wives, mainly from the Philippines, Sri Lanka, Thailand and other Asian countries, due to a lack of interest from Japanese women living a farming life. Migrant wives often travel as mail-order brides as a result of arranged marriages with Japanese men.

Foreign residents as of 2015

There was an increase of 110,358 foreign residents from 2014 to 2015. Vietnamese made the largest proportion of these new foreign residents, whilst Nepalese, Filipino, Chinese and Taiwanese are also significant in numbers. Together these countries makes up 91,126 or 82.6% of all new residents from 2014 to 2015. However, the majority of these immigrants will only remain in Japan for a maximum of five years, as many of them have entered the country in order to complete trainee programmes. Once they complete their programmes, they will be required to return to their home countries.

As of December 2014 there were 2,121,831 foreigners residing in Japan, 677,019 of whom were long-term residents in Japan, according to national demographics figures. The majority of long-term residents were from Asia, totalling 478,953. Chinese made up the largest portion of them with 215,155, followed by Filipinos with 115,857, and Koreans with 65,711. Thai, Vietnamese, and Taiwanese long-term residents totaled 47,956, and those from other Asian countries totaled 34,274. The Korean figures do not include zainichi Koreans with *tokubetsu eijusha* ("special permanent resident") visas, of whom there were 354,503 (of a total of 358,409 of all nationalities with such visas). The total number of permanent residents had declined over the previous 5 years due to high cost of living.

Foreign residents on short term employment contracts

A significant number of foreign residents of Japan are employed on a short term contractual basis under programs administered by the Japanese government. Well known programs include:

- The JET Programme employing up to 5,000 foreign university graduates as native language teachers in Japanese schools and as international support staff in local government offices.
- The Technical Intern Training Program employing in excess of 200,000 mainly manual laborers in variety of industries including construction, ship building, manufacturing, agriculture, retail and food processing.

In the light of current demographic trends Japan is likely to experience a decrease in tax revenue without a corresponding decrease in welfare expenses for an increasingly elderly population. Given growing manpower shortages, immigrant workers continue to play an important role taking low skilled and manual labour jobs. A recent growth in blue collar employment using documented short term contractual labour from developing countries has also contributed to the rise in the resident foreign population. The government administered Technical Intern Training Program, first established in 1993, provided over 190,000 short term contracted workers in 2015. However, it has been claimed that many of these workers often work at reduced pay and are required to undertake significant amounts of overtime in order to make up for labor shortages. As trainees, labor standards law and minimum wage legislation has on occasion been ignored by unscrupulous employers. The Japanese government has begun to examine this problem and has sought to both strengthen the vocational training aspect of the work program oversight.

Koseki

Foreign residents were recorded only in an alien registration system separate from the *koseki* (family registry) and *jûminhyô*(resident registry) systems in which Japanese citizens were registered until a new registration system was enacted in July 2012. Since then, all residents are recorded by municipal offices in the *jûminhyô* system. The *koseki* system continues for Japanese citizens, while foreigners are recorded in a separate residency management system administered by immigration offices which combines the previous immigration status and local alien registration systems.

Foreigner-reporting website and hotline

The Japanese Ministry of Justice maintains a website and hotline for "receiving report on [*sic*] illegal stay foreigner." The criteria for reporting include "feeling anxious about a foreigner", and anonymous submissions are permitted. Japanese immigration authorities work in unison with police to investigate those reported, and human rights groups such as Amnesty International have argued that those reported do not receive proper legal protection.

The Daiyo Kangoku system allows police to detain suspects without charges, access to legal counsel or telephone calls for up to 23 days. In October 2006, the foreigner reporting hotline's operating hours were extended to include Saturday, Sunday and national holidays.

Fingerprinting foreigners when entering Japan

As of November 20, 2007, all foreigners entering Japan must be biometrically registered (photograph and fingerprints) on arrival; this includes people living in Japan on visas as well as permanent residents, but excludes people with special permanent resident permission, diplomats, and those under 16.

Religion

Shinto and Buddhism are Japan's two major religions. They have co-existed for more than a thousand years. However, most Japanese identify as either atheists, irreligious, or do not identify themselves as adherents of one religion, but rather incorporate various elements in a syncretic fashion. There are small Christian and other minorities as well, with the Christian population dating to as early as the 1500s, as a result of European missionary work before sakoku was implemented from 1635–1853.

AGING OF JAPAN

The aging of Japan is thought to outweigh all other nations, as the country is purported to have the highest proportion of elderly citizens. Not just in rural, but also in urban areas, Japan is experiencing a "super-aging" society. According to 2014 estimates, 33.0% of the Japanese population is above the age of 60, 25.9% are aged 65 or above, 12.5% are aged 75 or above.People aged 65 and older in Japan make up a fifth of its total population, estimated to reach a third by the year 2050.

Japan had a postwar baby boom between 1947 and 1949. However, the law of 1948 led to easy access to abortions, followed by a prolonged period of low fertility, resulting in the aging population of Japan. The dramatic aging of Japanese society as a result of sub-replacement fertility rates and high life expectancy is expected to continue, and the population began to decline in 2011. Japanese citizens view Japan as comfortable and modern, resulting in no sense of a population crisis. The government of Japan has responded to concerns about the stress that demographic changes place on the economy and social serviceswith policies intended to restore the fertility rate and make the elderly more active in society.

Aging dynamics

The number of Japanese people with ages 65 years or older nearly quadrupled in the last forty years, to 33 million in 2014, accounting for 26% of Japan's population. In the same period, the number of children (aged 14 and younger) decreased from 24.3% of the population in 1975 to 12.8% in 2014. The number of elderly people surpassed the number of children in 1997, and sales of adult diapers surpassed diapers for babies in 2014. This change in the demographic makeup of Japanese society, referred to as population aging , has taken place in a shorter span of time than in any other country.

According to projections of the population with the current fertility rate, over 65s will account for 40% of the population by 2060, and the total population will fall by a third from 128 million in 2010 to 87 million in 2060. Economists at Tohoku University established a countdown to national extinction, which estimates that Japan will have only one remaining child in 4205. These predictions prompted a pledge by Prime Minister Shinzô Abe to halt population decline at 100 million.

Causes

The aging of the Japanese population is a result of one of the world's lowest fertility rates combined with thehighest life expectancy.

High life expectancy

The reason for Japan's growing aging population is because of high life expectancy; Japan's life expectancy in 2016 was 85 years, similar to that of Singapore, and lower only than that of Monaco. The life expectancy is 81.7 for males and 88.5 for females. Since Japan's overall population is shrinking due to low fertility rates, the aging population is rapidly increasing. Factors such as improved nutrition, advanced medical and pharmacological technologies reduced the prevalence of diseases, improving living conditions. Also peace and prosperity post-World War II contributed to economic growth, leading to long life. Proportion of health care spending has dramatically increased as Japan's older population spends time in hospitals and visits physicians. 2.9% people aged 75–79 were in hospital and 13.4% visited physicians on a given day in 2011.

Life expectancy at birth has increased rapidly from the end of World War II, when the average was 54 years for women and 50 for men, as a result of improvements in medicine and nutrition, and the percentage of the population aged 65 years and older has increased steadily from the 1950s. The advancement of life expectancy translated into a depressed mortality rate until the 1980s, but mortality has increased again to 10.1 per 1000 people in 2013, the highest since 1950.

Low fertility rate

Japan's total fertility rate (the number of children born by each woman in her lifetime) has been below the replacement threshold of 2.1 since 1974 and reached a historic low of 1.26 in 2005. Experts believe that signs of a slight recovery reflect the expiration of a "tempo effect," as fertility rates accommodate a major shift in the timing and number of children, rather than any positive change. As of 2016, the TFR was 1.41 children born/woman.

A range of economic and cultural factors contributed to the decline in childbirth during the late 20th century: later and fewermarriages, higher education, urbanization, increase in nuclear family households (rather than extended family), poor work–life balance, increased participation of women in the workforce, a decline in wages and lifetime employment along with a highgender pay gap, small living spaces, and the high cost of raising a child.

Economic insecurity is a serious problem: about 40% of Japan's labor force is temporary workers.

Although most married couples have two or more children, a growing number of young people postpone or entirely reject marriage and parenthood. Conservative gender roles often mean that women are expected to stay home with the children, rather than work. Between 1980 and 2010, the percentage of the population who had never married increased from 22% to almost 30%, even as the population continued to age, and by 2035 one in four people will not marry during their childbearing years. The Japanese sociologist Masahiro Yamada coined the term parasite singles for unmarried adults in their late 20s and 30s who continue to live with their parents.

Effects

Demographic trends are altering relations within and across generations, creating new government responsibilities and changing many aspects of Japanese social life. The aging and decline of the working-age population has triggered concerns about the future of the nation's workforce, the potential for economic growth, and the solvency of the national pension and healthcare services.

Social

A smaller population could make the country's crowded metropolitan areas more livable, and the stagnation of economic output might still benefit a shrinking workforce. However, the low birthrate and high life expectancy has also inverted the standard population pyramid, forcing a narrowing base of young people to provide and care for a bulging older cohort even as they try to form families of their own. In 2014, the aged dependency ratio (the ratio of people over 65 to those age 15–65, indicating the ratio of the dependent elderly population to those of working age) was 40%, meaning two aged dependents for every five workers. This is expected to increase to 60% by 2036 and to nearly 80% by 2060.

Elderly Japanese have traditionally commended themselves to the care of their adult children, and government policies still encourage the creation of *sansedai kazoku* , where a married couple cares for both children and parents. In 2015, 177,600 people between the ages of 15 and 29 were caring directly for an older family member. However, the migration of young people into Japan's major cities, the entrance of women into the workforce, and the increasing cost of care for both young and old dependents have required new solutions, including nursing homes, adult daycare centers, and home health programs. Every year Japan closes 400 primary and secondary schools, converting some of them to care centers for the elderly.

There are special nursing homes in Japan that offer service and assistance to more than 30 residents. In 2008, it has been recorded that there were approximate 6,000 special nursing homes available that compensated 420,000 Japanese elders. With many nursing homes in Japan, the demand for more caregivers is high. In Japan, Family caregivers are preferred as the main caregiver, because it is a better support system if an elderly person is related to his/her caregiver. Therefore, it is possible that Japanese elderlies can perform ADL's with little assistance and live longer if his/her caregiver is a family caregiver. Many elderly people live alone and isolated, and every year thousands of deaths go unnoticed for days or even weeks, in a modern phenomenon known as *kodoku-shi* .

The disposable income in Japan's older population has made them to spend money on the new products for better looks and performances.

Political

The Greater Tokyo Area is virtually the only locality in Japan to see population growth, mostly due to internal migration from other parts of the country. Between 2005 and 2010 36 of Japan's 47 prefectures shrank by as much as 5%, and many rural and suburban areas are struggling with an epidemic of abandoned homes (8 million across Japan). Masuda Hiroya, a former Minister for Internal Affairs and Communications who heads the private think tank Japan Policy Council, estimated that about half the municipalities in Japan could disappear between now and 2040 as young people, especially young women, move from rural areas into Tokyo, Osaka, and Nagoya, where around half of Japan's population is already concentrated. The government is establishing a regional revitalization task force and focusing on developing regional hub cities, especially Sapporo, Sendai, Hiroshima, and Fukuoka.

Internal migration and population decline have created a severe regional imbalance in electoral power, where the weight of a single vote depends on where it was cast. Some depopulated districts send three times as many representatives per voter to the National Diet as their growing urban counterparts. In 2014, the Supreme Court of Japan declared the disparities in voting power violate the Constitution, but the ruling Liberal Democratic Party, which relies on rural and older voters, has been slow to make the necessary realignment.

The increasing proportion of elderly people has a major impact on government spending and policies. As recently as the early- 1970s, the cost of public pensions, health care and welfare services for the aged amounted to only about 6% of Japan's national income. In 1992 that portion of the national budget was 18%, and it is expected that by 2025 28% of national income will be spent on social welfare. Because the incidence of chronic disease increases with age, the health care and pension systems are expected to come under severe strain. In the mid-1980s the government began to reevaluate the relative burdens of government and the private sector in health care and pensions, and it established policies to control government costs in these programs. The large share of elderly inflation averse voters may also hinder the political attractiveness of pursuing higher inflation consistent with the evidence that ageing may lead to lower inflation.

Economic

Since the 1980s, there has been an increase of older-age workers and a shortage of young workers in Japan's workforce, from employment practices to benefits to the participation of women. The U.S. Census Bureau estimated in 2002 that Japan would experience an 18% decrease of young workers in its workforce and 8% decrease in its consumer population by 2030. TheJapanese labor market is already under pressure to meet demands for workers, with 125 jobs for every 100job seekers at the end of 2015, as older generations retire and younger generations become smaller in quantity.

Japan made a radical change in how healthcare system is regulated by introducing long-term care insurance in 2000. The proportion of old Japanese citizens will soon level off, however; there is a decline in young population due to zero growth, death exceeding the births. For example, number of young people under the age of 19 in Japan will constitute only 13 percent in the year 2060, which used to be 40 percent in the year 1960. Interestingly, Japan's aging population is considered economically prosperous profiting the large corporations. Lawson Inc., a Japanese convenience store chain has salons for senior citizens that feature adult wipes and diapers, strong detergents to eliminate urine on bed mats, straw cups, gargling basins, and even rice and water. However, on the downside, the decline in the working population is impacting the national economy. The government therefore, has focused on medical technologies such as regenerative medicines and cell therapy to recruit and retain more older population into the work force.

Mounting labor shortages in the 1980s and 90s led many Japanese companies to increase the mandatory retirement agefrom 55 to 60 or 65, and today many allow their employees to continue working after official retirement. The growing number of retirement age people has put strain on the national pension system. In 1986, the government increased the age at which pension benefits begin from 60 to 65, and shortfalls in the pension system have encouraged many people of retirement age to remain in the workforce and have driven some others into poverty. The retirement age may go even higher in the future if Japan continues to have older age populations in its overall population. A study by the UN Population Divisionreleased in 2000 found that Japan would need to raise its retirement age to 77 (or allow net immigration of 17 million by 2050) to maintain its worker-to-retiree ratio. Consistent immigration into Japan may prevent further population decline, therefore, it is encouraged that Japan develops policies that will support large influx of young immigrants.

Less desirable industries, such as agriculture and construction, are more threatened than others. The average farmer in Japan is 70 years old, and while about a third of construction workers are 55 or older, including many who expect to retire within the next ten years, only one in ten are younger than 30.

The decline in working-aged cohorts may lead to a shrinking economy if productivity does not increase faster than the rate of Japan's decreasing workforce. The OECD estimates that similar labor shortages in Austria, Germany, Greece, Italy,Spain, and Sweden will depress the European Union's economic growth by 0.4 percentage points annually from 2000 to 2025, after which shortages will cost the EU 0.9 percentage points in growth. In Japan labor shortages will lower growth by 0.7 percentage points annually until 2025, after which Japan will also experience a 0.9 percentage points loss in growth.

GOVERNMENT POLICIES

The Japanese government is addressing demographic problems by developing policies to encourage fertility and keep more of its population, especially women and elderly, engaged in the workforce. Incentives for family formation include expanded opportunities for childcare, new benefits for those who have children, and a state-sponsored dating service.Some policies have focused on engaging more women in the workplace, including longer maternity leave and legal protections against pregnancy discrimination, known in Japan as *matahara* . However, "Womenomics," the set of policies intended to bring more women into the workplace as part of Prime MinisterShinzô Abe's economic recovery plan, has struggled to overcome cultural barriers and entrenched stereotypes.

Work-life balance

Japan has focused its policies on the work-life balance with the goal of improving the conditions for increasing the birth rate. To address these challenges, Japan has established goals to define the ideal work-life balance that would provide the environment for couples to have more children with the passing of the Child Care and Family Care Leave Law, which took effect in June 2010.

The law provides both mothers and fathers with an opportunity to take up to one year of leave after the birth of a child (with possibility to extend the leave for another 6 months if the child is not accepted to enter nursery school) and allows employees with preschool-age children the following allowances: up to five days of leave in the event of a child's injury or sickness, limits on the amount of overtime in excess of 24 hours per month based on an employee's request, limits on working late at night based on an employee's request, and opportunity for shorter working hours and flex time for employees.

The goals of the law would strive to achieve the following results in 10 years are categorized by the female employment rate (increase from 65% to 72%), percentage of employees working 60 hours or more per week (decrease from 11% to 6%), rate of use of annual paid leave (increase from 47% to 100%), rate of child care leave (increase from 72% to 80% for females and .6% to 10% for men), and hours spent by men on child care and housework in households with a child under six years of age (increase from 1 hour to 2.5 hours a day).

COMPARISONS WITH OTHER COUNTRIES

Japan's population is aging faster than any other country on the planet. The population of those 65 years or older roughly doubled in 24 years, from 7.1% of the population in 1970 to 14.1% in 1994. Life expectancy for women in Japan is 87 years, five years more than that of the U.S. Men in Japan with a life expectancy of 81 years, have surpassed U.S. life expectancy by four years. The same increase took 61 years in Italy, 85 years in Sweden, and 115 years in France. Japan also has more centenarians than any other country (58,820 in 2014, or 42.76 per 100,000 people). Almost one in five of the world's centenarians live in Japan, and 87% of them are women.

In contrast to Japan, a more open immigration policy has allowed Australia, Canada, and the United States to grow their workforce despite low fertility rates. An expansion of immigration is often rejected as a solution to population decline by Japan's political leaders and people. Reasons include a fear of foreign crime, a desire to preserve cultural traditions, and a belief in the ethnic and racial homogeneity of the Japanese nation.

Japan is leading the world in aging demographics, but the other countries of East Asia are following a similar trend. In China, after decades of modernization and a one-child policy, the population could peak by as early as 2020. In South Korea, where the fertility rate often ranks among the lowest in the OECD (1.21 in 2014), the population is expected to peak in 2030. The smaller states of Singapore and Taiwan are also struggling to boost fertility rates from record lows and to manage aging populations. More than a third of the world's elderly (65 and older) live in East Asia and the Pacific, and many of the economic concerns raised first in Japan can be projected to the rest of the region. India's population is aging exactly like Japan, but with a 50-year lag. A study of the populations of India and Japan for the years 1950 to 2015 combined with median variant population estimates for the years 2016 to 2100 shows that India's is 50 years behind Japan on the aging process.

9

Culture and Society

CULTURE OF JAPAN

The culture of Japan has evolved greatly over the millennia, from the country's prehistoric time Jômon period, to its contemporary modern culture, which absorbs influences from Asia, Europe, and North America. Strong Chinese influences are still evident in traditional Japanese culture as China had historically been a regional powerhouse, which has resulted in Japan absorbing many elements of Chinese culture first through Korea, then later through direct cultural exchanges with China. The inhabitants of Japan experienced a long period of relative isolation from the outside world during theTokugawa shogunate after Japanese missions to Imperial China, until the arrival of "The Black Ships" and the Meiji period.

Language

Japanese is the official and primary language of Japan. Japanese is relatively small but has a lexically distinct pitch-accent system. Early Japanese is known largely on the basis of its state in the 8th century, when the three major works of Old Japanesewere compiled. The earliest attestation of the Japanese language is in a Chinese document from 252 AD.

Japanese is written with a combination of three scripts: hiragana, derived from the Chinese cursive script, katakana, derived as a shorthand from Chinese characters, and kanji, imported from China. The Latin alphabet, rômaji, is also often used in modern Japanese, especially for company names and logos, advertising, and when inputting Japanese into a computer. TheHindu-Arabic numerals are generally used for numbers, but traditional Sino-Japanese numerals are also very common.

Literature

Early works of Japanese literature were heavily influenced by cultural contact with China and Chinese literature, often written in Classical Chinese. Indian literature also had an influence through the spread of Buddhism throughout Japan. Eventually, Japanese literature developed into a separate style in its own right as Japanese writers began writing their own works about Japan. Since Japan reopened its ports to Western trading and diplomacy in the 19th century, Western and Eastern literature have strongly affected each other and continue to do so.

Music

The music of Japan includes a wide array of performers in distinct styles bothtraditional and modern. The word for music in Japanese is ongaku, combining the kanji "on" (sound) with the kanji "gaku" (enjoyment). Japan is the second largest music market in the world, behind the United States, and the largest in Asia,and most of the market is dominated by Japanese artists.

Local music often appears at karaoke venues, which is on lease from the record labels. Traditional Japanese music is quite different from Western Music and is based on the intervals of human breathing rather than mathematical timing. In 1873, a British traveler claimed that Japanese music, "exasperate(s) beyond all endurance the European breast."

Visual arts

Painting

Painting has been an art in Japan for a very long time: the brush is a traditional writing and painting tool, and the extension of that to its use as an artist's tool was probably natural. Japanese painters are often categorized by what they painted, as most of them constrained themselves solely to subjects such as animals, landscapes, or figures. Chinese papermaking was introduced to Japan around the 7th century. Later, washi was developed from it. Native Japanese painting techniques are still in use today, as well as techniques adopted from continental Asia and from the West. Schools of painting such as the

Kano school of the 16th century became known for their bold brush strokes and contrast between light and dark, especially after Oda Nobunaga and Tokugawa Ieyasu began to use this style. Famous Japanese painters includeKanô Sanraku, Maruyama Ôkyo, and Tani Bunchô.

Calligraphy

The flowing, brush-drawn Japanese rendering of text itself is seen as a traditional art form as well as a means of conveying written information. The written work can consist of phrases, poems, stories, or even single characters. The style and format of the writing can mimic the subject matter, even to the point of texture and stroke speed. In some cases, it can take over one hundred attempts to produce the desired effect of a single character but the process of creating the work is considered as much an art as the end product itself.

This calligraphy form is known as 'shodô' which literally means 'the way of writing or calligraphy' or more commonly known as 'shûji' 'learning how to write characters'. Commonly confused with Calligraphy is the art form known as 'sumi-e' literally means 'ink painting' which is the art of the paintings a scene or object.

Sculpture

Traditional Japanese sculptures mainly focused on Buddhist images, such asTathagata, Bodhisattva, and Myô-ô. The oldest sculpture in Japan is a wooden statue of Amitâbha at the Zenkô-ji temple. In the Nara period, Buddhist statues were made by the national government to boost its prestige. These examples are seen in present-day Nara and Kyoto, most notably a colossal bronze statue of the BuddhaVairocana in the Tôdai-ji temple.

Wood has traditionally been used as the chief material in Japan, along with traditional Japanese architecture. Statues are often lacquered, gilded, or brightly painted, although there are little traces on the surfaces. Bronze and other metals are also used. Other materials, such as stone and pottery, have had extremely important roles in the plebeian beliefs.

Ukiyo-e

Ukiyo-e, literally "pictures of the floating world", is a genre of woodblock prints that exemplifies the characteristics of pre-MeijiJapanese art. Because these prints could be mass-produced, they were available to a wide cross-section of the Japanese populace —

those not wealthy enough to afford original paintings — during their heyday, from the 17th to 20th century.

Ikebana

Ikebana is the Japanese art of flower arrangement. It has gained widespread international fame for its focus on harmony, color use, rhythm, and elegantly simple design. It is an art centered greatly on expressing the seasons, and is meant to act as a symbol to something greater than the flower itself.

Religion

Buddhism and Shintoism are the primary religions of Japan.

Shintoism

Shintoism is an ethnic religion that focuses on ceremonies and rituals. In Shintoism, followers believe that kami, a Shinto deity or spirit, are present throughout nature, including rocks, trees, and mountains. Humans can also be considered to possess a kami. One of the goals of Shintoism is to maintain a connection between humans, nature, and kami. The religion developed in Japan prior to the sixth century C.E., after which point followers built shrines to worship kami.

Buddhism

Buddhism developed in India around the 6th and 4th centuries BCE and eventually spread through China and Korea. It arrived in Japan during the 6th century C.E., where it was initially unpopular. Most Japanese people were unable to understand the difficult philosophical messages present in Buddhism, however they did have an appreciation for the religion's art, which is believed to have led to the religion growing more popular. Buddhism is concerned with the soul and life after dying. In the religion a person's status was unimportant, as every person would get sick, age, die, and eventually be reincarnated into a new life, a cycle called saCsâra. The suffering people experienced during life was one way for people to gain a better future. The ultimate goal was to escape the cycle of death and rebirth by attaining true insight.

Performing arts

The four traditional theatres from Japan are *noh* (or *nô*), *kyôgen*, *kabuki*, and*bunraku*. Noh had its origins in the union of the *sarugaku*, with music and dance made by Kanami and Zeami Motokiyo. Among the characteristic aspects of it are the masks, costumes, and the stylized gestures, sometimes accompanied by a fanthat can represent other objects. The *noh* programs are presented in alternation with the ones of *kyôgen*, traditionally in number of five, but currently in groups of three.

The *kyôgen*, of humorous character, had older origin, in 8th century entertainment brought from China, developing itself in *sarugaku*. In *kyôgen*, masks are rarely used and even if the plays can be associated with the ones of noh, currently many are not.

Kabuki appears in the beginning of the Edo period from the representations and dances of Izumo no Okuni in Kyoto. Due to prostitution of actresses of *kabuki*, the participation of women in the plays was forbidden by the government in 1629, and the feminine characters had passed to be represented only by men (*onnagata*). Recent attempts to reintroduce actresses in*kabuki* had not been well accepted. Another characteristic of kabuki is the use of makeup for the actors in historical plays (*kumadori*).

Japanese puppet theater *bunraku* developed in the same period, that *kabuki* in a competition and contribution relation involving actors and authors. The origin of *bunraku*, however is older, lies back in the Heian period. In 1914, appeared theTakarazuka Revue a company solely composed by women who introduced the revue in Japan.

Architecture

Japanese architecture has as long of a history as any other aspect of Japanese culture. Originally heavily influenced by Chinese architecture, it has developed many differences and aspects which are indigenous to Japan. Examples of traditional architecture are seen at temples, Shinto shrines, and castles in Kyoto and Nara. Some of these buildings are constructed with traditional gardens, which are influenced from Zen ideas.

Some modern architects, such as Yoshio Taniguchi and Tadao Ando are known for their amalgamation of Japanese traditional and Western architectural influences.

Gardens

Garden architecture is as important as building architecture and very much influenced by the same historical and religious background. A primary design principle of a garden is the creation of the landscape based on, or at least greatly influenced by, the three-dimensional monochrome ink (*sumi*) landscape painting,*sumi-e* or *suibokuga*.

In Japan, the garden has the status of artwork.

Traditional clothing

Traditional Japanese clothing distinguishes Japan from all other countries around the world. The Japanese word kimono means "something one wears" and they are the traditional garments of Japan. Originally, the word kimono was used for all types of clothing, but eventually, it came to refer specifically to the full-length garment also known as the naga-gi, meaning "long-wear", that is still worn today on special occasions by women, men, and children. The earliest kimonos were heavily influenced by traditional Han Chinese clothing, known today as hanfu (kanfuku in Japanese), through Japanese embassies to China which resulted in extensive Chinese culture adoptions by Japan, as early as the 5th century AD. It was during the 8th century, however, that Chinese fashions came into style among the Japanese, and the overlapping collar became particularly women's fashion.Kimono in this meaning plus all other items of traditional Japanese clothing is known collectively as wafuku which means "Japanese clothes" as opposed to yofuku (Western-style clothing). Kimonos come in a variety of colors, styles, and sizes. Men mainly wear darker or more muted colors, while women tend to wear brighter colors and pastels, and, especially for younger women, often with complicated abstract or floral patterns.

The kimono of a woman who is married (tomesode) differs from the kimono of a woman who is not married (furisode). The tomesode sets itself apart because the patterns do not go above the waistline. The furisode can be recognized by its extremely long sleeves spanning anywhere from 39 to 42 inches, it is also the most formal kimono an unwed woman wears. The furisode advertises that a woman is not only of age but also single.

The style of kimono also changes with the season, in spring kimonos are vibrantly colored with springtime flowers embroidered on them. In Autumn, kimono colors are not as bright, with Autumn patterns. Flannel kimonos are most commonly worn in winter; they are made of a heavier material and are worn mainly to stay warm.

One of the more elegant kimonos is the uchikake, a long silk overgarment worn by the bride in a wedding ceremony. The uchikake is commonly embellished with birds or flowers using silver and gold thread. Kimonos do not come in specific sizes as most western dresses do. The sizes are only approximate, and a special technique is used to fit the dress appropriately.

The obi is a very important part of the kimono. Obi is a decorative sash that is worn by Japanese men and women, although it can be worn with many different traditional outfits, it is most commonly worn with the kimono.

Most women wear a very large elaborate obi, while men typically don a more thin and conservative obi.

Most Japanese men only wear the kimono at home or in a very laid back environment, however it is acceptable for a man to wear the kimono when he is entertaining guests in his home. For a more formal event a Japanese man might wear the haoriand hakama, a half coat and divided skirt.

The hakama is tied at the waist, over the kimono and ends near the ankle. Hakama were initially intended for men only, but today it is acceptable for women to wear them as well. Hakama can be worn with types of kimono, excluding the summer version, yukata. The lighter and simpler casual-wear version of kimono often worn in Japanese summer festival is called yukata.

Formal kimonos are typically worn in several layers, with number of layers, visibility of layers, sleeve length, and choice of pattern dictated by social status, season, and the occasion for which the kimono is worn. Because of the mass availability, most Japanese people wear western style clothing in their everyday life, and kimonos are mostly worn for festivals, and special events. As a result, most young women in Japan are not able to put the kimono on themselves. Many older women offer classes to teach these young women how to don the traditional clothing.

Happi is another type of traditional clothing, but it is not famous worldwide like the kimono. A happi (or happy coat) is a straight sleeved coat that is typically imprinted with the family crest, and was a common coat for firefighters to wear.

Japan also has very distinct footwear.

Tabi, an ankle high sock, is often worn with the kimono. Tabi are designed to be worn with geta, a type of thonged footwear.Geta are sandals mounted on wooden blocks held to the foot by a piece of fabric that slides between the toes. Geta are worn both by men and women with the kimono or yukata.

Cuisine

Through a long culinary past, the Japanese have developed sophisticated and refined cuisine. In more recent years, Japanese food has become fashionable and popular in the United States, Europe, and many other areas. Dishes such as sushi,tempura, noodles, and teriyaki are some of the foods that are commonly known. The Japanese diet consists principally of rice; fresh, lean seafood; and pickled or boiled vegetables. The healthy Japanese diet is often believed to be related to thelongevity of Japanese people.

Sports and leisure

In the long feudal period governed by the samurai class, some methods that were used to train warriors were developed into well-ordered martial arts, in modern times referred to collectively as koryû. Examples include kenjutsu, kendo, kyûdô, sôjutsu,jujutsu, and sumo, all of which were established in the Edo period. After the rapid social change in the Meiji Restoration, some martial arts changed into modern sports, called gendai budô. Judo was developed by Kanô Jigorô, who studied some sects of jujutsu. These sports are still widely practiced in present-day Japan and other countries.

Baseball, Association football, and other popular western sports were imported to Japan in the Meiji period. These sports are commonly practiced in schools, along with traditional martial arts.

Baseball, soccer, football, and ping pong are the most popular sports in Japan. Association football gained prominence in Japan after the J League (Japan Professional Football League) was established in 1991. Japan also co-hosted the 2002 FIFA World Cup. In addition, there are many semi-professional organizations, which are sponsored by private companies: for example, volleyball, basketball, rugby union, table tennis, and so on.

POPULAR CULTURE

Japanese popular culture not only reflects the attitudes and concerns of the present day, but also provides a link to the past. Popular films, television programs, manga, music,anime and video games all developed from older artistic and literary traditions, and many of their themes and styles of presentation can be traced to traditional art forms. Contemporary forms of popular culture, much like the traditional forms, provide not only entertainment but also an escape for the contemporary Japanese from the problems of an industrial world. When asked how they spent their leisure time, 80 percent of a sample of men and women surveyed by the government in 1986 said they averaged about two and a half hours per weekday watching television, listening to the radio, and reading newspapersor magazines. Some 16 percent spent an average of two and a quarter hours a day engaged in hobbies or amusements. Others spent leisure time participating in sports, socializing, and personal study. Teenagers and retired people reported more time spent on all of these activities than did other groups.

Many anime and manga are very popular around the world and continue to become popular, as well as Japanese video games, fashion, and game shows.

In the late 1980s, the family was the focus of leisure activities, such as excursions to parks or shopping districts. Although Japan is often thought of as a hard-working society with little time for leisure, the Japanese seek entertainment wherever they can. It is common to see Japanese commuters riding the train to work, enjoying their favorite manga, or listening through earphones to the latest in popular music on portable music players.

A wide variety of types of popular entertainment are available. There is a large selection of music, films, and the products of a huge comic book industry, among other forms of entertainment, from which to choose. Game centers, bowling alleys, andkaraoke are popular hangout places for teens while older people may play shogi or go in specialized parlors.

Together, the publishing, film/video, music/audio, and game industries in Japan make up the growing Japanese content industry.

National character

The Japanese "national character" has been written about under the term *Nihonjinron*, literally meaning "theories/discussions about the Japanese people" and referring to texts on matters that are normally the concerns of sociology, psychology, history, linguistics, andphilosophy, but emphasizing the authors' assumptions or perceptions of Japanese exceptionalism; these are predominantly written in Japan by Japanese people, though noted examples have also been written by foreign residents, journalists and even scholars.

Priest-painter Josetsu, marks a turning point in Muromachi painting. In the foreground a man is depicted on the bank of a stream holding a small gourd and looking at a large slithery catfish. Mist fills the middle ground, and the background, mountains appear to be far in the distance. It is generally assumed that the "new style" of the painting, executed about 1413, refers to a more Chinese sense of deep space within the picture plane

By the end of the 14th century, monochrome landscape paintings had found patronage by the ruling Ashikaga family and was the preferred genre among Zen painters, gradually evolving from its Chinese roots to a more Japanese style.

The foremost artists of the Muromachi period are the priest-painters Shûbun andSesshû. Shûbun, a monk at the Kyoto temple of Shôkoku-ji, created in the painting*Reading in a Bamboo Grove* (1446) a realistic landscape with deep recession into space. Sesshû, unlike most artists of the period, was able to journey to China and study Chinese painting at its source. *Landscape of the Four Seasons* (*Sansui Chokan*; c. 1486) is one of Sesshu's most accomplished works, depicting a continuing landscape through the four seasons.

In the late Muromachi period, ink painting had migrated out of the Zen monasteries into the art world in general, as artists from the Kanô school and the Ami school adopted the style and themes, but introducing a more plastic and decorative effect that would continue into modern times.

Important artists in the Muromachi period Japan include:
- Mokkei (c. 1250)
- Mokuan Reien (died 1345)
- Kaô Ninga (e.14th century)
- Mincho (1352–1431)
- Josetsu (1405–1423)
- Tenshô Shûbun (died 1460)
- Sesshû Tôyô (1420–1506)
- Kanô Masanobu (1434–1530)
- Kanô Motonobu (1476–1559)

Azuchi–Momoyama period (1573–1615)

In sharp contrast to the previous Muromachi period, the Azuchi-Momoyama periodwas characterized by a grandiose polychrome style, with extensive use of gold andsilver foil, and by works on a very large scale. The Kanô school, patronized by Oda Nobunaga, Toyotomi

Hideyoshi, Tokugawa Ieyasu, and their followers, gained tremendously in size and prestige. Kanô Eitoku developed a formula for the creation of monumental landscapes on the sliding doors enclosing a room. These huge screens and wall paintings were commissioned to decorate the castles and palaces of the military nobility. This status continued into the subsequent Edo period, as theTokugawa bakufu continued to promote the works of the Kano school as the officially sanctioned art for the Shogun, *daimyôs*, and Imperial court.

However, non-Kano school artists and currents existed and developed during the Azuchi–Momoyama period as well, adapting Chinese themes to Japanese materials and aesthetics. One important group was the Tosa school, which developed primarily out of the *yamato-e* tradition, and which was known mostly for small scale works and illustrations of literary classics in book or *emaki* format.

Important artists in the Azuchi-Momoyama period include:
- Kanô Eitoku (1543–1590)
- Kanô Sanraku (1559–1663)
- Kanô Tan'yû (1602–1674)
- Hasegawa Tôhaku (1539–1610)
- Kaihô Yûshô (1533–1615)

Edo period (1603–1868)

Many art historians show the Edo period as a continuation of the Azuchi-Momoyama period. Certainly, during the early Edo period, many of the previous trends in painting continued to be popular; however, a number of new trends also emerged.

One very significant school which arose in the early Edo period was the Rinpa school, which used classical themes, but presented them in a bold, and lavishly decorative format. Sôtatsu in particular evolved a decorative style by re-creating themes from classical literature, using brilliantly colored figures and motifs from the natural world set against gold-leaf backgrounds. A century later, Korin reworked Sôtatsu's style and created visually gorgeous works uniquely his own.

Another important genre which began during Azuchi–Momoyama period, but which reached its full development during the early Edo period was *Namban* art, both in the depiction of exotic foreigners and in the use of the exotic foreigner style in painting. This genre was centered around the port of Nagasaki, which after the start of the national seclusion policy of the Tokugawa shogunate was the only Japanese port left open to foreign trade, and was thus the conduit by which Chinese and European artistic influences came to Japan. Paintings in this genre includeNagasaki school paintings, and also the Maruyama-Shijo school, which combine Chinese and Western influences with traditional Japanese elements.

A third important trend in the Edo period was the rise of the *Bunjinga* (literati painting) genre, also known as the Nanga school (Southern Painting school). This genre started as an imitation of the works of Chinese scholar-amateur painters of the Yuan dynasty, whose works and techniques came to Japan in the mid-18th century. Master Kuwayama Gyokushû was the greatest supporter of creating the *bunjin* style. He theorised that polychromatic landscapes were to be considered at the same level of monochromatic paintings by Chinese literati. Furthermore, he included some Japanese traditionalist artists, such as Tawaraya Sôtatsuand Ogata Kôrin of the Rinpa group, among major Nanga representatives. Later *bunjinga*artists considerably modified both the techniques and the subject matter of this genre to create a blending of Japanese and Chinese styles. The exemplars of this style are Ike no Taiga, Uragami Gyokudô, Yosa Buson, Tanomura Chikuden, Tani Bunchô, and Yamamoto Baiitsu.

Due to the Tokugawa shogunate's policies of fiscal and social austerity, the luxurious modes of these genre and styles were largely limited to the upper strata of society, and were unavailable, if not actually forbidden to the lower classes. The common people developed a separate type of art, the *fûzokuga*, in which painting depicting scenes from common, everyday life, especially that of the common people, *kabuki* theatre, prostitutes and landscapes were popular. These paintings in the 16th century gave rise to the paintings and woodcut prints of ukiyo-e.

Important artists in the Edo period include:
- Tawaraya Sôtatsu (died 1643)
- Tosa Mitsuoki (1617–1691)
- Ogata Kôrin (1658–1716)
- Gion Nankai (1677–1751)
- Sakaki Hyakusen (1697–1752)
- Yanagisawa Kien (1704–1758)
- Yosa Buson (1716–1783)

- Itô Jakuchû (1716–1800)
- Ike no Taiga (1723–1776)
- Suzuki Harunobu (c. 1725–1770)
- Soga Shôhaku (1730–1781)
- Maruyama Ôkyo (1733–1795)
- Okada Beisanjin (1744–1820)
- Uragami Gyokudô (1745–1820)
- Matsumura Goshun (1752–1811)
- Katsushika Hokusai (1760–1849)
- Tani Bunchô (1763–1840)
- Tanomura Chikuden (1777–1835)
- Okada Hankô (1782–1846)
- Yamamoto Baiitsu (1783–1856)
- Watanabe Kazan (1793–1841)
- Utagawa Hiroshige (1797–1858)
- Shibata Zeshin (1807–1891)
- Tomioka Tessai (1836–1924)
- Kumashiro Hi (Yûhi) (c. 1712–1772)

Prewar period (1868–1945)

The prewar period was marked by the division of art into competing European styles and traditional indigenous styles.

During the Meiji period, Japan underwent a tremendous political and social change in the course of the Europeanization and modernization campaign organized by theMeiji government. Western-style painting (*yôga*) was officially promoted by the government, who sent promising young artists abroad for studies, and who hiredforeign artists to come to Japan to establish an art curriculum at Japanese schools.

However, after an initial burst of enthusiasm for western style art, the pendulum swung in the opposite direction, and led by art critic Okakura Kakuzô and educatorErnest Fenollosa, there was a revival of appreciation for traditional Japanese styles (Nihonga). In the 1880s, western style art was banned from official exhibitions and was severely criticized by critics. Supported by Okakura and Fenollosa, the *Nihonga*style evolved with influences from the European pre-Raphaelite movement and European romanticism.

The Yôga style painters formed the *Meiji Bijutsukai* (Meiji Fine Arts Society) to hold its own exhibitions and to promote a renewed interest in western art. In 1907, with the establishment of the *Bunten* under the aegis of the Ministry of Education, both competing groups found mutual recognition and co-existence, and even began the process towards mutual synthesis.

The Taishô period saw the predominance of *Yôga* over *Nihonga*. After long stays in Europe, many artists (including Arishima Ikuma) returned to Japan under the reign of Yoshihito, bringing with them the techniques of impressionism and early Post-Impressionism. The works of Camille Pissarro, Paul Cézanne and Pierre-Auguste Renoir influenced early Taishô period paintings. However, *yôga* artists in the Taishô period also tended towardseclecticism, and there was a profusion of dissident artistic movements. These included the Fusain Society (*Fyuzankai*) which emphasized styles of post-impressionism, especially fauvism. In 1914, the *Nikakai* (Second Division Society) emerged to oppose the government-sponsored Bunten Exhibition.

Japanese painting during the Taishô period was only mildly influenced by other contemporary European movements, such as neoclassicism and late post-impressionism.

However, interestingly it was resurgent *Nihonga*, towards mid-1920s, which adopted certain trends from post-impressionism. The second generation of *Nihonga* artists formed the Japan Fine Arts Academy (*Nihon Bijutsuin*) to compete against the government-sponsored *Bunten*, and although *yamato-e* traditions remained strong, the increasing use of westernperspective, and western concepts of space and light began to blur the distinction between *Nihonga* and *yôga*.

Japanese painting in the prewar Shôwa period was largely dominated by Sôtarô Yasui and Ryûzaburô Umehara, who introduced the concepts of pure art and abstract painting to the *Nihonga* tradition, and thus created a more interpretative version of that genre. This trend was further developed by Leonard Foujita and the Nika Society, to encompass surrealism. To promote these trends, the Independent Art Association (*Dokuritsu Bijutsu Kyokai*) was formed in 1931.

During the World War II, government controls and censorship meant that only patriotic themes could be expressed. Many artists were recruited into the government propaganda effort, and critical non-emotional review of their works is only just beginning.

Important artists in the prewar period include:

* Harada Naojirô (1863–1899)
* Yamamoto Hôsui (1850–1906)
* Asai Chû (1856–1907)
* Kanô Hôgai (1828–1888)
* Hashimoto Gahô (1835–1908)
* Kuroda Seiki (1866–1924)
* Wada Eisaku (1874–1959)
* Okada Saburôsuke (1869–1939)
* Sakamoto Hanjirô (1882–1962)
* Aoki Shigeru (1882–1911)
* Fujishima Takeji (1867–1943)
* Yokoyama Taikan 1868-1958
* Hishida Shunsô 1874-1911
* Kawai Gyokudô 1873-1957
* Uemura Shôen (1875–1949)
* Maeda Seison (1885–1977)
* Takeuchi Seihô (1864–1942)
* Tomioka Tessai (1837–1924)
* Shimomura Kanzan (1873–1930)
* Takeshiro Kanokogi (1874–1941)
* Imamura Shiro (1880–1916)
* Tomita Keisen (1879–1936)
* Koide Narashige (1887–1931)
* Kishida Ryûsei (1891–1929)
* Tetsugorô Yorozu (1885–1927)
* Hayami Gyoshû (1894–1935)
* Kawabata Ryûshi (1885–1966)
* Tsuchida Hakusen (1887–1936)
* Murakami Kagaku (1888–1939)
* Sôtarô Yasui (1881–1955)
* Sanzô Wada (1883–1967)
* Ryûzaburô Umehara (1888–1986)
* Yasuda Yukihiko (1884–1978)
* Kobayashi Kokei (1883–1957)

- Leonard Foujita (1886–1968)
- Yuzô Saeki (1898–1928)
- Itô Shinsui (1898–1972)
- Kaburaki Kiyokata (1878–1972)
- Takehisa Yumeji (1884–1934)

Postwar period (1945–present)

In the postwar period, the government-sponsored Japan Art Academy (*Nihon Geijutsuin*) was formed in 1947, containing both *nihonga* and *yôga* divisions. Government sponsorship of art exhibitions has ended, but has been replaced by private exhibitions, such as the *Nitten*, on an even larger scale. Although the *Nitten* was initially the exhibition of the Japan Art Academy, since 1958 it has been run by a separate private corporation. Participation in the *Nitten* has become almost a prerequisite for nomination to the Japan Art Academy, which in itself is almost an unofficial prerequisite for nomination to theOrder of Culture.

The arts of the Edo and prewar periods (1603–1945) was supported by merchants and urban people. Counter to the Edo and prewar periods, arts of the postwar period became popular. After World War II, painters, calligraphers, and printmakersflourished in the big cities, particularly Tokyo, and became preoccupied with the mechanisms of urban life, reflected in the flickering lights, neon colors, and frenetic pace of their abstractions. All the "isms" of the New York-Paris art world were fervently embraced. After the abstractions of the 1960s, the 1970s saw a return to realism strongly flavored by the "op" and "pop" art movements, embodied in the 1980s in the explosive works of Ushio Shinohara. Many such outstanding avant-garde artists worked both in Japan and abroad, winning international prizes. These artists felt that there was "nothing Japanese" about their works, and indeed they belonged to the international school. By the late 1970s, the search for Japanese qualities and a national style caused many artists to reevaluate their artistic ideology and turn away from what some felt were the empty formulas of the West. Contemporary paintings within the modern idiom began to make conscious use of traditional Japanese art forms, devices, and ideologies. A number of *mono-ha* artists turned to painting to recapture traditional nuances in spatial arrangements, color harmonies, and lyricism.

Japanese-style or *nihonga* painting continues in a prewar fashion, updating traditional expressions while retaining their intrinsic character. Some artists within this style still paint on silk or paper with traditional colors and ink, while others used new materials, such as acrylics. Many of the older schools of art, most notably those of the Edo and prewar periods, were still practiced.

For example, the decorative naturalism of the *rimpa* school, characterized by brilliant, pure colors and bleeding washes, was reflected in the work of many artists of the postwar period in the 1980s art of Hikosaka Naoyoshi.

The realism of Maruyama Ôkyo's schooland the calligraphic and spontaneous Japanese style of the gentlemen-scholars were both widely practiced in the 1980s. Sometimes all of these schools, as well as older ones, such as the Kanô school ink traditions, were drawn on by contemporary artists in the Japanese style and in the modern idiom. Many Japanese-style painters were honored with awards and prizes as a result of renewed popular demand for Japanese-style art beginning in the 1970s. More and more, the international modern painters also drew on the Japanese schools as they turned away from Western styles in the 1980s. The tendency had been to synthesize East and West. Some artists had already leapt the gap between the two, as did the outstanding painter Shinoda Toko. Her bold sumi ink abstractions were inspired by traditional calligraphy but realized as lyrical expressions of modern abstraction.

There are also a number of contemporary painters in Japan whose work is largely inspired by anime sub-cultures and other aspects of popular and youth culture. Takashi Murakami is perhaps among the most famous and popular of these, along with and the other artists in his Kaikai Kiki studio collective. His work centers on expressing issues and concerns of postwar Japanese society through what are usually seemingly innocuous forms. He draws heavily from anime and related styles, but produces paintings and sculptures in media more traditionally associated with fine arts, intentionally blurring the lines between commercial and popular art and fine arts.

JAPANESE SCULPTURE

The sculpture of Japan started from the clay figure. Japanese sculpture received the influence of the Silk Road culture in the 5th century, and received a strong influence from Chinese sculpture afterwards. The influence of the Western world was received since the

Meiji era. The sculptures were made at local shops, used for sculpting and painting. Most sculptures were found at areas in front of houses and along walls of important buildings.

Most of the Japanese sculptures derived from the idol worship in Buddhism or animistic rites of Shinto deity. In particular, sculpture among all the arts came to be most firmly centered on Buddhism. Materials traditionally used were metal — especially bronze — and, more commonly, wood, often lacquered, gilded, or brightly painted.

History

Primitive arts

Interest in primitive arts is seeing a wide ascendancy and spontaneity and seek to produce a similar artless artistry in their own works. In every instance examples of ancient primitive art have been found to possess characteristics identical to modern arts; and the ancient Japanese clay figures known as dogû and haniwa are no exceptions to this rule.

No scholar has been able to determine absolutely just when human life moved over into the Japanese archipelago. It was these early inhabitants who eventually evolved the first crude Japanese native art in rough earthenware and in strange clay figures called dogû, which are probably fetishes of some religious nature. Some may have been used in fertility rites, and some in exorcism or other forms of primitive ritual.

The dogû figures are impressive in their grotesque and mysterious symbolism; and there is a crude sense of primitive force and passion in the strongly engraved lines and swirls with which the figures are decorated.

Legend, as recorded in the *Nihon Shoki* (Chronicles of Japan) which is an ancient history of Japan compiled in 720, states that thaniwa was ordered at the time of an empress's death by the emperor who regretted the custom of servants and maids of the deceased following their master in death, and ordered that clay figures be molded and placed around the kofun burial mound instead of the sacrifice of living beings. Scholars doubt the authenticity of this story and contend that plain cylindrical clay pipes were the first haniwa forms, and that they were used in the manner of stakes to hold the earth of the burial mound in place. Later these plain cylindrical haniwa came to be decorated and to take various forms, including the shapes of houses and domestic animals as well as human beings. They have been found arranged in a circle around the mound, lending credence to the scholars' theory. However, the haniwa figures no doubt came to take on some sort of religious symbolism later, aside from their original practical purpose as stakes.

Asuka and Hakuhô periods

Japanese emergence from her period of native primitive arts was instigated mainly by the introduction of Buddhism from the mainland Asian continent about the middle of the 6th century. Together with the new religion, skilled artists and craftsman from China came to Japan to build its temples and sculptic idols, and to pass on artistic techniques to native craftsmen.

Earliest examples of Buddhist art may be seen in accumulated splendor at the seventh-centuryHoryû-ji temple in Nara, whose buildings themselves, set in a prescribed pattern with main hall, belfy, pagodas, and other buildings enclosed within an encircling roofed corridor, retain an aura of the ancient era, together with the countless art treasures preserved within their halls.

Nara and its vicinity contain the vast majority of the nation's treasures of the early period of Buddhist art, known in art history as the Asuka period. The sculpture of this period shows, as do most all subsequent sculpture, the influence of continental art. Noted Asuka sculptor Tori Busshi followed the style of North Wei sculpture and established what has come to be known as the Tori school of sculpture. Notable examples of Tori works are the Sakyamuni Triad which are the main icons of the Golden Hall of Horyû-ji temple and the Kannon Boddhisatva of Yumedono Hall of the same temple, also known as Guze Kannon. Some of the most important Buddhist sculptures belong to the ensuing Hakuho art period when the sculpture came to show predominantly Tang influence. The mystic unrealistic air of the earlier Tori style came to be replaced by a soft supple pose and a near sensuous beauty more in the manner of the Maitreya with long narrow slit eyes and gentle effeminate features which in spite of their air of reverie have about them an intimate approachability. The aloofness of the earlier Asuka sculpture is softened into a more native form; and there is to be seen in them a compromise between the divine and the human ideal.

Representative sculptures of this period are the beautiful Sho Kannon of Yakushiji temple, and the Yumatagae Kannon of Horyû-ji, both showing the fullness of rounded flesh within the conventionalized folds of the garments, reflecting in their artistry features of the Gupta art are transmitted to Japanese through Tang.

Nara period

In 710–793, Japanese sculptors learned high Tang style and produced a style "Tenpyô sculpture", which shows realistic face, massive solid volume, natural drapery, and delicate representation of sentiment. Emperor Shômu ordered the colossal gilt bronze Virocana Buddha in Tôdai-ji temple and completed in 752. Although the statue has been destroyed twice and repaired, the minor original part has survived. Among many original works, the Asura in Kôfukuji temple is attractive, which is a dry lacquer statue and show delicate representation of sentiment. The four guardians in Kaidanin: a division of Tôdai-ji temple are masterpiece, which are clay statues. A national official factory *Zô Tôdai-ji shi* ("Office to build Tôdai-ji Temple") produced many Buddhism sculptures by division of the work for Tôdai-ji and other official temples and temples for novelties. Gilt bronze, dry lacquer, clay, terracotta, repousee, stone, and silver sculptures were made in the factory. Generally the sculptors are secular and got official status and salary. Some private ateliers offered Buddhist icons to people, and some monks made it themselves.

Heian period

With the moving of the imperial capital from Nara to Kyoto in 794, big temples did not move to Kyoto. Government fed new esoteric Buddhism imported from Tang china. The official factory *Zo Tôdai-ji shi0*was closed in 789. Fired sculptors worked under patronage of big temples in Nara, new temples of esoteric sect, the court, and the novelties. Sculptors got temple clergy status whether or not they were members of the order.

Wood became the primary medium. On the style, Heian period was divided two: the early Heian period and the later. In the early Heian period (794 to about the mid-10th century), statues of esoteric Buddhism flourished. Kûkai,Saichô and other members of Imperial Japanese embassies to China imported the high to later Tang style. The statue bodies were carved from single blocks of wood and appear imposing, massive, and heavy when compared to Nara period works. Their thick limbs and severe, almost brooding facial features imbue them with a sense of dark mystery and inspire awe in the beholder, in keeping with the secrecy of Esoteric Buddhist rites. Heavily carved draperies, in which rounded folds alternate with sharply cut folds are typical of the period. Among esoteric Buddhism deities, Japanese like Acala and have produced enormous Acala images.

In the later Heian period (the mid-10th century to the 12th century), the sophistication of court culture and popularity of Amida Worship gave rise to a new style: gentle, calm, and refined features with more attenuated proportion. Sculptors Japanized faces of images. Pure Land sect(Amida Worship) leader Genshin and his work *Ôjôyôshû* influenced many sculpture. The masterpiece is the Amida Buddha in Byôdô-in in Uji by the master Jôchô. He established a canon of Buddhist sculpture. He was called the expert of yosegi zukuri technique: sculptors became working with multiple blocks of wood, too. This technique allowed masters atelier production with apprentices. It led the style more repetitious and mediocre afterJôchô. In school, a grandson of Jôchô established an atelier which worked with the Imperial Court in Kyoto. En school (ja) a discipline of Jôchô, also established Sanjyô-Atlier in Kyoto.

Kamakura period

This Kamakura period is regarded as the "Renaissance era of Japanese sculpture". Kei school sculptures led this trend; they are descendants of Jôchô.0They succeeded in the technique called "yosegi-zukuri" (woodblock construction) and represented a new sculpture style: realism, representation of sentiment, solidity, and movement, for which they studied early Nara period masterpieces and Chinese Song dynasty sculptures and paintings. On the other side, clay, dry-lacquer, embossing, and terracotta sculptures did not revive. They used mainly wood and sometimes bronze.

The Kei school took root in Nara-city, which was the former capital (710-793), and worked in large temples in Nara. In the Kamakura period, the Kyoto court and Kamakura shogunatemilitary government reconstructed large temples burned in late-12th-century wars. Many sculptures were repaired and many buildings were rebuilt or repaired. The "renaissance" character is reflected in the project.

Among the sculptors of the Kei school, Unkei is the most famous. Among his works, a pair of colossal Kongô-rikishi in Tôdai-ji are most famous, and the portrait-like statues of Indian priests in Kôfuku-ji are elaborate masterpieces. Unkei had six sculptor sons and their work was also imbued with the new humanism. Tankei, the eldest son and a brilliant sculptor, became the head of the studio. Kôshô, the 4th son, produced a remarkable sculpture of the 10th-century Japanese Buddhist teacher Kuya (903–972). Kaikei was a collaborator of Unkei. He was a devout adherent of the Pure Land sect. He worked with the priest Chôgen (1121–1206), the director of the Tôdai-ji reconstruction project. Many of his figures are more idealized than those of Unkei and his sons, and are characterized by a beautifully finished surface, richly decorated with pigments and gold. More than 40 of his works have survived, many of which are signed by him. His most important work is Amitabha Triad of Ono Jôdo-ji(1195).

Sculptors also worked for the Kamakura shogunate and other military clans. They produced Buddhist and portrait sculptures for them. The colossal bronze Amitabha Buddha in Kamakura Kôtoku-in was made in 1252. All classes of society contributed funds to make this colossal bronze. Such patronage raised and sometimes replaced the former patronage of wealthy and powerful men.

Muromachi period and Sengoku period

Buddhist sculptures declined in quantity and quality. The new Zen Buddhism deprecated images of Buddha. Big temples of the old sects were depressed under civil wars. Portrait sculptures of Zen masters became a new genre during this period. The art of carving masks for Noh theatre flourished and improved from the 15th to 17th centuries.

Edo period

The reconstruction of Buddhist temples burned in the civil wars required sculptors. The new sculptures were mostly conservatively carved from wood and gilt or polychromed. They mostly lack artistic power. However, some Buddhist monk sculptors produced unpainted, roughly hewn images of wood. Enkû (1632–1695) and Mokujiki (1718–1810) are representative. They traveled through Japan and produced enormous works for missionary and ceremonial purposes. Their archaic and spiritual styles were reevaluated in the 20th century. The art of carving masks for Noh also continued to produce better works in the 17th century.

MODERN ARTS

Introduction of the Western techniques

The stimulus of Western art forms returned sculpture to the Japanese art scene and introduced the plaster cast, outdoor heroic sculpture, and the school of Paris concept of sculpture as an "art form". Such ideas adopted in Japan during the late 19th century, together with the return of state patronage, rejuvenated sculpture. After World War II, sculptors turned away from the figurative French school ofRodin and Maillol toward aggressive modern and avant-garde forms and materials, sometimes on an enormous scale. A profusion of materials and techniques characterized these new experimental sculptures, which also absorbed the ideas of international "op" (optical illusion) and "pop" (popular motif) art. A number of innovative artists were both sculptors and painters or printmakers, their new theories cutting across material boundaries.

1970s onwards

In the 1970s, the ideas of contextual placement of natural objects of stone, wood, bamboo, and paper into relationships with people and their environment were embodied in the mono-ha school. The mono-ha artists emphasized materiality as the most important aspect of art and brought to an end the antiformalism that had dominated the avant-garde in the preceding two decades. This focus on the relationships between objects and people was ubiquitous throughout the arts world and led to a rising appreciation of "Japanese" qualities in the environment and a return to native artistic principles and forms. Among these precepts were a reverence for nature and various Buddhist concepts, which were brought into play by architects to treat time and space problems. Western ideology was carefully reexamined, and much was rejected as artists turned to their own environment—both inward and outward—for sustenance and inspiration. From the late 1970s through the late 1980s, artists began to create a vital new art, which was both contemporary and Asian in sources and expression but still very much a part of the international scene. These artists focused on projecting their own individualism and national styles rather than on adapting or synthesizing Western ideas exclusively.

Outdoor sculpture, which came to the fore with the advent of the Hakone Open-Air Museum in 1969, was widely used in the 1980s. Cities supported enormous outdoor sculptures for parks and plazas, and major architects planned for sculpture in their buildings and urban layouts. Outdoor museums and exhibitions burgeoned, stressing the natural placement of sculpture in the environment. Because hard sculpture stone is not native to Japan, most outdoor pieces were created from stainless steel, plastic, or aluminum for "tension and compression" machine constructions of mirror-surfaced steel or for elegant, polished-aluminum, ultramodern shapes. The strong influence of modern high technology on the artists resulted in experimentation with kinetic, tensile forms, such as flexible arcs and "info-environmental" sculptures using lights. Video components and video art developed rapidly from the late 1970s throughout the 1980s. The new Japanese experimental sculptors could be understood as working with Buddhist ideas of permeability and regeneration in structuring their forms, in contrast to the general Western conception of sculpture as something with finite and permanent contours.

In the 1980s, wood and natural materials were used prominently by many sculptors, who now began to place their works in inner courtyards and enclosed spaces. Also, a Japanese feeling for rhythmic motion, captured in recurring forms as a "systematic gestural motion", was used by both long-established artists like Kyubei Kiyomizu and Hidetoshi Nagasawa and the younger generation led by Shigeo Toya.

10

Tourism

Japan attracted 24.03 million international tourists in 2016. Japan has 21 World Heritage Sites, including Himeji Castle, Historic Monuments of Ancient Kyoto andNara. Popular foreigner attractions include Tokyo and Hiroshima, Mount Fuji, ski resorts such as Niseko in Hokkaido, Okinawa, riding the shinkansen and taking advantage of Japan's hotel and hotspring network.

The *Travel and Tourism Competitiveness Report 2017* ranks Japan 4th out of 141 countries overall, which was the best in Asia. Japan gained relatively high scores in almost all aspects, especially health and hygiene, safety and security, cultural resources and business travel.

HISTORY

The origins of early traditions of visits to picturesque sites are unclear, but early sight-seeing excursions was Matsuo Basho's 1689 trip to the then "far north" of Japan, which occurred not long after Hayashi Razan categorized the Three Views of Japan in 1643. During the Edo era of Japan, from around 1600 to the Meiji Restoration in 1867, travel was regulated within the country through the use ofshukuba or post stations, towns where travelers had to present appropriate documentation. Despite these restrictions, porter stations and horse stables, as well as places for lodging and food were available on well-traveled routes. During this time, Japan was a closed country to foreigners, so no foreign tourism existed in Japan.

Following the Meiji Restoration and the building of a national railroad network, tourism became more of an affordable prospect for domestic citizens and visitors from foreign countries could enter Japan legally. As early as 1887, government officials recognized the need for an organized system of attracting foreign tourists; the *Kihinkai* , which aimed to coordinate the players in tourism, was established that year with Prime Minister Ito Hirobumi's blessing. Its early leaders included Shibusawa Eiichi and Ekida Takashi. Another major milestone in the development of the tourism industry in Japan was the 1907 passage of the Hotel Development Law, as a result of which the Railways Ministry began to construct publicly owned hotels throughout Japan.

TOURISM TODAY

Domestic tourism remains a vital part of the Japanese economy and Japanese culture. Children in many middle schools see the highlight of their years as a visit to Tokyo Disneyland or perhaps Tokyo Tower, and many high school students often visit Okinawa or Hokkaido. The extensive rail network together with domestic flights sometimes in planes with modifications to favor the relatively short distances involved in intra-Japan travel allows efficient and speedy transport.

In inbound tourism, Japan was ranked 28th in the world in 2007. In 2009, the *Yomiuri Shimbun* published a modern list of famous sights under the name *Heisei Hyakkei* (the Hundred Views of the Heisei period).

Neighbouring South Korea is Japan's most important source of foreign tourists. In 2010, the 2.4 million arrivals made up 27% of the tourists visiting Japan.

Chinese travelers are the highest spenders in Japan by country, spending an estimated 196.4 billion yen (US$2.4 billion) in 2011, or almost a quarter of total expenditure by foreign visitors, according to data from the Japan Tourism Agency.

The Japanese government hopes to receive 40 million foreign tourists every year by 2020.

Major tourist destinations

Hokkaido

- Niseko Ski Resort
- Shiretoko Peninsula (WHL)
- Teshikaga — Lake Mashû, Lake Kussharo

- Tôya Caldera and Mount Usu Geopark
- Daisetsuzan Volcanic Group
- Hakodate
- Otaru

Tôhoku region

- Shirakami-Sanchi (WHL)
- Mount Osore
- Lake Towada
- Hirosaki — Hirosaki Castle, Nakacho Samurai District
- Hiraizumi — Chûson-ji, Môtsû-ji, Kanjizaiô-in, Takkoku-no-Iwaya
- Semboku — Kakunodate Samurai District, Lake Tazawa, Nyuto Onsen
- Yamagata — Yama-dera Temple, Zaô Onsen
- Matsushima

Kantô region

- Edo Wonderland Nikko Edomura
- Nikkô - Shrines and Temples of Nikkô (WHL), Kegon Falls
- Tokyo - Imperial Palace, Asakusa, Akihabara, Ginza, Harajuku/Omotesando,Shibuya, Shinjuku, Tsukiji Fish Market, Ueno Park
- Tokyo Disney Resort
- Kamakura - Tsurugaoka Hachiman-gû, Kôtoku-in, Kenchô-ji, Engaku-ji,Meigetsu-in, Hase-dera
- Kusatsu Onsen
- Hakone Onsen

Chûbu region

- Mount Fuji
- Japanese Alps — Tateyama Kurobe Alpine Route(Mount Tate), Hida Mountains,Kiso Mountains, Akaishi Mountains
- Shiga Kôgen
- Matsumoto - Matsumoto Castle, Mount Hotaka, Kamikôchi
- Shirakawa-gô and Gokayama (WHL)
- Takayama - Sanmachi Traditional Street, Ôshinmachi Traditional Street, Higashiyama Temple Area
- Kanazawa - Kenroku-en Garden, Kanazawa Castle, Higashi

Geisha District, Nagamachi Samurai District

- Sakai - Tôjinbô, Maruoka Castle
- Nagoya - Nagoya Castle, Atsuta Shrine, Sakae, Nagoya Station (Meieki), Ôsu Kannon temple

Kansai region

- Kyoto — Kinkaku-ji, Ginkaku-ji, Kiyomizu-dera, Ryôan-ji, Sanjûsangen-dô, etc., they are parts of Historic Monuments of Ancient Kyoto (WHL)
- Uji — Byôdô-in and Ujigami Shrine (WHL), Relation of *The Tale of Genji*
- Ôtsu — Lake Biwa, Hiyoshi Taisha, Sakamoto Temple District, Mount Hiei,Enryaku-ji (WHL)
- Ômihachiman — Traditional Riverside District
- Nara — Tôdai-ji, Tôshôdai-ji, Kôfuku-ji, Yakushi-ji, Heijô Palace, Kasuga-taishaand Nara Park, etc. They are parts of the Historic Monuments of Ancient Nara(WHL).
- Ikaruga — Hôryû-ji and Hôki-ji are Buddhist Monuments in the Hôryû-ji Area(WHL).
- Yoshino (Mount Yoshino) — Kimpusen-ji, Yoshimizu Shrine, Yoshino Mikumari Shrine, etc. They are parts of the Sacred Sites and Pilgrimage Routes in the Kii Mountain Range (WHL).
- Shingû — Kumano Hayatama Taisha and Kumano River (WHL)
- Nachikatsuura — Nachi Falls, Kumano Kodô, etc., they are parts of Sacred Sites and Pilgrimage Routes in the Kii Mountain Range (WHL)
- Mount Kôya — Kongôbu-ji (WHL)
- Osaka — Osaka Castle, Umeda, Namba, Dôtonbori, Shinsekai, Shitennô-ji,Universal Studios Japan, Rinku Town
- Himeji — Engyô-ji, Koko-en Garden, and Himeji Castle (WHL)
- Kobe — Port of Kobe, Rokkô Mountains, Kitano-chô, Arima Onsen, Kobe Luminarie
- San'in Kaigan Geopark — Toyooka, Izushi, Kinosaki Onsen, Yumura Onsen

Chûgoku region

- Hiroshima Prefecture — Atomic Bomb Dome (WHL), Itsukushima Shrine (WHL),Onomichi, Tomonoura

- Okayama Prefecture — Kurashiki, Kôrakuen Garden, Okayama Castle
- Tottori Prefecture — Tottori Sand Dunes, Mount Daisen, Mount Hyôno, San'in Kaigan Geopark
- Shimane Prefecture — Iwami Ginzan Silver Mine (WHL), Izumo-taisha, Matsue Castle, Oki Islands, Tsuwano
- Yamaguchi Prefecture — Hagi

Shikoku

- Shikoku Pilgrimage (Zentsû-ji, Motoyama-ji, etc.)
- Ehime Prefecture — Dôgo Onsen, Matsuyama Castle
- Kagawa Prefecture — Kotohira-gû Shrine, Ritsurin Garden, Shôdo Island,Naoshima Island
- Tokushima Prefecture — Naruto whirlpools, Awa Dance Festival in Tokushima
- Kôchi Prefecture — Kôchi Castle, Cape Muroto (Muroto Geopark), Cape Ashizuri

Kyushu and Okinawa

- Fukuoka Prefecture — Mojiko Retro Town, Kokura Castle, Dazaifu Tenman-gû, Remains of Dazaifu (government)
- Ôita Prefecture — Many types of hot springs in Beppu, Ôita or Yufuin, Ôita, Usa jingû, stone bridges, small stonehenge on the top of Komekamiyama (mountain), Hello Kitty Harmonyland
- Nagasaki Prefecture — Ôura Church, Higashi-Yamate, Minami-Yamate, Huis Ten Bosch (theme park)
- Kagoshima Prefecture — Yakushima (WHL), Sakurajima, Amami Ôshima
- Miyazaki Prefecture — Kirishima-Yaku National Park, Takachiho, Old Exculibur on the top of Takachiho-kyo mountain,Nichinan, Miyazaki,0Chambered barrows of Saitobaru kofungun, Heiwadai Park
- Kumamoto Prefecture — Kumamoto Castle,0Mount Aso
- Saga Prefecture — Pre-400 BC Yayoi archaeological site in Yoshinogari site
- Okinawa Prefecture — Shuri Castle, Nakagusuku Castle, Nakijin Castle etc. They are parts of the Gusuku Sites and

Related Properties of the Kingdom of Ryukyu. (WHL), Ishigaki Island, Miyako Island, Iriomote Island, Traditional Ryukyuan Houses in Taketomi Island

Tourism after the Fukushima disaster

After the triple melt-down of the nuclear reactors in Fukushima, the number of foreign visitors declined for months. In September 2011 some 539,000 foreign people visited Japan, this was 25 percent down compared with the same month in 2010. This decline was largely attributed to the Fukushima nuclear accident and the stronger yen made a visit to Japan more expensive.

To boost tourism the Japanese Tourism Agency announced in October 2011 a plan to give 10,000 round-trip air tickets to Japan to encourage visitors to come. In 2012 free tickets would be offered if the winners would write online about their experiences in Japan. They also would need to answer some questions about how they felt while visiting Japan after the earthquake and how the interest in tourism in Japan could be renewed. About US$15 million would be spent on this program. On December 26, 2011, The Japan Tourism Agency reported on their site that the "Fly to Japan! Project", which would have given out 10,000 round-trip tickets to Japan, was not approved by the government for fiscal year 2012.

11

Education

Education in Japan is compulsory at the elementary and lower secondary levels. Most students attend public schools through the lower secondary level, but private education is popular at the upper secondary and university levels.

Education prior to elementary school is provided at kindergartens and day-care centers. Public and private day-care centers take children from under age 1 on up to 5 years old. The programmes for those children aged 3–5 resemble those at kindergartens. The educational approach at kindergartens varies greatly from unstructured environments that emphasize play to highly structured environments that are focused on having the child pass the entrance exam at a private elementary school. The academic year starts from April and ends in March, having summer vacation in August and winter vacation in the end of December to the beginning of January. Also, there are few days of holidays between academic years. The period of academic year is same all through elementary level to higher educations nationwide.

Japanese students consistently rank highly among OECD students in terms of quality and performance in reading literacy, math, and sciences. The average student scored 540 in reading literacy, maths and science in the OECD's Programme for International Student Assessment (PISA) and the country has one of the world's highest-educated labour forces among OECD countries. Its populace is well educated and its society highly values education as a platform for social mobility and for gaining employment in the country's high-tech economy. The country's large pool of highly educated and skilled individuals is largely responsible for ushering Japan's post-war economic growth. Tertiary-educated adults in Japan, particularly graduates in sciences and engineering benefit economically and socially from their education and skills in the country's high tech economy. Spending on education as a proportion of GDP is below the OECD average. Although expenditure per student is comparatively high in Japan, total expenditure relative to GDP remains small. In 2015, Japan's public spending on education amounted to just 3.5 percent of its GDP, below the OECD average of 4.7%. In 2014, the country ranked fourth for the percentage of 25- to 64-year-olds that have attained tertiary education with 48 percent. In addition, bachelor's degrees are held by 59 percent of Japanese aged 25–34, the second most in the OECD after South Korea. As the Japanese economy is largely scientific and technological based, the labor market demands people who have achieved some form of higher education, particularly related to science and engineering in order to gain a competitive edge when searching for employment opportunities. About 75.9 percent of high school graduates attended a university, junior college, trade school, or other higher education institution.

Japan's education system played a central part in Japan's recovery and rapid economic growth in the decades following the end of World War II. After World War II, the Fundamental Law of Education and the School Education Law were enacted. The latter law defined the school system that would be in effect for many decades: six years of elementary school, three years of junior high school, three years of high school, and two or four years of university. Although Japan ranks highly on the PISA tests, its educational system has been criticized for its focus on standardized testing and conformity; its aforementioned bullying problem; and its strong academic pressure on students.

HISTORY

Formal education in Japan began with the adoption of Chinese culture, in the 6th century. Buddhist and Confucian teachings as well as sciences, calligraphy,divination and literature were taught at the courts of Asuka, Nara and Heian. Scholar officials were chosen through an Imperial examination system. But contrary to China, the system never fully took hold and titles and posts at the court remained hereditary family possessions. The rise of the *bushi*, the military class, during theKamakura period ended the influence of scholar officials, but Buddhist monasteries remained influential centers of learning.

In the Edo period, the Yushima Seidô in Edo was the chief educational institution of the state; and at its head was the *Daigaku-no-kami*, a title which identified the leader of the Tokugawa training school for shogunate bureaucrats.

Under the Tokugawa shogunate, the daimyô vied for power in the largely pacified country. Since their influence could not be raised through war, they competed on the economic field. Their warrior-turned-bureaucrat Samurai elite had to be educated not only in military strategy and the martial arts, but also agriculture and accounting. Likewise, the wealthy merchant class needed education for their daily business, and their wealth allowed them to be patrons of arts and science. But temple schools (terakoya) educated peasants too, and it is estimated that at the end of the Edo period 50% of the male and 20% of the female population possessed some degree of literacy. Even though contact with foreign countries was restricted, books from China and Europe were eagerly imported and Rangaku ("Dutch studies") became a popular area of scholarly interest.

Meiji Restoration

After the Meiji Restoration of 1868, the methods and structures of Western learning were adopted as a means to make Japan a strong, modern nation. Students and even high-ranking government officials were sent abroad to study, such as theIwakura mission. Foreign scholars, the so-called *o-yatoi gaikokujin*, were invited to teach at newly founded universities and military academies. Compulsory education was introduced, mainly after the Prussian model. By 1890, only 20 years after the resumption of full international relations, Japan discontinued employment of the foreign consultants.

A modern concept of childhood emerged in Japan after 1850 as part of its engagement with the West. Meiji period leaders decided the nation-state had the primary role in mobilizing individuals - and children - in service of the state. The Western-style school was introduced as the agent to reach that goal. By the 1890s, schools were generating new sensibilities regarding childhood. After 1890 Japan had numerous reformers, child experts, magazine editors, and well-educated mothers who bought into the new sensibility. They taught the upper middle class a model of childhood that included children having their own space where they read children's books, played with educational toys and, especially, devoted enormous time to school homework. These ideas rapidly disseminated through all social classes.

Post-WWII

After the defeat in World War II, the allied occupation government set an education reform as one of its primary goals, to eradicate militarist teachings and "democratize" Japan. The education system was rebuilt after the American model.

A number of reforms were carried out in the post-war period. They aimed at easing the burden of entrance examinations, promoting internationalisation and information technologies, diversifying education and supporting lifelong learning.

The Ministry of Education, Culture, Sports, Science and Technology (MEXT) is responsible for educational administration.

In successive international assessment tests, Japan's fourth- and eighth-grade students have consistently ranked in the top five globally in both mathematics and science.

Despite concerns that academic skills for Japanese students may have declined since the mid-1990s, Japan's students showed a significant improvement in math and science scores in the 2011 TIMSS survey, compared to the 2007 scores.

School grades

The school year in Japan begins in April and classes are held from Monday to either Friday or Saturday, depending on the school. The school year consists of two or three terms, which are separated by short holidays in spring and winter, and a six-week-long summer break.

THE JAPANESE EDUCATIONAL SYSTEM

The schooling years in the Japanese education system are segmented along the lines of 6-3-3-4: 6 years of primary or elementary school; 3 years of middle or junior high school; 3 years of high school; and 4 years of university. However, the government announced (October 2005, Daily Yomiuri) that it intended to make changes in the Education Law to allow schools to merge the 6-3 division between elementary and middle schools and to create an integrated curriculum. The key purpose for this change is to allow elementary and middle schools to pool or share their resources, with special regard to making available specialist teachers of middle schools to elementary schools.

Many private schools, however, offer a six year programme incorporating both junior high school and high school. Specialized schools may offer a five year programme comprising high school and two years of junior college. There are two options for tertiary education: junior college (two years) and university (four years).

A school year has three terms: summer, winter and spring, which are each followed by a vacation period. The school year begins in April and ends in March of the following year.

An elementary school (from 6 years) and junior high school (3 years) education, i.e. nine years of schooling are considered compulsory.

This system, implemented by the School Education Law enacted in March 1947 after WWII, owes its origin to the American model 6-3-3 plus 4 years of university. Many other features of the Japanese educational system, are however, based on European models.

Compulsory education covers elementary school and junior high school. A break from the past, modern public schools in Japan today are mostly co-ed(more than 99% of elementary schools). The Japanese school year begins in April and students attend school for three terms except for brief spring and winter breaks and a one month long summer holiday.

Looking at the statistics

Japan has 23,633 elementary schools, 11,134 junior high schools, 5,450 senior high schools, 995 schools for the handicapped, 702 universities, 525 junior colleges, and 14,174 kindergartens (May 2003 figures). School attendance rate for the nine years of compulsory education is 99.98%.

About 19.2 million students (MEXT 2012 figures) were enrolled in educational institutions in Japan from the kindergarten to university levels.

Japanese children enter primary school from age 6. The average class size in suburban schools is between 35-40 students, though the national average had dropped to 28.4 pupils per class in 1995. 70% of teachers teach all subjects as specialist teachers are rare in elementary schools. 23.6% of elementary school students attend juku (mostly cozy family-run juku).

Suburban schools tend to be large with student populations ranging from around 700 to over 1,000 pupils, while remote rural schools (19% of schools) can be single-class schools.

From age 12, children proceed to middle schools. At this point, about 5.7% of students attend private schools. The main reasons why parents choose such schools are high priority on academic achievement or because they wish to take their children out of the high school selection rat-race since such schools allow their students direct entry into their affiliated high schools (and often into the affiliated universities).

2005 results of a survey-questionnaire sent to schools of 6th grade parents in 2 Tokyo wards showed:

Parents who select a private junior high school for their child tend to be parents with time and economic influence (home-makers or self-employed with one child) base their decisions and place top priority on academic achievement. The most common reason for sending their children to a private junior high school was that they wanted their children to achieve a higher level of academic achievement.

Parents who select public junior high schools make their choice on the basis of location, incidence of bullying, and personal guidance. Among parents who selected a public school outside the school district, 45% reported that a particularly important criterion was little incidence of bullying and truancy, indicating that bullying was a crucial consideration. The most important criteria for these parents in selection were distance to school, environment and whether good friends also attended the school.

A large percentage of parents (65.1%) tend to select the school based on hearsay.

90.8% of the parents send their children to a juku or cram school, and those whose children attended cram school four or more days a week accounted for 65.2%.

98% of 15 year-old middle-school graduates go on to high schools or private specialist institutions. A high-school diploma is a considered the minimum for the most basic jobs in Japanese societies. The rate of students who advance on to senior high schools was 97.0% in 2002.

One-fourth of students attend private high schools, a small number of which are elite academic high schools. Over 97% of high-school students attend day high schools, about three-fourths are enrolled in academic courses. Other students are enrolled in the one or other of the 93 correspondence high schools or the 342 high schools that support correspondence courses.

There are 710 universities (not counting junior colleges). Almost three-fourths of university students are enrolled at private universities. The rate of students who went on to universities and junior colleges was 44.8 %. Special education institutions exist: 70 schools for the deaf (rougakko); 107 for the blind (mougakko); 790 for those with disabilities (yougogakko). This number is considered to be inadequate.

The National School Curriculum

The elementary school curriculum covers Japanese, social studies, mathematics, science, music, arts and handicrafts, homemaking and physical education. At this stage, much time and emphasis is given to music, fine arts and physical education.

Once-a-week moral education classes were re-introduced into the curriculum in 1959, but these classes together with the earlier emphasis on non-academic subjects are part of its "whole person" education which is seen as the main task of the elementary school system. Moral education is also seen as more effectively carried on through the school routine and daily interactions that go on during the class cleaning and school lunch activities.

The middle curriculum includes Japanese, mathematics, social studies, science, English, music, art, physical education, field trips, clubs and homeroom time. Students now receive instruction from specialist subject teachers. The pace is quick and instruction is textbook bound because teachers have to cover a lot of ground in preparation for high-school entrance examinations.

High schools adopt highly divergent high school curricula, the content may contain general or highly specialized subjects depending on the different types of high schools. More on the curriculum of high schools, visit the following link.

High schools may be classed into one of the following types:

Elite academic high schools collect the creme de la creme of the student population and send the majority of its graduates to top national universities.

Non-elite academic high schools ostensibly prepare students for less prestigious universities or junior colleges, but in reality send a large number of their students to private specialist schools (senshuugakko), which teach subjects such as book-keeping, languages and computer programming. These schools constitute mainstream high schooling.

Vocational High Schools that offer courses in commerce, technical subjects, agriculture, homescience, nursing and fishery. Approximately 60% of their graduates enter full-time employment.

Correspondence High Schools offers a flexible form of schooling for 1.6% of high school students usually those who missed out on high schooling for various reasons.

Evening High School which used to offer classes to poor but ambitious students who worked while trying to remedy their educational deficiencies. But in recent times, such schools tend to be attended by little-motivated members of the lowest two percentiles in terms of academic achievement.

The national curriculum and number of hours of study have been in a state of flux, having transitioned recently from the earlier Yutori hoiku educational philosophy, curriculum and Integrated Study Periods, to the currently restructured and padded courses of study and textbooks. Read more about the curriculum development and the national curriculum here:

About School Life

School life often receives bad press on delinquency, bullying (ijime) or behavioral problems or the spate of horrendous and baffling crime knifings and killings taking place in schools in the past decade that were once unheard of in the country. Student life in public elementary schools in general is however acknowledged by most Japanese to be largely enjoyable, except for some students that can set in during the transition to junior high school.

Rigorous swotting for entrance exams is said to characterise student life in Japanese schools beginning just before entry to middle schools. To secure entry to most high schools, universities, as well as a few private junior high schools and elementary schools, applicants are required to sit entrance exams and attend interviews.

As a result, a high level of competitiveness (and stress) is often observed among students (and their mothers) during pre-high to high school years. In order to pass entrance exams to the best institutions, many students attend private afterschool study sessions (juku or gakken) that take place after regular classes in school, and/or special private preparation institutions for one to two years between high school and university (yobiko).

Higher education

Children learn early on (beginning in preschool) to maintain cooperative relationships with their peers; to follow the set school routines; and to value punctuality (from their first year in elementary school). Classroom management emphasizes student responsibility and stewardship through emphasis on daily chores such as cleaning of desks and scrubbing of classroom floors. Students are encouraged to develop strong loyalties to their social groups, e.g. to their class, their sports-day teams, their after-school circles, e.g. baseball and soccer teams. Leadership as well as subordinate roles, as well as group organization skills are learnt through assigned roles for lunchtime (kyushoku touban), class monitor or class chairperson and other such duties.

Despite the assigned leadership-subordinate roles, group activities are often conducted in a surprisingly democratic manner. Teachers usually delegate authority and responsibility to students. Small-group (han) activities often foster caring and nurturing relationships among students.

The teaching culture in Japan differs greatly from that of schools in the west. Teachers are particularly concerned about developing the holistic child and regard it as their task to focus on matters such as personal hygiene, nutrition, sleep that are not ordinarily thought of as part of the teacher's duties in the west. Students are also taught proper manners, how to speak politely and how to address adults as well as how to relate to their peers in the appropriate manner. They also learn public speaking skills through the routine class meetings as well as many school events during the school year.

Noisy and lively classrooms, the absence of teacher supervision along with the effective use of peer supervision are most often noted of elementary school classrooms. Homework workload is not overly heavy at this stage, daily portions typically comprise kanji (Chinese characters) or kokugo (Japanese language) worksheets and one or two pages of arithmetic worksheets. Various after-school hamako or club activities or remedial classes may be held by individual home-room teachers (or schools) as they see fit.

Middle-school (i.e. junior school) instruction of academic subjects shifts gear into intense, structured, fact-filled learning and routine-based school life. Small-group han are dispensed with during academic classes. Hierarchical teacher-peer and senior-to-junior relationships as well as highly organized, disciplined and hierarchical work environments such as various established student committees, are observed at middle schools.

Bibliography

Aaron Moore, *Constructing East Asia: Technology, Ideology, and Empire in Japan's Wartime Era, 1931–1945* (2013)

Beasley, W. G. :*Select Documents on Japanese Foreign Policy 1853-1868* (1960)

Beasley, William G. *Japanese Imperialism, 1894–1945* (Oxford UP, 1987)

Borg, Dorothy: *Pearl Harbor as History: Japanese American Relations, 1931-1941* (1973).

Buckley, Roger. *US-Japan Alliance Diplomacy 1945-1990* (1992)

Chalmers Johnson, *Miti and the Japanese Miracle: The Growth of Industrial Policy, 1925-1975* (1982)

Dickinson, Frederick R. *War and National Reinvention: Japan in the Great War, 1914-1919* (1999).

Dorothy Borg and Shumpei Okamoto, eds. *Pearl Harbor as History: Japanese-American Relations, 1931-1941* (1973).

Dower, John W. *Empire and aftermath: Yoshida Shigeru and the Japanese experience, 1878-1954* (1979) for 1945-54.

Frederick W. Mote, *Japanese-Sponsored Governments in China, 1937–1945* (1954)

Gerald E. Bunker, *Peace Conspiracy: Wang Ching-wei and the China War, 1937–41* (1972)

Haruo Tohmatsu and H. P. Willmott, *A Gathering Darkness: The Coming of War to the Far East and the Pacific* (2004)

Hilary Conroy, *The Japanese seizure of Korea, 1868-1910: a study of realism and idealism in international relations* (1960).

Hook, Glenn D. : *Japan's international relations: Politics, economics and security, 1945-2010.*

Ian Nish, *Alliance in Decline: A Study of Anglo-Japanese Relations, 1908-23* (1972).

Inoguchi, Takashi. *Japan's Foreign Policy in an Era of Global Change* (2013).

Iriye, Akira, ed. *Pearl Harbor and the Coming of the Pacific War: A Brief History with Documents and Essays* (1999)

Iriye, Akira. *Japan and the wider world: from the mid-nineteenth century to the present* (1997)

Izumi Hirobe, *Japanese pride, American prejudice: Modifying the exclusion clause of the 1924 Immigration Act* (2001).

Jansen, Marius B. ed. *The Cambridge History of Japan, : The Nineteenth Century* (1989)

Martha Byrd, *Chennault: Giving Wings to the Tiger* (2003).

Michael Auslin, *Negotiating with Imperialism: The Unequal Treaties and the Culture of Japanese Diplomacy* (2004)

Nish, Ian. *Japanese Foreign Policy, 1869-1942: Kasumigaseki to Miyakezaka* (1977)

O'Brien, Phillips Payson. *The Anglo-Japanese Alliance, 1902-1922* (2004).

Oliver Lindsay, *The Battle for Hong Kong, 1941–1945: Hostage to Fortune* (2009)

Peter Duus et al. eds. *The Japanese informal empire in China, 1895-1937* (2014).

Philip R. Piccigallo, *The Japanese on trial: Allied war crimes operations in the East, 1945–1951* (1980).

Richard B. Finn, *Winners in peace: MacArthur, Yoshida, and postwar Japan* (1992).

Sayuri Shimizu, *Creating People of Plenty: The United States and Japan's Economic Alternatives, 1950-1960* (2001)

Shimamoto, Mayako, Koji Ito and Yoneyuki Sugita, eds. *Historical Dictionary of Japanese Foreign Policy* (2015) excerpt

Sugita, "Enigma of U.S.-Japan Relations in the 1950s", *Reviews in American History* (2002)

Togo, Kazuhiko. *Japan's Foreign Policy 1945-2003* (Brill, 2005)

Treat, Payson J.H. *The Far East, a Political and Diplomatic History* (1935)

Index

❑❑❑